The
Private Gardens
of England

The
Private Gardens
of England

Edited by

Tania Compton

CONSTABLE

First published in Great Britain in 2015 by Constable

1 3 5 7 9 8 6 4 2

A CIP catalogue record for this book
is available from the British Library.

ISBN 978-1-47212-101-1 (Royal hardback)
ISBN: 978-1-47212-102-8 (ebook)

Designed by carrdesignstudio.com

Printed and bound in China

Constable
is an imprint of
Little, Brown Book Group
Carmelite House
50 Victoria Embankment
London EC4Y 0DZ
An Hachette UK Company

www.hachette.co.uk
www.littlebrown.co.uk

Every effort has been made to obtain the necessary permissions with reference
to copyright material, both illustrative and quoted. We apologise for any
omissions in this respect and will be pleased to make the appropriate
acknowledgements in any future edition.

PAGE I: Spilsbury
TITLE PAGE: The Barn

Contents

Introduction

I NTRIGUED BY THE gridlock of cars heading for a garden opening on behalf of a local village church, the publisher Nick Robinson joined the queue.

He had walked through Ferne Park a decade earlier but there had been no trace of a garden. The transformation he beheld left him wondering how many other private horticultural miracles were hidden behind the lanes and hedges of England. I assured Nick there were certainly enough to merit an updated and more sumptuous version of *The Englishwoman's Garden*. That had been one of the first books Nick had commissioned; this has turned out to be his last.

In her preface to *The Englishwoman's Garden* in 1980 Alvilde Lees-Milne lamented that 'many lovely gardens are shrinking, and may well end up like the dodo'. Far from presaging any sort of impending horticultural extinction Lees-Milne's words heralded a new golden age of garden creation and patronage. Drop a pin in a map of England today and manifold earthly visions of paradise could be found within any five-mile radius.

Gardens however are transient; their fortunes and atmosphere ebb and flow depending on the care being lavished upon them. We wanted to bring together a collection of the private gardens of both men and women that are at an acme of attention and dedication.

What had struck Nick and me rereading the original book was its sense of immediacy and intimacy; after thirty-five years each contribution read like a recording of the owner's voice bringing them, and their gardens, back to life with astonishing vibrancy. As the world's first archive devoted to gardens and garden design is being created at London's Garden Museum, we asked owners and photographers who have been active in supporting the museum to contribute to this book. Their generosity of spirit and devotion to this most ephemeral of art forms, the private garden, shines from each page. So I dedicate this book to them and to the late Nicholas Robinson.

OPPOSITE: Ferne Park
OVERLEAF: The Barn

New Garden:
Field to Paradise

Ferne Park

BERWICK ST JOHN, WILTSHIRE

THE VISCOUNTESS ROTHERMERE

'DON'T MAKE IT too obvious when you look out of the window,' advised the estate agent as I climbed into the back of the muddy Land Rover. We were being taken to see an estate that was, well, *not quite yet* for sale, but my husband Jonathan had been talking with excitement lately about his dreams of building an entirely new house, so we decided to take a look. For my part I had never thought of building a new home, and the notion of creating a garden from nothing had simply never crossed my mind.

'This is the North Lodge entrance,' said our guide, and I glanced out to see a battered and broken gate hanging off its hinges, propped on one pier with a great tangle of orange string: not the most inspiring of thresholds. An old abandoned tractor deepened the general sense of dereliction. Hoping for a glimpse of the Secret Garden, I was seeing something more like the detritus of a gypsy camp. This impression was confirmed by the baleful presence of a dead sheep on the edge of the drive. Then again, as the shepherd would later remind me, 'where there's livestock, there's dead stock'.

'The old house used to sit up there,' the estate agent told us, and I looked where he was pointing – there was no trace of a house at all now, and yet, all of a sudden, I was captivated by the beauty of the landscape that was unfolding before me. Ancient rolling hills spread across the whole horizon: this was Cranborne Chase. My eyes were drawn to a crown of beech trees at the apex. This, I was to discover, was Win Green, a Bronze Age bowl barrow situated at the highest point in Wiltshire. It seemed to be connected by a track which ran along the horizon: this was the Ox Drove, an ancient drovers' road, which connected the countryside of Dorset – Thomas Hardy's famous Wessex – with Salisbury. I gazed in delight, then turned to see an equally entrancing vista to the north – the Vale of Wardour. I realised I was looking at an almost uninterrupted 360-degree view of the Wiltshire and Dorset countryside: Ferne's location was sublime.

OPPOSITE: Looking down on the south façade of Ferne Park from the ancient ox drove that runs along the summit of Cranborne Chase

OVERLEAF: Beyond the box parterre a double avenue of more than 400 lime trees *Tilia* x *europaea* 'Pallida' leads the eye up towards Cranborne Chase

ABOVE: The north-facing
front of Ferne Park
illuminated by the
setting sun

I could tell by the way Jonathan was gripping my hand that he felt the same way. The rest is a blur in my memory – a village called Berwick St John, driving through the Rushmore estate, our guide saying 'Cecil Beaton used to live nearby . . .'

I didn't even get out of the car that day. But we had found a place that was to change our lives. We didn't so much feel that we had chosen Ferne so much as Ferne had chosen us. Looking back on it, I can hardly believe that Jonathan had so much faith in me – I didn't think of myself as a person with a strongly aesthetic or creative background, I had no horticultural knowledge whatsoever, and we knew hardly anyone who lived hereabouts.

But youth is never daunted and, a few weeks later, around the end of March 1999, we were driving our own car through that same North Lodge entrance and parking on the site of the old house. We were now the owners of the remnants of Ferne Park estate. We had engaged Quinlan Terry to design a new home for us and had decided to restore the derelict farm buildings: what could be simpler? As for the grounds – one could hardly call it a garden at this point – they had scarcely entered my mind.

Since 1225 there has been a settlement at Ferne. Two houses are recorded on the estate, and ours was to be the third. The last family to have lived there, the Douglas-Hamiltons, left during the 1920s, having bequeathed the land to an animal sanctuary. The wife of the Thirteenth Duke of Hamilton had in 1912 founded the Scottish Society for the Prevention of Vivisection. Therefore the most notable recent residents of Ferne were the pet dogs of well-off Londoners, evacuated from the city in the teeth of the Blitz to the relative safety of the Wiltshire–Dorset border. But the sanctuary fell into disrepair, the old house was demolished, and the estate went into terminal decline.

I spent my first years at Ferne planning the new house. I had no thoughts whatever about the garden; I knew next to nothing about horticulture. In 1996 my father-in-law had sponsored a Chelsea Garden that had won 'Best in Show', but I remember being constantly drawn to the show garden that was beside it. This garden fascinated me and I spent hours looking closely at it. Most show gardens are – well, exactly that. But the garden of Rupert Golby was different. I had never forgotten its beauty, nor how, in response to my amateur's questions – 'What are those lovely flowers in the meadow?' and so on – Rupert had answered kindly and patiently: 'Those are ox-eye daisies . . . that's a tree peony' and so, when in 2001 I contemplated the enormous work that would have to be done on this grand and thoroughly neglected estate, it was Rupert to whom I turned. And even he was sceptical at first, clearly recognising that I had not the faintest idea how much blood, sweat and tears I was letting myself in for.

For the ten years before we arrived at Ferne, it had functioned largely as a rubbish dump. Before we could embark upon anything resembling a garden, we would have to remove mountains of rubble, glass and bricks, dig up concrete yards, demolish barns that were riddled with asbestos, make war on acres and acres of Japanese knotweed, tame the rampaging laurel. Before a single creative act we would be facing several months of destructive struggle. For it soon became blindingly clear to me that underneath all this chaos there lay no trace of a former garden, no ancient bedrock to build upon, no lost Eden to unearth. We would need to start absolutely from scratch.

Houses, like people, generally look better when clothed. Our new home looked bare and exposed without a garden, intimidated by the natural beauty surrounding it as far as the eye could see. One listened in vain for birdsong. I had fallen in love with a magnificent landscape, and I felt it was demanding of me a garden of comparable splendour.

So I went back to school. I enrolled at Rosemary Alexander's English Gardening School to learn as much as I could as quickly as I could. I devoured as many gardening books as I could get my hands on, and drew strength and inspiration from their lore and wisdom. There was Russell Page's *The Education of a Gardener* – 'A garden really lives only insofar as it is an expression of faith, the embodiment of a hope and a song of praise' – and the reassuring counsel of Christopher Lloyd – 'Because you are inexperienced, your mistakes will be numerous, but experienced gardeners do and indeed should make many mistakes also.' Toiling in the endless weeds and brambles I could turn to the words of Gertrude Jekyll for support: 'There is no spot of ground, however arid, bare or ugly, that cannot be tamed into such a state as may give an impression of beauty and delight.'

Along with these most generous mentors in my mind, I had the amazing good fortune to live not far from some of the loveliest gardens in the country, and whiled away many an afternoon in the magnificent grounds of Cranborne Manor, Shute House, Heale House and many others.

Gradually, a plan for the garden started to evolve. I came to understand that what mattered most to me was what Nancy Lancaster described as 'bone structure and abundance'. A double avenue of more than 400 lime trees – *Tilia* x *europaea* 'Pallida' – would stretch away to the south to embrace the hills of Win Green and Cranborne Chase. I would restore the stone parterre to the north and plant a set of yew pyramids, influenced by the topiary garden at Athelhampton

in Dorset, a house where Jonathan's father had lived as a child. Rupert had taught me how reclaimed York stone could be used to soften the look of a terrace. I would introduce a water feature that I had admired, at the Radcliffe Infirmary in Oxford, itself inspired by Bernini's Fontana Del Tritone on the Piazza Barberini in Rome.

The East and West Gardens were designed by Rupert to help anchor the house to the landscape and, most importantly, to bring nature right up to the windows. Two orchards were planted. Rupert somehow conjured from a disused coalyard a magical potager with glasshouses: this now supplies the house with an abundance of fruit and vegetables, as well as freshly cut flowers.

I found the practical side of gardening thoroughly engrossing. The building of a new house had created the inevitable problems of soil erosion and compaction. It turned out there was no quick or easy way to deal with this problem. Blessed with a wonderful team of young and enthusiastic gardeners under the guidance of brothers Jeremy and Brendan Long, we set about digging in well-rotted compost twice a year for several years, thereby slowly restoring the structure of the soil. Every spring we thickly mulched the borders, and any newly placed trees or shrubs, in order to suppress the weeds and help with water retention during the summer: this is work that can never really stop.

Above all it was the trees that demanded attention. No serious or considered attempt at tree planting had been made since the Douglas-Hamilton family had left over eighty years ago. It was later explained to me by Sarah Cook that the life of trees is generational, that trees need continually to be planted. The veteran trees that remained in the Park were – and are – magnificent, but nothing had ever been planted to succeed them. And yet the woodlands were worse. There the hardwoods had been cut for profit and not restocked. This meant that the woods were in a very sorry state, populated with exceedingly sticky self-seeded sycamores. Of all the tasks that had to be undertaken, this was the most daunting. How could we restore the Park without damaging its late eighteenth-century atmosphere? And how could we restore the woods without making them look devastated? All we could do was get our heads down and work, tackle one thing at a time, and try not to contemplate how daunting was the task that lay ahead.

I have learned so much from my long, absorbing and enriching work on the garden at Ferne. I know now that there is great comfort and peace to be gained from a close affinity with nature. Proximity to its cycles and seasons, a growing sensitivity to its harmonies and habits: these things have taught me practical wisdom, like the value of eating local and seasonal produce. I believe we should foster this love and respect in our young, so that it

ABOVE: The mist settling in the Vale of Wardour beyond the Topiary Garden inspired by Athelhampton House in Dorset. Stephen Pettifer's Triton fountain is based on the Radcliffe Infirmary statue that itself was modelled on the top part of Bernini's Triton fountain in Rome

becomes second nature. These days my own children know that around mid-February they are likely to taste Jerusalem artichoke soup at some point, and that there's a good chance there'll be leeks, spinach and cauliflower on the table at our family Sunday lunch. I also have high hopes for my purple sprouting broccoli next spring...

And February is, of course, prime time for the Galanthophile. How I love those brave, exquisite flowers, so beautiful and heart-warming when placed in a bud vase! And how I look forward to checking the rebirth of the *Galanthus nivalis* Sandersii Group – the special yellow snowdrops that grow in Mari's grave garden.

Already my garden has become a treasury of beloved influences, a repository of recollected arcadias – such as the landscape of the Gods at Rousham and the heartbreakingly nostalgic garden of ruins at Ninfa near Rome. I cannot walk past a *Fagus sylvatica* 'Tricolor' without remembering the first time I saw those pink-fringed, green-feathered leaves set against a backdrop of dark evergreens at Stourhead, or the first time I strolled at Heale House and smelled the delicious burnt-sugar aroma of the champion *Cercidiphyllum japonicum* floating on the fresh autumn air.

OPPOSITE ABOVE: Looking towards Cranborne Chase over a meadow planted with camassias for spring and roses for summer

I treasure the memory of certain lectures I attended, such as those of the brilliant horticulturist Ken Burrows. I cannot walk through my viburnum collection without thinking of Ken, who taught me a great deal about those beautiful shrubs, just as the great rosarian Charles Quest-Ritson comes to mind when the hybrid musk roses break into flower, or I see a vase of the velvety red *Rosa* 'Ingrid Bergman'. And the sight of a *Davidia involucrata* cannot fail to remind me of Roy Lancaster, with his one brown eye and one blue-green, recounting the story of poor legendary botanist Ernest Wilson, searching to find that very tree in China but pipped to the post by Père David...

OPPOSITE BELOW: White Park cattle, a rare breed of beef cattle kept in Britain for more than 2000 years, graze the park

I think that what I am most interested in is what Mary Keen described as 'the other-worldly nature of gardens'. It is this transcendental quality that inspires me to keep gardening at Ferne. Through horticulture I try to create an atmosphere of peace and tranquility where one might cast off daily anxiety and enter a more spiritual dimension, a natural place where one might arrive perhaps at some deeper understanding of one's own nature. It is clear to me that memories embedded deep in the subconscious have influenced the creation of the garden at Ferne. Moreover, to walk in a beautiful garden is to realise how inadequate are our conceptions of time and space: gardening has the power to enliven and enrich both words, compressing here, elongating there. Space resonates in a garden; time quickens and slows and pauses; it can even stop altogether. Perhaps it is no coincidence that in *The Four Quartets* T. S. Eliot's meditations on past and present occur beside a rose garden.

For a fine garden achieves a fusion of the melancholy and the sublime: sublime because it is ineffable, melancholy because its heights of beauty are always transitory, temporary, caught on the wing. The loveliest compliment I have ever received about the garden was that of an English professor who wrote to me after her visit. She said she had been reminded of 'the Lost Estate' in Alain-Fournier's *Le Grand Meaulnes*, that strange enduring hymn to evanescence, in which a young man is haunted by a beauty he recollects. As he grows to adulthood he yearns to recreate that 'far-away time . . . the mysterious love-dream of adolescence . . .' It is a book I loved as a girl but had almost forgotten. Perhaps all of us who experience the profound delight of creating, preserving and tending a beloved garden are searching too, for a deeply remembered innocence and sweetness, another glimpse of that Lost Estate.

ABOVE: The old coalyard has been transformed into a walled kitchen garden

BELOW: A gate with an assortment of garden tools and carvings is framed by rose 'Albéric Barbier' and flanked by pruned fig trees

ABOVE: Fruit trees are trained against the kitchen garden walls and the hazel supports are covered in sweet peas and *Cobaea scandens* in summer

BELOW LEFT: Stone planters are filled with white *Tulipa* 'Purissima' for spring in the East Garden

BELOW RIGHT: *Hesperis matronalis* and tree peonies surround an urn

LEFT: Multi-stemmed ivory *Staphylea colchica* flower with *Camassia quamash* lining a path to the Walled Garden

BELOW: A multitude of ferns line a stone path below the lake

OVERLEAF: Golden evening light streaming onto the topiary pyramids and Stephen Pettifer's Triton fountain with the Vale of Wardour in the distance. *Verbascum bombyciferum*, originally from Chatsworth, and *Eryngium giganteum* seed themselves in the gravel drive

The Barn

HERTFORDSHIRE

❧

Tom Stuart-Smith

OPPOSITE: *Genista aetnensis, Salvia nemorosa* 'Amethyst' and *Euphorbia seguieriana* subsp. *niciciana* in the courtyard at The Barn

I WAS BORN 150 yards from where I now live and in the same year that the M1 sliced its way through Hertfordshire, the county that E. M. Forster had once referred to as 'England at its quietest'. A motorway half a mile from your door sometimes makes your grip on the land feel a little provisional: if everyone else is in a hurry to get away then why not you? Scotland beckons one way and the bright lights of London the other. Living at The Barn has been a half-a-lifetime effort to fight this sense of being a 'place not worth stopping for'.

Converting the old farm buildings was my father's idea, and he started rebuilding them without even knowing which of us six children might live here. Two years later Sue and I moved in with our newborn daughter Rose, about three pieces of furniture and a grand piano. This sparse furnishing extended to the outside as well. In contrast to my childhood home over the road where there was a mature garden with good old trees, at The Barn there was a decrepit elder bush in the corner of the farmyard and a five-yard strip of grass. Beyond that: fifty acres of wheat. This has perhaps been the greatest excitement of gardening here over the last twenty-seven years: forging a place with a sense of anchorage in the landscape where nothing much existed before.

The garden began slowly. First the courtyard, a modest enclosed space, was terraced and planted with a pioneer's combination of flowers and vegetables. My father and I laid the bricks; my mother propagated the plants. At weekends family and friends were enlisted to dig, plant and sow (we were quite shameless). As we were able to acquire more land the outlines of a more ambitious project began to take shape on the other side of The Barn, in the teeth of the north-westerly wind and a great open panorama. We sowed five acres of meadow and planted yew and hornbeam hedges to give protection and enclosure. By now we had three children; campanulas and roses were vying for space with sandpits, plastic tractors and a climbing frame. In one important sense the whole garden was conceived as a

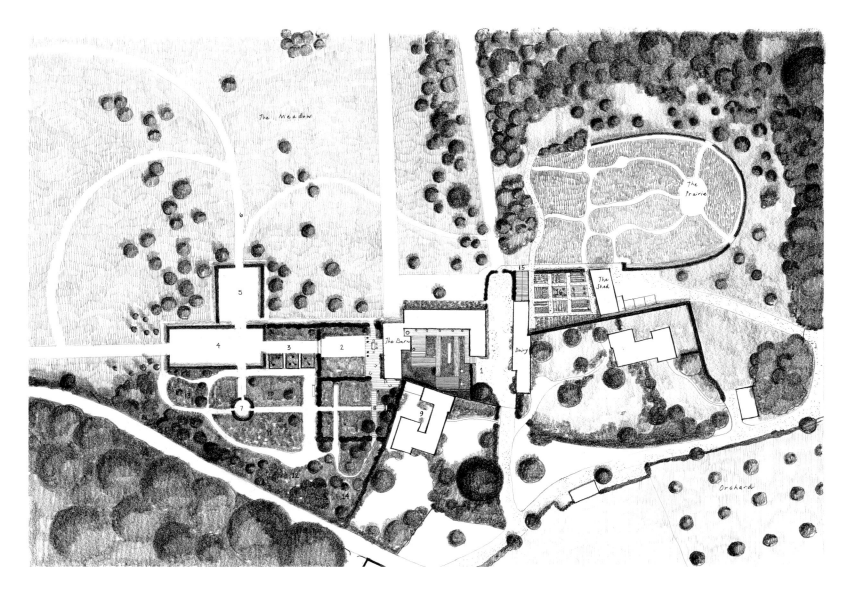

ABOVE: An aerial drawing by Tom of The Barn, its gardens and buildings with the Prairie in a horseshoe shape

playground for the children, somewhere to explore, with small intricate and intimate spaces and then quite open places to charge about in. Always changing – and never too neat.

The greatest challenge of those early years of garden making was how to find some kind of frame and shape to the thing. There were fortunately still just enough hedges left in the landscape for that to be the guiding motif, and we made enclosures that I envisaged filled with plants over the years. But by the time they were half full it was quite obvious to Sue and me that some remaining green rooms should be left empty.

Now The Barn begins to feel rooted in its setting. It is developing a grain; the cowslips, narcissi and cranesbills are naturalising in the meadow; the snowdrops, at first just a bucket or two that we dug up from over the road, have spread into carpets of thousands. The oaks are just about worth climbing and can support a hammock. I think these incalculable blessings of natural increase matter to me more than anything I effect more directly by digging, snipping and cajoling.

When we started we had only occasional help so I gardened about thirty hours a week in the summer, sometimes using a miner's head torch so I could continue on into the dark. In retrospect it probably wasn't a very balanced way of carrying on, and over time Sue and I have shared more and more to do with the garden. It has changed from being a crazed project in a windy waste to something more intrinsically therapeutic. Also there was something to see rather than just dream about.

The vegetable garden is where Sue spends most time. Five years ago we swopped our ten-foot aluminium greenhouse for a wonderful purpose-built wooden structure and this has rapidly become a spiritual home where Sue tends vegetable seedlings, pelargoniums and auriculas. We mix up the flowers and the veg and sometimes I get above myself and sneak some tulips into what should be her early potato patch. Sue has added delphiniums in another bed and cowslips are seeding like cress in a third. Sometimes it feels that the whole vegetable enterprise is at risk, but then there is a bounty of lettuce and beans and we realise we have the balance about right. We now have a full-time gardener, Brian Maslin, who has been with us five years, and part-time help in the summer. Most of my gardening is done at weekends and in the evening, so the place has two masters and Brian and I communicate largely by email, which might seem a little prosaic, but it seems to work well.

What about the flower garden? When I started off, I was so influenced by all the great Arts and Crafts gardens I had seen when I was a teenager that I began by gardening in compartments: a little herb garden here, a rose garden in the next space; a succession of contrasting plantings. I collected plants as quickly as I could afford and experimented in a cottagey sort of style. With time I became much more interested in the emotional and theatrical effect the garden had rather than in collecting plants, and started to simplify and unify the planting so that now there aren't sudden changes in character, more a subtle shifting. The planting is used to intensify the mood created by the space. Some favourites such as the little umbellifer *Cenolophium denudatum*, white foxgloves or *Geranium psilostemon* pop up pretty much anywhere, whereas other self-sowers have limits imposed on them. I have tried to create something that has the character of a very stylised meadow with very abundant growth,

ABOVE: Tom's perspective drawing shows Serge Hill, the house he grew up in, across the lane from where he and Sue now live at The Barn

The entrance courtyard at The Barn has a palette of repeated plants. Flowering in June are *Genista aetnensis*, *Salvia nemorosa* 'Amethyst' and *Euphorbia seguieriana* subsp. *niciciana* with *Astrantia major* 'Hadspen Blood' and bottom left *Origanum laevigatum* 'Herrenhausen'. The rectangular and cubed water tanks act like reflective mirrors to the surrounding plants and structure

A view from the main barn door the length of the original garden with its enfilade of spaces, some planted, others left plain. Tall plants such as the plume poppy *Macleaya microcarpa* tower over *Stipa calamagrostis*, *Geranium* 'Patricia' and *Veronicastrum virginicum* 'Fascination'

which creates an intense contrast between the bareness of winter, when the hedges and dead silhouettes create most of the interest, and high summer when you can hardly see where you are going amongst the towering veronicastrums, inulas, eupatoriums and grasses that fill the central part of the garden.

The ground was pretty rough in the main bit of the garden, all stones and sand. I piled it high with manure and compost, and as a result the plants now grow very tall. As the hedges have matured the main part of the flower garden has become very sheltered, but we still have to do a lot of staking to prevent things falling over in a dry and windy July. It's a ritual I enjoy, although it's easy for me to say that now since Brian and Fabian do most of it. I love going out into the fields and woods in January to cut the hazel rods and pea sticks. That moment feels more like the turning point of the year than any other. In April when all the neat and hummocky cat's cradles are woven over the emerging poppies, campanulas and asters this part of the garden has a brief moment when the husbandry of it all is at its most evident. It feels deliciously antiquated with its clustered, twiggy mounds dotted about; the uninitiated might think that we are engaged in catching moles by some trusty Hertfordshire method or making some strange obeisance to the moon god.

By June the garden is transformed and is all around my ears. I feel it change from a place that I just think about a lot and do stuff in to a place that I completely inhabit and which inhabits me. For two months in midsummer there are wonderful moments when I feel more than any other time of the year I am an inmate of this place. I almost don't know where the garden ends and I begin. The silphiums are towering at ten or twelve feet. The rampant plume poppy is waving around at about the same height, and the white eremurus grows at several inches a day. It is wonderfully engrossing. I stand in the middle of the garden and feel I can hear the roar of the growing grass.

We have tried to keep the garden in scale with both the barn and the landscape. I remember the architect Peregrine Bryant, who helped with the conversion, telling me that as an agricultural building it shouldn't really have a garden at all. In a way he was right but, having decided to ignore his advice, I have always been conscious of not occluding the connection between building and landscape. So on one side the barn faces immediately on to the meadow, and on the main garden side there is a glimpse of the same meadow at the end of the main axis to the west. The garden in one sense becomes just a way of mediating between the intimacy of the home and the openness of the horizon; from the hearth to the heath.

There is another quality of the place that runs across this; a sense that the garden and the landscape immediately around it are patches stitched together to form a multi-coloured fabric, each patch managed slightly differently. The woods, the garden, the meadow, several smaller meadows beyond the garden and then closer at hand the vegetable garden and, most recently, an exotic prairie.

The prairie is definitely the most outlandish of our garden patches. It covers about half an acre of a paddock where we used to keep sheep. I had collaborated with James Hitchmough on a number of projects making exotic meadows for other people and had seen enough to know that I wanted to look after one myself. In the winter of 2011 we covered the bare ground with three inches of sand and sowed a kilogramme of the most expensive seed you

can imagine, selected by James. Over the summer lots of interesting things started to come up, but so too did thousands of willows, blown in on the sand from the local gravel pit, and then countless buttercups that germinated on the worm casts. All were removed and it was worth it. From June to November there is now an extraordinary succession of flower and texture. It begins with *Dianthus carthusionorum* and species penstemons and is then joined by thousands of *Echinacea pallida*, kniphofias and the steely foliage and bobbly flowers of *Eryngium yuccifolium*. Spires of various liatris species and the towering stems of several silphiums then come into play, jostling with *Rudbeckia fulgida* var. *maxima* in their thousands and coreopsis up to eight feet tall. A grand finale of asters combines with great drifts of *Rudbeckia deamii*. So many of the plants are just a bit unfamiliar to me that the meadow feels like something from a fairy story where things are just a bit bigger and bolder. It is unexpected, joyously spectacular at its best and gets thoroughly into its stride just as the rest of the garden quietens down.

I write this as the daffodils and magnolias are in flower, the prairie is neat and muted, the first bluebells are appearing in the woods, Sue's auriculas are starting into flower and there are carrots coming up thick and fast in the greenhouse. The motorway still roars away when the wind is in the east, but we hear it less these days.

ABOVE: A view of The Barn with coloumnar Irish yews adding height and punctuation amongst an abundance of flowering plants

Other ingredients in the meadow as well as *Liatris spicata* and *Eryngium yuccifolium* include (top right) *Silphium laciniatum* with beautifully cut leaves and rudbeckias *R. hirta* and *R. maxima* (seen below)

The damper part of the prairie with more clay is home to a higher proportion of yellow-flowered prairie dwellers including Black-eyed Susan *Rudbeckia fulgida* var. *deamii* and California coneflower *Rudbeckia hirta* (seen overleaf with *Eryngium yuccifolium*)

Plaz Metaxu

WITHERIDGE, DEVON

Alasdair Forbes

P LAZ METAXU IS a garden in north Devon that has been created since 1992. It occupies a west-facing valley, and extends over thirty-two acres, nearly half of which is a pastoral landscape grazed by sheep. A stream flows east/west through the valley, entering the garden in the orchard, then taking the form of a canal in front of the house, where it is flanked by a gently terraced lawn. Behind the house there is a series of enclosed gardens: a walled garden, and two courtyards that were formerly the farmyards. The main garden unfolds to the west of the house and is centred on the lake, made in 1994. The extensive lawns around the lake are fringed by areas of woodland, hedged enclosures, and (sometimes parallel) sheltered walks, themselves linking adjacent groves. Below the lake dam a last formal area is bounded by a ha-ha. The stream, which is diverted around the lake in the main garden, here returns to its original course before flowing on down the centre of the valley to a final pond with a cascade. While open to the west, and to the sky, the valley, from within the garden, is largely self-contained. Extensive panoramas do, however, occur, from either side of the valley, on the high walk that has been landscaped within the encircling pastures. This expansiveness adds an important dimension to the garden, as does the reciprocity of contact (which is vital) between the garden and its surrounding fieldscape.

As poetry is the remembrance of language, so a garden is a remembrance of space. My own garden's version of this remembrance takes the form of a meditation on the landform of the valley. Plaz Metaxu is situated in a self-contained valley covering an area of thirteen hectares. My ideal has been to create a garden that responds to its site in as tactful and meaningful a way as possible.

OPPOSITE: Plaz Metaxu means 'The Place that is Between'. This stone, expertly cut by Nicholas Sloan, like all the others in the garden, is to the left of the drive as you enter the garden (Plan 1)*

---

* 'Plan' references are to the numbers and letters on the plan of Plaz Metaxu on page 37

The top of the walled garden (Plan 3) and part of the house can be seen above

The granite footprints are positioned to either side of the drive (Plan J)

When visitors arrive at the garden, the first thing that puzzles them is the garden's name. Plaz Metaxu means the 'place that is between', which acknowledges the valley as an interval between two hillsides. But why the need for a foreign name instead of the traditional one of Coombe House? In fact the two names complement each other, and give a clue to the garden's dual nature, which is made up of both literal reality, and a more elusive one that appeals to the imagination. Although these two aspects of the garden are ultimately inseparable, this does not mean the surface appearance of the garden cannot be enjoyed for its own sake, and the plants and the walks and the atmospheres taken simply at face value. It can, and should be. But because the metaphorical aspect of the garden is only hinted at 'on the ground' I am going to speak mainly about that here.*

A sign near where visitors park their cars is inscribed with the words 'This both was and was not'. This suggests that the place you are entering has an ambiguous identity, similar to that of a fairy tale. It straddles two worlds, like the mythic figures of Orpheus and Persephone, who were familiar with Hades as well as the earth. In addition to the physical interval the valley creates, this transition between our familiar world and a more elusive complementary one is therefore also part of what is meant by 'the place that is between'.

This elusive other world that means so much to the garden does not have a single definite character. It is more a different perspective on things. I have referred to fairy tales and the Underworld as two examples of it. I might just as well have mentioned the Buddhist's nirvana or the poet Wallace Stevens' 'necessary fiction' or the *mundus imaginalis* of the Sufis and archetypal psychology. Visitors to the garden will have their own intuitions to bring.

---

* Many areas of the garden are not discussed or illustrated here. These include all the more intricately planted areas of the garden, such as Auxo, the walled garden (Plan 3), Pothos, the orchard (plan 7), Kedalion (Plan 2) and the whole area to the south of the lake

What I want to emphasise is that there is this constant dialogue going on in the garden between the apparent certainties of our everyday world, and the persistent rumours of another dimension. These rumours both heighten the poignancy and question the exclusivity of our literal sense of belonging here, and give the garden its 'poetic' edge.

As you walk down the drive, you notice the images of a bare and a shod foot cut into two granite stones. This hints at the best way to approach the garden. The shod foot represents our habitual behaviour. But the bare foot suggests both a more intimate contact with the earth and a more imaginative predisposition. In the ancient world, when Jason arrived at Iolkos wearing only one sandal, it was apparent to everyone that his bare foot connected him to a more mysterious world. Wherever you go in the garden you will be presented with these two faces of reality. Each space you enter will lead a metaphorical life as well as a literal one.

Let us begin with the garden's response to the valley as a whole. Among the physical attributes of the valley which haunt the garden are the contrasts it presents us with between its axial direction and its bilaterality, and its convergence on depth and its openness to height. On the garden's terms, such spatial gestures parallel the human predicament, with far-reaching imaginative consequences.

Such a parallel seems implicit in the plural meanings we attach to such phenomena as depth and height. For example, height, and forward momentum are often identified with the aspirations of the human spirit, and are characterised in the garden by spatial references

OPPOSITE RIGHT: Coombe House and front lawn with votive terrace (Plan 5). A house has been here since before the seventeenth century. In this photograph, we are looking *at* the house, but the deeper function of the space works the other way round, as if the house were curtseying towards its surroundings. The house faces the field Eos, seen across the lake on page 42-3. The diminutive grass terrace relates the house to the hillside opposite in a humble gesture of tribute, which, together with the crescent-shaped windows, forms part of the dedication to the virginal moon goddess Artemis. The contrast with the courtyards behind the house could not be greater. Until 1994, the drive came right up to the house

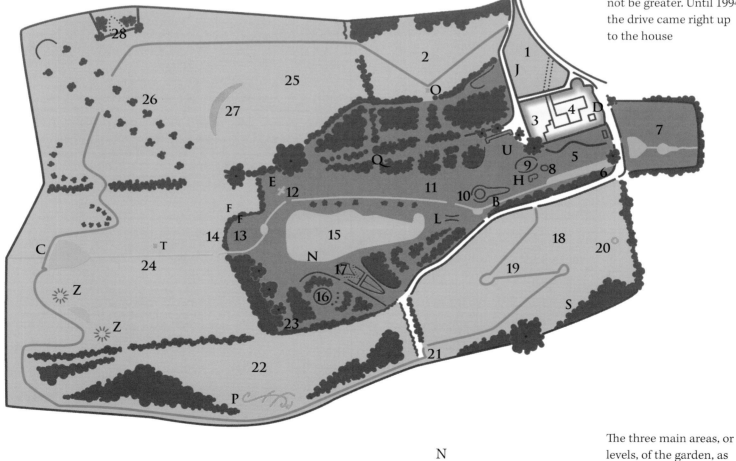

DISTRESS RETORT   LYRIC MOTIVE   PASTORAL LOOP

N

The three main areas, or levels, of the garden, as mentioned on page 39, are clearly visible on the plan

BELOW: The canal
which carries the axis
of the valley across the
front garden's votive
space, looking towards
Mnemosyne (Plan 6).
Its straight lines, highly
unusual at Plaz Metaxu,
are continued in the
'runway' of The Bolt
(Plan B)

to the *puer aeternus* (or eternal youth) in various guises. Yet, in many traditions, valleys are also the home of the soul (or Psyche), and here the essential association is one of depth. The tension between the reaching for height, and the plumbing of depth, is an archetypal one and is given mythic expression in Apuleius' tale of *Eros and Psyche* which explores the tragic courtship, and eventual marriage, between the soul and the spirit. At Plaz Metaxu this myth occupies centre stage, but is expressed in terms of the spatial tensions inherent in the valley: both through changes in momentum and the different claims made upon us by depth and height.

For example, depth is present in the garden's lake, dedicated to Narcissus, a well of sometimes troubling introspection. By contrast, the sky inspires a more elated and extrovert freedom. So the sky and the lake often pull in different directions and, as you follow the course of the stream down the garden, the axial momentum also eventually gives way, at the far end of the lake, to an alternative cross-play between the two sides of the valley. These shifting spatial gestures act like destinies in the garden, with the power to change our perspective on things.

The garden is a polytheistic place. Individual areas also create their own spatial idioms in deference to the gods who are manifest there. Examples would be the *votive* space for Artemis in front of the house, the *reflexive* space for Hermes in the main courtyard, and the *kenotic* space for Hades across the lake. A votive space pays tribute, with piety. A reflexive space draws strength from being enclosed; and a kenotic space invites us to become empty.

There is not room here to detail the ways in which the character of an individual god and the style of a specific space come to intermingle their identities. Nonetheless, these 'spatial epiphanies' have been an indispensable inspiration in the making of the garden.

What I want to emphasise is that when a space is visited by a god it is no longer inert, but starts to 'behave', to act on us. To become aware of this we need to make ourselves correspondingly passive, thus reversing our normal understanding of how perception works. Yet just this kind of reversal is what is proposed to us by the deeper levels of mythic and poetic experience. In a garden we are often more open to such reversals.

Between spaces also favour reversals, and the best way to negotiate them is by a kind of unhurried and rhythmic to-and-fro movement, or poetic shuttling. This movement is not usually the one we adopt when first visiting a garden, since our inclination is naturally to cover the ground. But, ideally, a more patient response emerges, which lets us imagine how the garden *dwells*. This concerns how the garden endures through time and spreads out to take respectful possession of its terrain. Dwelling, for the philosopher Heidegger, relates us to the 'fourfold' of earth and sky and mortals and immortals. This wider perspective, a kind of spatial caring for the human situation, may well be the proper 'element' of gardening.

The double life the garden leads is also reflected in its attitude to 'emptiness'. A phenomenon of the valley not yet mentioned is the cradle of empty space at its heart, which plays a vital role in the imaginative as well as the physical life of the garden. Eastern philosophies have generally been more receptive than Western ones to the creative values of emptiness. The emptiness at the heart of Plaz Metaxu easily slips from being the literal gap between the two sides of the valley into something ineffable, like the Taoist's 'ravine under everything that is'.

The between space is empty. Because of this it is *conductive*. The whole garden is nothing but a theatre of conduction that puts no limits on the nature of what can be transmitted. I call the sign for the place of transmission a *caesura*. A caesura (typographically rendered as | |) marks the break in rhythm in a line of verse. The garden advocates a caesural *form of attentiveness*, which means a way of noticing things that is unusually hospitable to interruptions or suspensions, giving rise to 'threshold' experiences. The caesural intuition alerts us to those instances of spatial discontinuity (when a part of space seems to jump out from its surroundings) that stop space being taken for granted and encourage us to value space for its own sake. This caesural remembrance of space is the central loyalty of the garden.

The *fabled* space out of which the garden is made is inseparable from this act of remembrance. The garden's method is an *in-laying out* that responds to both the 'inscape' and landscape of reality. In this method, neither inscape nor landscape is privileged above the other, but both work mutually to reveal space anew. The input of the fable, or meaning, grows out of the garden's gratitude for space.

The structure of the garden operates on three interrelating 'levels'. The first of these is composed of the enclosed gardens around the house, collectively given the name of *Distress Retort* ('retort' in the double sense of alembic and antidote). It is here that the work of the garden was founded, and the first connections ventured between the garden's interiority and its outward expansion into the landscape. The reflexive intuitions stirred in the *Distress Retort* are not discarded once outside its walls, but transferred to the wider garden at large.

OPPOSITE: A view of the lake at the centre of the garden facing west down the valley. From this vantage point, the axis of the valley is dominant. Fastigiate oaks line the new course of the stream. It is into this view that the *puer aeternus* soars, emerging from the corridor of The Bolt (Plan B). The lake, often bringing the sky down to earth, helps reveal the valley's emptiness. In the foreground, an engraved caesura is laid into the lawn. The lines curve inwards, in sympathy with the natural contours, and to parry the shock of Zeus' thunderbolt in the field above (Plan L, 19). The gap at the heart of the caesura holds the two sides of the valley in balance, and also weighs the mortal and immortal options of the garden. Lake and caesura together combine to lay the valley open as an offering

ABOVE AND BELOW LEFT: Two views of the Hermes courtyard (Plan 4) looking both ways across the 'Labyrinth of the Broken Heart', shaped as a question mark and an ear. The planting is mainly evergreen, including magnolias, phillyreas and stauntonia. This was still a working farmyard in 1992. The barns form the garden's ricetto. It is within this 'reflexive' space that the garden found its poetic courage. A blacksmith's mandrel doubles as a wizard's hat. A white granite drip-stone represents Hestia. A coiled chain rings the trunk of an arbutus. Hermes was known as 'the magic darkness in the midst of bright sunlight', as figured in the mouth of the oracular pot, above right. Across the lake, a group of gardens surrounds a yew circle, Hades (Plan 16). The entrance to Hades is shown below left. Hermes escorted the soul to Hades after death, and the pattern of the Labyrinth in the courtyard is echoed in the layout around Hades. Much else that happens in the garden at large is already predicted in the courtyard. The gravel is not walked on, giving rise to an 'intransitive' space, like that of the lake. There are many such hermetic connections in the garden

BELOW RIGHT AND OPPOSITE: Two details of the smaller courtyard (Plan D), which is like a dungeon in winter, but a suntrap in summer. Enclosed spaces are prisons as well as paradises. The turn of the year is marked in this courtyard when the mimosa, *Acacia pravissima*, comes into flower in April. Zeus appeared to Danaë, in her dungeon, as a shower of gold. The rustic Greek pot, planted up in summer, stands on a pavement of Italian porphyry. The 'harem' window is from northern India

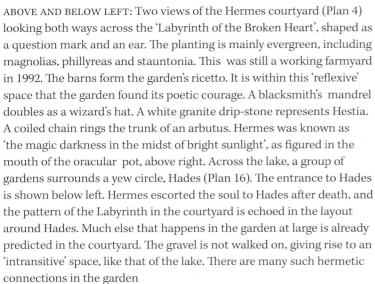

OPPOSITE: Orexis (Plan E) is a figure for Eros, and the focus of Psyche's pining (next page). The view is south-east across the lake to Eos (Plan 18), where the zigzag path (Zeus' thunderbolt) is clearly visible (Plan 19). Cutting the path into the hillside transformed the field from being an inert background and made it an integral part of the theatre of the garden. Garden and landscape are here at one. The 'mount' of Orexis was made from the spoils of the lake and is the best place from which to experience the rhythmic cradling action of the valley

ABOVE: Two reciprocal cross views of the garden taken from opposite sides of the valley along the Pastoral Loop. TOP: The 60m figure of Pan (Plan P) can be seen at the top of the hillside. ABOVE: One again looks across Hesperos (Plan 24) to Themis (Plan 25) with Atlantic Bow (Plan 27) and the Avenue of the Hours (Plan 26). Ananke (Plan 13), with curved beech hedge and ha-ha (Plan 14) is visible, lower right. These expansive views help situate the garden in the wider landscape. Elevation lends the garden new forms of entitlement

LEFT: This is a view down the valley over Ananke (Plan 13) and the ha-ha to Hesperos (Plan 24), with Zen Bens (Plan Z) and Trakl stone (Plan T). This stone marks the ebbing away of *puer* ambitions, and the decline of the axis. The shrine to Ananke, goddess of necessity, is centre left. Ananke's garden is shaped like a noose

Four different views of the lake, Narcissus (Plan 15), presided over by Psyche in the form of a stainless steel 'alarm sail' (Plan N). The lake here centres the landscape and gives it reflective depth. Its moods change. Formally, the shape of the sail bends back to gather the run of the slope behind it before referring the space on across the water to the Orexis slates (Plan E, page 42). The spatial gesture re-enacts the famous *outremer* 'prayer across the water' of the Troubadours. The sail is the garden's antenna. Narcissus does well to heed its reflection rather than his own. Hedges, as shown here on the south shore of the lake, are of paramount importance throughout the garden. They are used to articulate betweenness: 'every separation is a link'. Like so much else at Plaz Metaxu, they are cared for by Cyril Harris, who has been the indispensable gardener here since 1992

ABOVE: A 'ready-made' (upside down snatch block) in the Rudiweg

ABOVE: 'Garden Logo' slate with 'Vishnu Asleep on the Serpent Ananta between the Creation of Universes' (Plan Q). Gardens are open to all kinds of visions. The alder woods were planted in 1993, with tens of thousands of bulbs added since then

The main garden, in the centre of the valley, is grouped around the axis of the stream, known as the *Lyric Motive*. This axial momentum is, by turn, aspirational and entropic, describing the trajectory of the rise and fall of the *puer aeternus,* giving way, as suggested, to the counterpoint vantages of Psyche, who is represented at the side of the lake in the form of a *Notsegel* (derived from the poet Paul Celan) or 'Alarm Sail'. The complex interconnections between the open and planted areas around the lake cannot be elaborated here, but serial development is generally less important, as a means of spatial organisation, than the use of echoing patterns, reciprocal gestures or surprise adjacencies. The *Lyric Motive* cuts through the garden, but it forms no more than one of several possible itineraries.

From the main garden, at key junctions, one can look out to the surrounding fields, which together form the third level of the *Pastoral Loop*. A high landscaped walk through these fields, which are grazed by sheep, gives views down over the garden on both sides of the valley, and out to the surrounding countryside. This Olympian vantage is integral to the overall conception of the garden, both balancing the intensity of the garden's many enclosed areas and providing fresh perspective on the valley as the garden's containing vessel.

The figure of the vessel is important at all three levels of the garden, whether that of its valley framework, its inner 'retort', or its central cradle around the lake. Vessels provide asylum yet, optimally, remain vulnerable to many different kinds of exposure, which is what may turn gardens from being defensive refuges into vessels of transformation, and from places of consolation into active offerings – but offerings to what, or to whom?

I would say, to the remembrance of space; but also perhaps to the figure of the 'paredros', who appears in the inscription *Ut Paredros Poesis* on the garden's leave-taking stone. Who, then, is this numinous companion for whom the 'poetic' experiment of the garden is made? Is the paredros not the mysterious figure who makes a garden's spaces responsible to distress, to meaning and to beauty and gives them their distinctive voice – also, when the signs are propitious, making that voice heard in the heart of the visitor?

Hilborough House

Thetford, Norfolk

Mrs Hugh van Cutsem

WHEN MY HUSBAND Hugh acquired the Hilborough estate in 1985 it was purely for sporting purposes. We had no intention then to live here. Ten years down the line, however, it became clear that we and our four sons much preferred being at Hilborough to being at our previous home on a stud farm at Newmarket. So we decided to build a house here, and it seemed sensible to create a garden at the same time.

OPPOSITE: The flint and brick Norfolk house, the work of the architect Francis Johnson, is set in a garden designed by Arne Maynard

Despite having a virgin site, creating the house and garden was not going to be easy, so we looked for someone to help us and chose Francis Johnson to design the house and Arne Maynard to design the garden. The project took us the three years up to 1999 to complete.

Arne came into our lives purely by chance. My father had a consignment of trees delivered to him from Holland and the lorry carrying them also contained some for Arne, who was described to us as 'an amazing garden designer'. He wasn't then the famous designer he is now, but the description was so enthusiastic that I got in touch with him.

The design of the flint-and-brick house had the balanced formality characteristic of the Anglo-Dutch style redolent of the reign of William and Mary, and we wanted a garden in a similar style. That is, one which was formal and structured, with the 'good bones' of evergreen hedges and topiarised shapes, which would look good throughout the year. But I also love flowers, so we asked for the planting in the main beds within that formal structure to be relatively loose and lush. It was a total pleasure to work on the details of the design with Arne. He always listened to what we wanted and was always open to suggestions. I'm afraid we didn't abide by Hugh's instruction that this had to be a 'one gardener' garden and in fact we now have two, both of them full time! I should add that Derek Smith, our current head gardener, is the most dedicated, knowledgeable and organised perfectionist, and that the garden as it looks today is a great tribute to his skill and devoted hard work.

The garden covers approximately five acres, our soil is a light sandy Norfolk loam, and since this is a hilltop site we are subject to frequent severe winds, another good practical

reason for making the garden one of hedged compartments. The front of the house faces directly north, the back directly south, and there are major areas of the garden on both sides, the larger being on the south that is flanked by east and west gardens.

Beyond a broad terrace along the front of the house and an entrance court, the north garden descends in a series of 'steps' to a sunken box parterre, which is centred on a three-tiered fountain surrounded by *Verbena bonariensis* and *Stipa tenuissima*, with the inner pattern filled with lavender and santolina. At the level of the house and terrace, the three sides are hedged with double rows of pleached beech, which were installed as quite large specimens, already semi-trained. The next 'step' down has yew hedges on all three sides and at the lowest level, the level of the parterre, are densely planted hollies, their tops cut flat so that they create a 'table-like' effect from which rise ornamental vases. This composition has subsequently become something of an Arne 'trademark'.

At least, that is how the garden *used* to look – and how, we hope, it will eventually look again. Because a few years ago we found we had two serious problems. No garden is without problems, of course, and since I confess I always like to hear about other people's I won't try to hide ours!

The first problem we discovered was that yew roots were reaching down the slope and strangling the hollies, which as a result died back further each year. In the end we decided that the only thing to do was to remove all the hollies and prune back the yew roots, a huge task that had to be carried out by special machines. We then installed sunken edge-on concrete pavers next to the remaining roots, so that they will not be able to grow down the slope again. New hollies have been planted but it will be several more years before they again produce that solid, flat, 'tabletop' look.

The second problem also involved invading roots, this time those of the miniature box hedges in the parterre, which have been stealthily sucking the life out of the lavender and santolina. Apparently the box roots should have been cut back each year. By the time I learned about this, when Derek Smith arrived, it was too late to save them. So they are all being removed to enable us to deal with the roots, as we did the yew. Then new lavender and santolina will be planted.

We almost had a more serious problem in the south garden, but not this time to do with the plants. We had approved Arne's final

LEFT: The feather grass *Stipa tenuissima* catches light and wind in tandem with the water flowing in the tiered fountain

design that looked wonderful on paper: a broad paved terrace along the width of the house leading on to a lawn that stretched away to a circular pool with a central fountain as a distant focal point. The pool is framed by a central upward-slanting golden yew topiary in the shape of a *fleur-de-lys*, positioned so that the pattern can be read from both the house and the terrace. A scrollwork pattern in box stretched to the edge of this garden on either side of the *fleur-de-lys* with the lawn framed by two rows of six standard *Quercus ilex*.

Just before the diggers moved in to begin the construction work a friend advised us to measure out the design on the ground. We all then realised that the scale was too small in relation to the house, so it was back to the drawing board and the design was expanded by at least another fifty per cent. At this point Hugh became so anxious about how much was being added so he gave instructions for a ha-ha to be put in to stop any further extensions! I think the proportions as they are today are near perfect, so all was well in the end.

Incidentally a word of advice here: make absolutely certain that your contract with builders contains a clause specifying that no rubble or concrete can be dumped where you will want to make your garden. So often the last thing builders do at the end of a big job is bring in soil to hide everything they want to leave behind – something the gardener only discovers a few years down the line, when plants either die or fail to perform as they should.

On both sides of this garden to the south of the house, between the flanking holm oaks

and the outer yew hedges (whose tops are 'scalloped' at regular intervals, with each 'scallop' featuring a standard beech, clipped alternately either to the same shape as the holm oaks or into a cone) are areas which provide good examples of what I meant by saying that I wanted the formal structure of the garden to be softened by more relaxed and colourful planting. These two outer gardens, which have mirror planting of eight lavender-edged beds, contain hundreds of old roses, the shrub roses grown on hazel tripods and dozens of that endlessly flowering favourite 'Madame Alfred Carrière' grown over all the arches which span the central paths. The colours of the roses and herbaceous underplanting, which includes salvias, alliums, geraniums, irises, Japanese anemones and asters, are deliberately soft and subdued because those are the sorts of colours I prefer. There is nothing hard or strident; the predominant colours are purple and pink, with relieving dashes of white.

Beyond the rose gardens there is more mirroring, but now the mirroring becomes less exact and, gradually, the formality less rigorous. To the west there is an informally arranged 'pip' orchard, devoted to pears and apples, with a central copper beech maze. To the east is the 'stone' orchard of plums, cherries, gages and a few pip quinces because we couldn't resist them. This orchard has a copper beech labyrinth rather than a maze.

The mirroring finally breaks down completely as you move from the 'stone' orchard through a yew hedge towards the house, since here you find two long and relatively narrow

ABOVE AND PAGES 58–9: Scrolls of box, clipped domes of *Quercus ilex* and obelisks of copper beech *Fagus sylvatica* 'Purpurea' looking through to the lavender-edged rose and salvia beds arched by rose 'Madame Alfred Carrière'

ABOVE AND BELOW: Urns that emerge from platforms of neatly-clipped beech are seen through narrow arches of yew and are framed by wider arches covered in free-flowering rose 'Madame Alfred Carrière'

RIGHT: Old-fashioned roses such as 'Isaphan' and 'Tuscany Superb' are supported by wigwams of hazel and planted with *Salvia nemorosa* 'Amethyst' and Geranium 'Ivan'

hedged areas running out from the side of the house, which have no echoing equivalent on the western side of the garden (yet!). We call one 'the putting green' though its main feature is a vardo, a beautiful Romany painted wagon that the grandchildren use as a playhouse. The other has a double herbaceous border designed to extend the flowering season by being at its best in *late* summer and even into early autumn, with just the sort of relaxed and colourful planting I enjoy within a firm hedged structure. The colours here are also soft, with more salvias but also acanthus, achillea, astrantia, astilbe, eupatorium, thalictrum and veronicastrum, monardas, miscanthus, hemerocallis and pink-flowered *Sanguisorba canadensis*. The tall purple-flowered aster-relative *Vernonia arkansana* (syn. *V. crinita*) is a lovely injection of bright purple right at the end of the season and the good, long-flowering blue geranium, G. 'Brookside', runs all along the front edge on both sides.

Firm though the structure is in this garden there is still room for change and experiment. In a small rectangular courtyard we have beds around the central oval that used to contain a mixed bag of shrubs. They never really thrived so recently I decided to try something completely different. Out went the old and in came what I proudly call my (very miniature!) white garden. There are star jasmines on the wall, and the new ingredients include philadelphus, *Weigela* 'Candida,' *Hydrangea* 'Annabelle,' *H. paniculata* 'Kyushu' and *Osmanthus* x *burkwoodii*. Herbaceous plants such as white forms of phlox, aster, dicentra, dictamnus, sidalcea, *Campanula persicifolia*, foxgloves and lupins congregate amongst them, together with the white-flowered form of *Geranium macrorrhizum* called 'White Ness' and a fine white-flowered toad lily, *Tricyrtis* 'White Towers'. It is still too early to say how successful this is going to be – but it has been something fun to try.

We are also having more fun with previously ungardened areas both to the west of the main garden and off to the side of the drive. To the side of the drive, around a cleared and extended pond, there is now a completely informal collection of trees from some of our favourite genera that so far includes cherries, birches, oaks, limes, maples, a sequoia and a gingko. The only element of formality here, if it can be called that, is a new curving walk around the far side of the pond, which is flanked by infant hazels, eventually to be trained into arches.

There is just as little formality to be found, at least at the moment, in the tentative developments to the west, beyond the pip orchard and beech maze, where we have planted trios of *Pyrus salicifolia* 'Pendula' among ox-eye daisies and cornflowers in a young wildflower meadow. A more ambitious plan, still very much only in its formative stage, is to make double herbaceous borders here or perhaps a long canal: no garden can have too much water! The house and shadows from surrounding trees would reflect beautifully on it. It sounds very tempting – but who knows if or when it will happen? I certainly don't. But what I do know is that the garden, both as it was originally planned and as it has since developed, has given all of us such enormous pleasure. And despite Hugh's death in September 2013 I also know that it will continue to be developed and looked after by the next generation.

OPPOSITE: The gilded finials of the copper beech obelisks complement the Anglo-Dutch style of the house redolent of the reign of William and Mary

Bury Court

BENTLEY, HAMPSHIRE

John Coke Esq

OST PEOPLE WHO are starting a new garden from scratch will, I would imagine, have a notion of what they want, and how they will end up with something approximating to their original concept. The garden here at Bury Court was an altogether more serendipitous process . . .

When we took on Bury Court in 1994, our primary aim was to create a display garden for the plants we then grew in our nursery, Green Farm Plants. The old farmyard, enclosed on three sides by house, barn and outbuildings, presented an apparently ideal site. The idea was to cut a series of long rectangular beds out of the concrete, into which we would line out one each of all the plants we sold to create a demonstration area for our customers. But fate had a different plan for us. By one of those happy coincidences, Piet Oudolf was staying with us on one of his visits to England just as the heavy machinery was moving in. 'What do you intend to do here?' he asked, and when I explained, he said 'Why don't I do you a drawing?'

It must be understood that, in those days, Piet was not recognised as a garden designer, having hitherto only completed a few private gardens in Holland, and was unknown in this country outside the small world of specialist nurserymen. We had met several years earlier and I had been immediately drawn to him, both as a person and for his totally committed and individual approach to a deeply appealing new style of gardening with a most original palette of plants. But the thought of asking him to design the new garden had not entered my head, and his suggestion caught me off guard. The initial sketch was duly produced – and was not what I had in mind at all. Firstly, because it was an 'artistic' concept poles apart from my essentially pragmatic idea, and secondly because it would be planted up with the typical range of plants that Piet then favoured, rather than what would politely be called the 'eclectic' range that filled our catalogue – anything from miffy alpines through tender pelargoniums to shrubs, trees, and botanical curiosities.

OPPOSITE: The façade of Bury Court overlooking the garden designed by Christopher Bradley-Hole in 1999. A mixture of ornamental grasses and perennials in beds with corten steel edging are laid out in a grid. *Calamagrostis* x *acutiflora* 'Karl Foerster', in the foreground with *Molina* 'Skyracer' on the right. *Miscanthus yakushimanum* and *M. gracillimus* with *Sanguisorba canadensis* behind

But Piet's range of plants had profound appeal. I was still flushed with the memory of my first visit to Piet's own garden in Hummelo, where his use of a whole range of unusual perennials, often very tall, rather wild-looking, and of course the profusion of grasses, created a mysterious beauty and a tangible atmosphere that I had never experienced in a garden before, and to which I was most attracted. A speedy decision had to be made. Piet has never been one for compromise: the design and planting were not up for negotiation — it was a 'take it or leave it' moment. Of course, it was not a difficult decision to go for the more adventurous option, but I little realised at the time that, as Piet Oudolf's first garden in this country, it would quickly start to attract visitors, not just from England but from all over the world as his career took off and his fame spread.

This style of planting, originally called 'The Dutch Wave' and subsequently 'The New Perennial Movement', has, over the last fifteen years, become something of a cliché, as so many designers and gardeners have adopted, or adapted, the style and palette — so much so that it is now hard to remember how exhilaratingly different and inspiring it once was — and Piet was its driving force. He believes strongly in our subconscious desire to connect with nature, and uses natural-looking perennials: plants which we might expect to see in meadows and woodland fringes, and which might have been dismissed as 'weeds' by the traditional English gardener, in particular, members of the umbellifer family, so reminiscent of the ubiquitous hedgerow 'cow parsley'. These perennials were not intermingled with woody plants as in the mixed border, partly because in nature this would not happen (these all being plants of the open meadow), but also, more practically, because woody plants would steal essential moisture and nutrients from the perennials. And then, of course, there are the grasses, in much greater variety and number than were hitherto used in gardens. Grasses are the most basic constituent of any open natural landscape, and bringing them into a garden situation enhances this connection with nature. But, just as important, they bring a rhythm and elegant movement and have an exceedingly long season of interest, remaining beautiful as senescent foliage and dry tawny stems until well into winter. Clumps also act as restful visual buffers between groups of other more showy flowering perennials.

Until well into the 1980s colour was the overriding factor in plant choice and border design. Piet, on the other hand, preferred to use plants which looked good throughout the growing season, and which remained statuesque and striking into winter; he also preferred form to colour, and carefully juxtaposed flowering heads of different shape. Thus the round-ball shape of echinops next to the pointed spike of veronicastrum next to the flat 'plates' of achillea next to the frothy haze of thalictrum. Seed heads also should play their part. Above all, the 'look' of every plant had to contribute to the overall aesthetic effect, and the collectors' plants and those of botanic interest only still favoured by the nursery were banished to the narrow wall borders around the garden perimeter.

All these plants and ideas were represented in the seven borders that comprise the courtyard garden at Bury Court, and each border has its own character. These range from the oval 'meadow' at the centre of the garden, planted with a single grass through which other bulbs and perennials emerge, to the Long Border running the length of the garden from north to south, which has a rich mix of classic Oudolf perennials. The oval meadow was originally planted with the beautiful *Deschampsia* 'Gold Dew' — at its best the most striking

ABOVE: The yew spiral
and large barn seen
beyond spires of indigo
Aconitum carmichaelii
'Arendsii' and *P.*
amplexicaule 'Firedance'

of all the shorter grasses when its massed tiny flower heads create a hazy golden cloud – but sadly whole areas died out each winter. Reluctantly this grass was replaced with the much stronger, if somewhat less picturesque, *Molinia* 'Paul Petersen'. Interest is added to this border from early spring until later summer with drifts of bulbs, including the tiny, scarlet-flowered *Tulipa linifolia*, the unusual greeny-yellow *Allium obliquum*, and *A. sphaerocephalon*, whose egg-shaped flower heads pierce the molinia, now (simultaneously) in full, hazy flower. I have been asked more than once by puzzled visitors why I have wasted the central area of the whole garden growing a few 'weeds'. To me it is most pleasing, a restful foil for other, busier parts of the garden, and always changing in subtle ways.

The Long Border contains many of the plants that Piet drew attention to in his first book, *Dream Plants*, some of which had been used in gardens since the 1950s but which Piet made new selections of to favour smaller flowers or more aesthetic colours, for example monarda, phlox, aster and helenium. Sparsely dotted here and there are the annuals or biennials that create a different look each year, the white-flowered *Verbascum lychnitis*, *Digitalis ferruginea* and the amazing umbellifer *Peucedanum verticillare*, striking from the moment its bronzy-purple foliage erupts out of the ground in spring till its statuesque two-metre-high skeleton becomes a feature of the winter garden. A quite new and telling feature of Piet's designs was the addition of wild species that would not hitherto have been considered garden-worthy, but which make a profound contribution to this subconscious connection with nature that we strive to achieve – plants like *Persicaria* x *fennica* 'Johanniswolke', *Artemisia lactiflora*, cirsium, sanguisorba and especially several umbellifers including *Angelica gigas* and *Selinum wallichianum*.

The use of very tall plants – eupatorium, veronicastrum, silphium and vernonia – sometimes at the front of the border, is another Oudolf trademark, splendidly effective but rigorous staking becomes essential. I well remember in the first year after planting: a combination of

fresh agricultural soil brought in from the neighbouring fields and over-zealous feeding by the owner produced staggering growth, magnificent until a summer storm flattened the lot. Wind – the gardener's worst enemy. Another memory, another time, is watching, helpless, as a momentary particularly strong gust brought down our three catalpas one after the other – the only trees in the garden and key elements of the design that had just begun to attain a decent size. Only afterwards did I read 'Not suitable for a windy site'!

Of course, gardens change over time. All the borders here have been replanted at least once, and some twice, and while I have tried to keep within the Oudolfian spirit, there have inevitably been changes, both to the design and to the planting. Some of the original plants simply did not thrive here – over-efficient drainage and constant winds make it a very dry garden, not conducive to growing good monardas or phlox, amongst others – although it has been noticeable how much stronger and long-lived than other colour forms are the scarlet monardas, especially the new *M.* 'Jacob Cline'. Achilleas, from a design point of view an important genus for their characteristic plate-shaped flat-flower cluster, proved almost invariably to be short-lived, and heleniums have not persisted.

More important than minor changes in the plant palette, however, have been design changes. The original design was very strong and not easily adaptable, and it is always a dilemma to know what right the garden owner has to change the design of someone with as classy a reputation as Piet Oudolf. However, the function of the garden changed radically ten years ago when the nursery closed, and the large barn forming one side of the garden was converted for use as a venue for large events. It was necessary to change the entire northern end of the garden – and, while Piet was hesitant for the balance of the garden to be so altered, he was won over to the necessity. Several borders, and a pond, have been replaced by a large terrace. I suspect that one increasingly craves simplicity with age; and, just as Piet has done with his own garden, I can imagine taking out the central lawn and dissolving the individual borders to create a meadow-like feeling throughout, retaining the original paths to lead the visitor through.

There was really no garden to speak of here when we arrived, and the area in front of and to the west of the house was a hideous *mélange* of grossly overgrown Victorian shrubbery, shapeless lawn, and even more shapeless tarmac drive. Surprisingly, I had been under the impression that a little minor tweaking here and there might be all that was needed to turn this into a semblance of paradise. I was corrected in this view by Christopher Bradley-Hole, to whom, on a visit to the nursery, I had shown this place, in the hope no doubt of a few (possibly free) tips on improvement. After a long and pregnant silence, it was pronounced that, in truth, the only possible answer was to hire in a very large excavator and start the entire thing again from scratch. Having spent all (and a bit more) of my gardening purse on the Oudolf garden I dismissed the project as unthinkable, but somehow (not least by finding a miraculous local jack of all trades who constructed the garden single-handedly for about half the lowest professional estimate) the garden was duly created in 2005.

I held Christopher in the highest regard, both for his several Chelsea gardens (which I thought exhibited an intensely singular and profoundly considered approach, with a meticulous eye for detail) and his minimalist aesthetic – the exclusion of all extraneous detail, and the reduction of the design to its essentials, for which he has become known.

The garden was to have an apparently simple grid pattern of paths cut through the space to create twenty-four metre-square beds, but which should read as one space divided by the

BELOW: A green oak timber summer house sits at the centre of the garden designed by Christopher Bradley-Hole. *Helianthus salicifolius* is left unstaked so that its characterful habit is given free rein

paths, rather than as twenty separate beds, and this effect would be greatly heightened by the planting, which would flow in multiple drifts from bed to bed. This sort of arrangement could have become tedious or predictable in lesser hands; but by using an asymmetric design, by incorporating subtle layers, or strata, in the landscaping, to echo the natural earth profile, with water, coarse stone, fine gravel and soil, and with Christopher's architect's sure eye for scale, the result is a deeply satisfying, atmospheric space, which sits beside and sets off the house in a most perfect way. It is also a private space – in a way that the inner courtyard garden could never be – and the green oak tea house that was constructed at a later date in the centre of the garden, beside the simple black square pond, is a contemplative and happy place to be.

A major difference between the creation of this garden and the earlier Oudolf garden is that by 2005 I had absorbed very much more both about gardening and about garden design, and so went into this project with a much clearer idea of the outcome I hoped for. We had made a number of visits to wild meadows and grasslands, in America, Armenia and Transylvania, in some cases untainted by agricultural practices and thus as created by nature, and it was striking and sometimes very moving how much better nature could create a garden than man. Clearly one could never copy, or replicate, nature, but I had wanted with this garden to evoke the idea, or spirit, of these wild places, perhaps in a dreamlike way. Thus, we used many grasses of all heights, some up to three metres or more, amongst which would be dotted carefully chosen flowering perennials, selected not just because they had the right 'look', but also to be as low maintainance as possible, and to be sufficiently robust to hold their own against strong-growing neighbours. Some also were very tall to add to the dreamlike effect – they might, for example, resemble the wild flowers to be be found in any hedgerow, but here in strange or different forms, or indeed be something altogether more mysterious on closer inspection. For example, the common red poppy of the cornfield is echoed in the garden, but here in a much larger form, with drifts of the glowing pure red oriental poppy 'Leuchtfeuer'. Or representatives of the genus *Sanguisorba*, such marvellous plants in their robustness, draught tolerance and ability to associate well with other plants and grasses – but here, in uncommon very late flowering forms, both red and white, collected in South Korea. There is also the beautiful but seldom seen pure white form of the common field scabious. In all, probably not more than eighty different species are used (and not a single woody plant), but all in multiple groups spanning several or many squares; and colour, apart from white, is restricted to the red spectrum, which covers anything from rusts and wine-red to scarlet. The garden is never particularly colourful, but there is always something to draw the eye, and the predominance of grasses means not just movement but also a long season of interest with buff, tan and ochre tints throughout autumn.

I have been remarkably fortunate to have had the opportunity to create not just one but two gardens, both starting with a blank canvas, and with two pre-eminent designers. There remains one undeveloped area, an outer farmyard, which might one day contain a third garden that would link the earlier two. Meanwhile my imagination leaps ahead to our next dwelling, which I dream will sit by a lake, backed by a wood, carpeted with bluebells, with no cultivated garden at all, with the wilderness allowed to come right up to the back door. Nature can, after all, do it so much better!

ABOVE: The yellowing autumn leaves of *Sanguisorba officinalis* 'Arnhem', are foil to the brown stems and seed heads that will remain all winter

BELOW: The towering and irregular inflorescences of *Sanguisorba tenuifolia* var. *alba* 'Korean Snow'

OVERLEAF: The formation of the beds filled with a tapestry of perennials and ornamental grasses seen from above with the green oak pavilion and rectangular pond whose footprint echoes that of the grid

Historic House
Renaissance Garden

Ven House

MILBORNE PORT, SOMERSET

Jasper Conran OBE

WHEN VEN CAME up for sale in 2007 it was a jewel that I couldn't let slip out of my hands. I have a passion for houses that are rare survivals with much of their original form intact, and Ven is a ravishing example of just such a house, and garden.

On the Dorset border of Somerset, Ven is in a part of England that I have found myself gravitationally pulled to since schooldays. The garden was not in a desperate state but in need of softening and cajoling back to life. In the entrance courtyard towering domes of yew, very likely as old as the house, frame the north façade with groups of later magnificent cedars, while on the south side the walled sunken parterre has strong echoes of the eighteenth-century landscape architect Richard Grange's layout for the garden. A long elegant orangery links the house to an exquisite tall conservatory, both elements of the additions Decimus Burton undertook in 1836 that are notably sympathetic to the architecture; no messing around with the façades other than a big new front door. There are large walled gardens to the east surrounded by tall walls of beautiful mellow brick. Water enlivens the garden. The River Yeo, cleverly diverted under the terrace to cool the adjacent cellars and stores in summer, creates canals, rills and runs around islands and under bridges, and there are stands of mature trees in the arboretum. All in all thirty-five acres of utterly irresistible house and garden.

Three hundred years before me, Ven proved equally tempting for the politically ambitious James Medlicott who, shall we say, 'purchased' what was then the rotten borough of Milborne Port. The Georgian house you see today was started during the reign of William and Mary but aggrandised forty years later and turned to face south by Nathaniel Ireson, the Somerset architect commissioned by Medlicott. Contemporary accounts show Ireson and Grange used half a million bricks in their transformation of the house and garden, bricks that appear to have been made from clay dug on site from the re-routing of the river and

THIS PAGE AND PREVIOUS PAGE: The sunken walled parterre has strong echoes of Richard Grange's eighteenth-century layout for the garden

myriad watercourses they created. It is an exceedingly pretty pale brick now and beautifully partnered by the local honey-coloured Ham stone that was used for all the architectural decoration and considerable lengths of balustrading. I have been busily training wisteria as camouflage around balustrading that was not repaired with Ham stone before I came to Ven.

The house and garden are very well documented. James Medlicott kept tabs on every penny spent in the garden: on the stairways and gate piers, balustrades and pedestals, vases and urns, many of which remain. The house stayed in the Medlicott family until the 1950s when it was used as a school (I have a soft spot for old houses that have been used as schools). Ven then went through various hands and in the 1990s it was Thomas Kyle who did a lot of replanting and restoration work in the garden. It was also he who handed Decimus Burton's Ven portfolio of working drawings down to me. These are a fascinating record showing the progression of Burton's thinking about where everything should go, from the stables to the turnip store.

I feel a sense of indebtedness to honour the spirit of this extraordinary place that has been touched by the past, so I tread carefully and aim to be sensitive to the uniqueness of Ven; but I am not a slave to historical accuracy in the garden. I'd need a team of twenty gardeners. Grange's original plan had formal gardens all around the house. My aim is to make it into a gentler, more romantic place than the one it had become. I like places with a slow momentum, so an orchard swiftly replaced a tennis court after I arrived. This is Somerset,

not Wimbledon. One of my happiest autumn rituals is to take boxes of apples to Patricia Thompson in Henstridge where she presses them into a year's supply of juice that tastes of apples just plucked from the tree.

To be honest I didn't think I'd end up with a grand country garden. My ideal garden is a cottage garden where you are engulfed in a riot of planting, or the heavenly garden nearby of my stepmother Caroline Conran, but a house like Ven demands a certain type of garden and my intention is to create a setting that suits both the house and our times. What could be prettier than pale-pink roses tumbling over a crumbling eighteenth-century brick wall and wide borders of luscious perennials? I like to soften the edges of rigid formality but where necessary to also give the planting an edge.

The garden at Ven is blessed with incredible structure. The south terrace is typical of the great thought that went into harmoniously matching proportions and the flow of space. It is the perfect width. And from early summer to the first nip of frost it is decked out by my collection of citrus trees. These treasures are treated with monthly doses of biological control akin to racehorse vet's fees and have their leaves regularly buffed and polished to remove sooty mould and aphids, but then they produce oranges sweeter than any I have ever tasted. In Somerset! As temperatures dip they go back to be overwintered in the orangery whose back wall has alcoves festooned with tender jasmine that when in blossom wafts scent

ABOVE: Decimus Burton's elegant orangery links the house to the double cube conservatory

through the entire house, almost to the attic.

The orangery leads into a conservatory that has an extraordinary quality of light in its tall double cube of glass, filled now with towering tree ferns and gargantuan sparmannias in pots. I line the west steps leading up to the back of the conservatory with more pots of ferns and ox-eye daisies: simple but exquisite, they glow like candles on midsummer nights.

The south terrace overlooks the parterre garden from a lofty height, but you descend the three metres or so effortlessly as the steps widen out on a generous curve. All the original steps at Ven are impeccably designed. In the fountain at the centre of the south parterre garden Neptune endures a continuous watery bombardment, but I am getting concerned that the splash might be affecting the box as, like so many other gardens at the moment, Ven is plagued by box blight. I almost have to cover my eyes walking through the devastation rampaging through the box hedges in the west rose garden so that may be in need of a dramatic overhaul quite soon. Fortunately most of the topiary in the south parterre is clipped yew and this year I am going to alter the heights of the yew columns. That is one of the things I most love about gardening: the constant looking, editing and reappraising.

The south parterre leads to a pleached lime walk and a new lime avenue planted at the correct width for future generations. The new avenue nods in homage to the elm avenue that once stretched for over a mile from the north entrance. I can't begin to imagine what the devastation of watching it succumb to Dutch elm disease must have been like in the 1970s. It's torture when just one of the old beech trees in the arboretum keels over, which seems to happen every year so I am busy replanting there too.

OPPOSITE: Citrus trees in pots overwinter in the conservatory where tree ferns, *Dicksonia antarctica*, tower over *Polystichum munitum*

Grange planned the arboretum as a formal eighteenth-century 'wilderness', and although the river still courses through it over weirs and under bridges it is no longer in the form of rectangular canals as he planned. This is a favourite place for my dogs, who stay here when I am away, and they hurry me to the arboretum the moment I arrive at Ven. I never cease to be astonished by the way life never stands still in the countryside; the seasons just never fail to surprise and you can't turn your back without plants seeding and growing. The boundary of the arboretum has suddenly become awash with ash saplings that need thinning out in patches, but not the brambles. They act as a windbreak and create hidden paths that I can pick fruit from as I walk the dogs; so long as it doesn't look messy there is nothing wrong with a bramble. The wilderness is also a sea of bulbs in spring.

There is a particularly fine pair of hop hornbeam, *Ostrya carpinifolia*, in the arboretum and an exceptionally old robinia whose winter silhouette traces out the shape of a mass of lightning forks. A majestic Wellingtonia rockets up to the sky with bark the colour of a fresh conker and the texture of a loofah. But possibly my favourite tree at Ven is the ancient walnut at the foot of the east steps, a wondrous character that does for the south side of the house what the cedars do on the north, creating that essential partnership between architecture and nature.

The walled gardens — yes plural, as joy of joys there are two of them — are havens. One is devoted to flowers for cutting and vegetables with wide and voluptuous mixed borders next to the walls that seem to blossom overnight into intricate arches of colour and stunning pattern. From one week to the next in summer this garden throws up a cornucopia of surprises; delphiniums go from bud to a rocketing explosion of breathtaking blues while I

blink. I like to fill the house with armfuls of peonies, roses, delphiniums, phlox and cosmos so there are large blocks of each for me to plunder. There are also row upon row of dahlias which I adore in every colour under the sun, except yellow. Yellow flowers are not my thing. The dahlias starting to bloom is as exciting for me as a Christmas tree is for a child, and I pick them by the barrow load to decorate the house. They, and the vegetables, are enclosed within a framework of waist-high clipped hedges so the swimming pool sits in a garden, not an allotment. The summerhouse that overlooks the pool was built with creamy grey stone that was once part of the great house at Bowood, demolished in the 1950s. There is a wonderful mulberry tree, a bowed and arching veteran that needs propping but survives despite a hollow core and leaning gait. It drops the messiest but most delicious fruit, an essential ingredient for cocktails and granitas.

The second walled garden is home to the orchard and an assortment of geese, ducks and Rhode Island Red chickens. I can't imagine having a garden without poultry and we live off the eggs. This is also where all the work goes on with compost heaps, potting sheds and greenhouses. I have got strawberry-growing down to a fine art in pots in the greenhouse, and defy anyone to find an early strawberry tastier than those from Ven. But they are now vying for space with my constantly increasing pelargonium collection, one of my favourite pot plants for the house, especially in winter. Fruit trees are trained against the walls; last summer's peaches, quite likely a once-a-decade treat, and the trugfuls of figs were spectacular. More reliable is the medlar I planted the year I arrived, delicious even when its bletted fruit starts to turn.

I feel that the garden at Ven, as much as the house, has been touched by the past and when I am in it I am acutely aware of, and so grateful for, the incredible patina of age that has built up within it. It feels as though the walls have some stored memory from the centuries of having fruit trees fan-pruned, tied and tended against them. There is a tremendous sense of continuity, a desire to keep it true to the spirit and times in which it was created but to make it sing with the present. The debt of honour and responsibility I feel to Ven is a joy rather than a burden.

OPPOSITE TOP: In the large walled gardens surrounded by tall walls of beautiful mellow brick, rows of delphiniums and peonies are followed by barrowloads of dahlias (opposite below)

OVERLEAF: The south-facing front of Ven and the voluminous black walnut with a traditional English border of catmint and cranesbills, oriental poppies, lupins and roses such as the pale pink climber 'Madame Caroline Testout'

Petworth House

Petworth, West Sussex

Caroline Egremont

WHAT IS THE point of gardening? Some see it as the most gigantic waste of time. Why not just mow a bit of lawn, plant a few trees and shrubs and forget about it? You would then have much more time to get on with other things. My husband, a writer, may secretly think this. His books will last and might be read in 100 years' time, whereas my gardening efforts of the past thirty-five years will be forgotten the moment my back is turned and I am no longer here.

In spite of this undeniable fact gardening is what I love more than anything. I never set out into my garden without a sense of excitement and anticipation. It may be on a lovely March morning with a tray of oxlip plugs to set into the long grass or to see if the *Cyclamen coum* planted last year have come up under the lime trees; or in early summer to encourage the new sweet woodruff plantings to hurry up and complete their circles under the crabapples. I want to be out of doors, and I like being out in all weather.

I grew up on the west coast of Scotland. Nobody in our family thought it was right to be indoors during daylight, particularly my father, the dominating force who believed that not only should we children be outside but also doing useful work. My brother, sister and I spent much of our time, under his direction, cutting down bracken and rhododendrons and making bonfires. The only escape was to pretend to want to go fishing. So I did a lot of fishing. My first efforts at digging were to look for worms in the windswept walled garden. After some experimental excavation I knew where to find them, usually under a heap of rotting seaweed piled in a corner for use as a mulch. These worms went into a rusty oatcake tin to be skewered later on a hook and dangled in the burn in the hope of luring a large brown trout.

To be alone in a garden as child with long idle hours ahead gave me a love of wild places. One absorbs with an intensity, never later recaptured, the colour of flowers seen at eye level, the smell of the earth, the cry of seabirds. The memory of enchantment at suddenly finding,

OPPOSITE: A glimpse of the South Downs in the distance through a window cut in an existing box and yew hedge is seen through a veil of cherry blossom from a mature *Prunus avium* 'Plena'

in a sunlit corner, a crowd of bright, spice-scented lupins as tall as myself has stayed with me always (particularly as I am sure I spoke to them).

I wanted to recreate something of these childhood memories in my gardening efforts at Petworth. When I came to live here in 1978 I knew very little about how to garden. I knew the names of a few rhododendrons and I knew that I did not want to plant any of those. My father spent thirty years growing them in Argyll. As he got older he thought they did not fit well into the soft landscape of the west coast. He found them gloomy, the leaves too heavy and the flowers too blowsy. So he spent the second half of his life digging them up. He concluded that native birch, oak woods carpeted with moss, bluebells and ferns looked best in that gentle, grey landscape, and I agreed. However, he did allow large plantings of deciduous azaleas *Rhododendron luteum*. These, he decided, sit happily among bluebells and are worth growing for one of the most delicious scents in the world.

I call my father's approach 'ungardening' and my guiding principle harks back to this. It is a question of what to impose on the landscape and what to leave out. A sense of place can easily be lost. How easy to strike a wrong note and to plant shrubs and trees, however beautiful in themselves, that do not fit with their surroundings. I am not a plantsman keen to plant anything and everything in every variety. I don't find such plantings harmonious. Mixed shrubs from China, New Zealand and Japan seem awkward in each other's company as if at an ill-conceived drinks party. I believe that what you don't plant is more important than what you do. I like the balance between calm and busy, open spaces among drifts of bold groupings of one species; or a single plant given room to display its particular beauty. You need space for this, but I would apply the same principle in a small garden. I accept that I am in a minority, and those who do not agree might find my garden a bit empty and lacking in 'interest'.

Equipped with these vague ideas I wanted to make something of the garden at Petworth that our young children would love, and that might give them their own 'lupin moment'. We live in the south end of the house, the rest of which is open to the public. The private garden close to the house had not changed since 1870 when Anthony Salvin worked on this end of Petworth. Wide gravel paths led a long way across a huge lawn, mown every week, which had the feel of a well-kept golf course. Children faltered halfway and there was nowhere to sit down. When you reached the walled garden a different world opened. High brick walls, some dating from the 1720s, enclose three large spaces of six acres. These walls, which once contained twenty glasshouses and employed thirty gardeners, were built to provide vegetables and fruit for the house

In 1978 when I came to Petworth two thirds of the walled garden had been grassed and turned into paddocks. The crumbling Victorian glasshouses, once expertly tended by Fred Streeter (the head gardener who became famous as a BBC radio broadcaster), had been taken down in the 1960s as they were no longer economical to run. A vegetable garden remained together with a couple of greenhouses, an abandoned tennis court and a sunken garden designed by Fred.

I loved these old walls and wanted to spend time inside them. As you go through the arched doorways the air feels different, the wind calms and there is an immediate sense of enclosure. I had no idea other than to plant climbing roses all over them. The ancient wiring

ABOVE: A lead statue under a cascade of white *Wisteria floribunda* 'Alba'

that once had held espaliered pears was still in place, with some of the lead labels attached. I had never ordered a rose and did not know one from another. A catalogue of Murrells Roses was given to me in which there were a few sketches but no photographs. Beguiled by the descriptions and a thought that buff, cream and white roses would look best against the brick, I ordered a dozen, which included 'Paul's Lemon Pillar', 'Reve d'Or', 'Desprez à Fleur Jaune', 'Mermaid, 'Gloire de Dijon', 'Seagull', 'Alister Stella Gray' and 'Maréchal Niel'. The last in this list soon died, but the others are here thirty years later. They like the soil, dug deep for many years by Fred Streeter and his men.

From this uncertain beginning I slowly made a series of garden rooms within these walls, trying to keep a sense of place and scale and to give a different atmosphere to each one. Atmosphere in a garden, that intangible sense, is something one remembers from other gardens and notices if it is not there.

A tennis court, perfectly fitted within the walls and the scene of tennis parties during my husband's childhood, had become pitted with holes. We decided that we had played enough tennis so took it away. In this space I have made a place for reading in a newly named Cloister Garden. A pair of pergolas of *Wisteria floribunda* 'Alba' underplanted with cream camassia form two sides of a square gravel garden planted with iris, lavender, cistus, romneya, yucca and Gallica roses. A spring, redirected from the park, bubbles in a pool in the middle.

John Brookes, the designer and author of many books (and with whom I once studied and worked), gave me this idea. He persuaded me that Mediterranean plants loosely planted thrive in gravel and it is good to walk among these rather than gaze sideways at massed blocks of plants in a traditional herbaceous border. Some, such as *Verbascum bombyciferum*, seed randomly in the gravel and give a jolly air of chance and asymmetry within the framework.

The long walk from the house presented a challenge. How could I make the scale more intimate and more interesting? Laurence Fleming, a writer and garden designer who was staying with us just after we married, came up with the solution. Take out the gravel paths, make huge sweeping curves of longer grass with mown paths cut through, plant thousands of bulbs and reposition three eighteenth-century urns. With Laurence's help and drawings this is what we did. His judgement was perfect. The urns that define the space are in the right place, the balance of long and short grass seems right and children love running through it. I have been lucky to have the space to plant many bulbs from snowdrops and aconites in January through to camassias and *Narcissus poeticus* var. *recurvus* in May. Not to inherit any large yellow daffodils was a blessing. (A friend who does not like their gaudy company has, in despair, taken to blazing them with a blowtorch, with little success.) We planted trees to allow this area to blend with the eighteenth-century park over the wall. Some of these, now sixty feet high, cast enough shade to grow big circles of cyclamen at their base. I look at them now and they make me feel old.

One of many good things about gardening for a long time in one place is that there has been time to make mistakes and undo them. I have tried to take out most of the 'superior' purple Dutch crocus put in with such enthusiasm at the beginning. It is nearly impossible to dig up 1000 naturalised Dutch crocus but this last wet year has been helpful. Not only charmless crocus but brutish docks have come out like well-extracted molars, complete with foot-long root attached.

ABOVE: House plants and staging for seedlings in a greenhouse against the kitchen garden wall

OVERLEAF: Within one of a sequence of walled enclosures rose 'Francis E Lester' is carefully trained so that it does not overpower its host apple trees

ABOVE: Ziggurat-shaped box topiary flanks steps leading down into the Sunk Garden pool, seen below in spring with plum and wine-coloured tulips 'Barcelona' and 'National Velvet'

It is lovely to live close to the South Downs, those ancient rounded hills that come between the Weald and the sea. To make a focal point I cut a round hole in a boundary hedge and discovered that I had opened a clear window on to the downs. In the foreground figures in white can sometimes be seen playing cricket. This lively picture makes a good contrast to a solemn urn or immobile statue. I have not gardened all of the walled garden and let a small flock of Southdown sheep keep half an acre. These woolly creatures with teddy-bear ears and smiling expressions belong to this part of Sussex. They keep the grass down, eat the spare apples, snooze under the trees and are generally no bother in their restful glade.

In 2001 we made one of the biggest changes. On the south façade we turned a window into a door and built a bridge out to a grass terrace. This new terrace, designed by the architect Peter Inskip and built from local stone by our estate craftsmen, gives us more pleasure than I could have imagined. It links the house, park and garden in a new way. We have more outdoor life and it is convenient for small children and dogs. To give shade to the terrace our architect son-in-law Adam Richards has built a painted arbour, modelled on a design by Soane. Now festooned with jasmine, it is perfect in scale and a masterpiece of elegance.

TOP LEFT: *Papaver* 'Alpha Centauri' with the self-sowing annual *Omphalodes linifolia*

BELOW LEFT: The single deep-red early herbaceous peony 'America'

ABOVE RIGHT: A stone disc set into a daisy-covered wall above a spring assortment of tulips 'Ballerina', 'Red Power' and 'Recreado', growing with *Fritillaria imperialis* 'Rubra', *Skimmia* x *confusa* 'Kew Green' and hellebores

RIGHT: The octagonal pond in the Cloister Garden where lavender is pruned at varying heights and roving *Verbascum bombyciferum* self-sows

OPPOSITE: The wall at the entrance to the wisteria tunnel is covered with the long-racemed *Wisteria floribunda* 'Alba'. The tunnel itself (above and below) is also shrouded in *Wisteria floribunda* 'Alba'

Two years ago I remodelled the kitchen garden. The large area under cultivation was unmanageable. To reduce this we dissected the space with brick-lined paths of Breedon gravel and grass and placed a nineteenth-century fountain basin in the middle. The large granite basin, which had once been on the South Lawn, was found abandoned in a shed. It is now filled with flowers rather than water and makes a sturdy central feature. Artichokes and crown imperials give it structure, foxtail lilies shoot up like rockets and *Crambe cordifolia* foams in the centre. Round the edge an annual mix from Pictorial Meadow gives us beloved cornflowers in jolly mixed colours at eye level.

As I grow older and watch the garden mature and grandchildren running about, I know I have been very lucky to realise a childhood dream. A stone disc set into the daisy-covered brick wall, a birthday present from my husband, is carved with a line from Andrew Marvell's poem. His words 'Fair Quiet Have I Found Thee Here' seem to hover in the air as the bees buzz around them.

LEFT: Openings throughout the walled garden are framed with *Trachelospermum asiaticum*. *Genista aetnensis* towers above a herbaceous border with hot flowers for summer including *Sanguisorba officinalis*, *Achillea filipendulina* 'Gold Plate', heuchera, hemerocallis and *Geum* 'Mrs J. Bradshaw'

ABOVE: The newly remodelled kitchen garden with fountain basin in the middle and *Eremurus robustus*

OVERLEAF: Seats in the private garden for watching the sun set over the Capability Brown landscape

Boughton

KETTERING, NORTHAMPTONSHIRE

The Duke of Buccleuch & Queensbury KBE

FOR 250 YEARS the immense formal gardens at Boughton gradually and almost entirely disappeared from view. Six wonderful decades of creativity and enthusiasm, beginning in 1684 shortly after my ancestor Ralph, First Duke of Montagu, inherited his Northamptonshire family seat, came grinding to a halt in 1749 with the death of his son John. Then, with house and estate passing twice in succession through the female line to different families – to the Earls of Cardigan at nearby Deene and then the Dukes of Buccleuch, already well endowed with great houses of their own – benign neglect took over. Waterways silted up, woodlands were adapted for shooting, and nature enveloped the terraces and parterres. Tantalising evidence of those initial decades, such as a curiously symmetrical, tree-covered hummock, or the majestic avenues of limes and of elms before they tragically succumbed to disease, remained. *Country Life* articles in 1909 talk wistfully of lost gardens and from early in the era of 'Listing', the system of planning rules intended to protect important heritage features, the Boughton landscape was recorded as Grade I.

In 1975 all this began to change. In a move of remarkable boldness my father, the Ninth Duke, had the great Broadwater Lake at the heart of the landscape dug out. With a new sluice gate to dam the modest River Ise, the transformation was astonishing. The Boughton west front had a proper setting once more, with a spectacular view across water and up the avenue to the distant A43 road and an equally eye-catching view from the road which, on a fine day, caused the heart to race and signalled to the family at least that we were almost home. Thus began the latest phase in the landscape story – one that has been under way for forty years now – of gradual reclamation and restoration. Gradual because, most obviously, of the expense, but in part too because the sometimes ruthless changes required could only be absorbed slowly.

As a family we all rather loved the natural, unmanaged maturity of English parkland with which we had grown up, with childhood memories of warm days, the smell of cut hay to play in, and peacefully grazing sheep in what was the domain of the Home Farm.

OPPOSITE : The west front of Boughton House with winter sun casting long reflections towards Orpheus

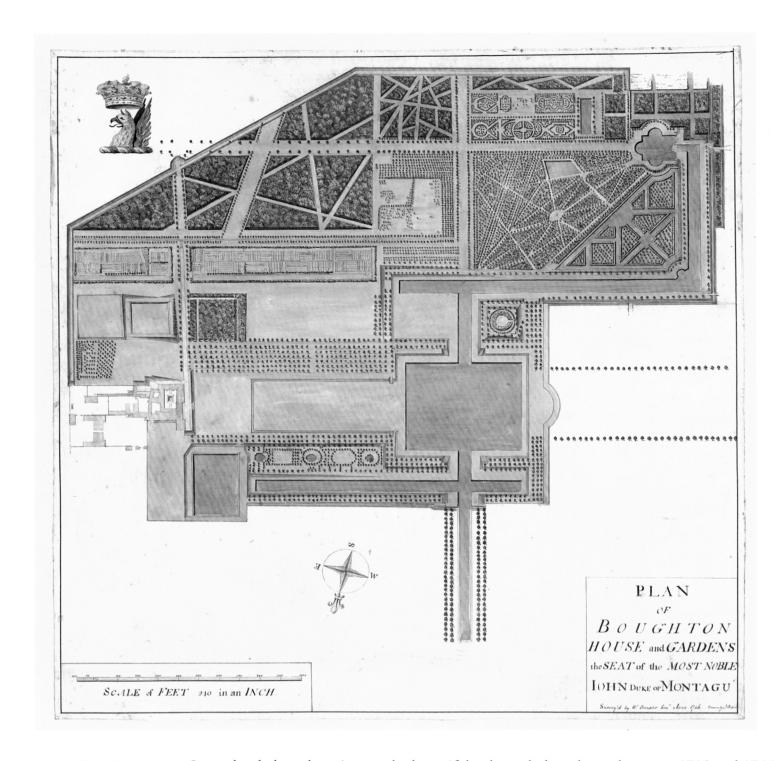

PLAN
OF
BOUGHTON
HOUSE and GARDENS
the SEAT of the MOST NOBLE
IOHN Duke of MONTAGU

Survey'd by W^r Bouvier Senr Anno 1716

SCALE of FEET 240 in an INCH

ABOVE: The 1746 plan of
Boughton that has been
a source of inspiration
for the restoration of
the garden

OPPOSITE ABOVE: An
overview of Orpheus
and its connection across
the canal to the Mount

OPPOSITE BELOW:
A corner of the mount
with a magnificent
Cedar of Lebanon
looking towards the
bridge over the River Ise
that feeds Boughton's
ponds and canals

It was hard, though, to ignore the beautiful coloured plans drawn between 1712 and 1746 or the *Vitruvius Britannicus* plan of 1724 that showed how very different it had once been. Their help in providing a clear roadmap of where we could or should be heading has been critical. They illustrate the evolving taste of the times, from the fine but fussy parterres, rigid and symmetrical, of the late seventeenth century to the free flow into the wider countryside which one feels the Second Duke was grasping at and which certainly echoed what his contemporaries were doing advised by Capability Brown and others. Known as John the Planter because of his obsession with establishing avenues, he appears to have been his own man in refashioning the Boughton landscape, although recent archive evidence shows that Bridgeman worked for him here as at his other houses. Even then he was being constrained by the template of canals and lakes, with their straight lines and right angles, and early avenues which his father had bequeathed him. Hugely influenced by what he had seen both at Versailles and elsewhere in Europe, Ralph had appointed a Dutchman, Leonard van der Meulen, as his head gardener at the outset and they were to work together for quarter of a century. Without

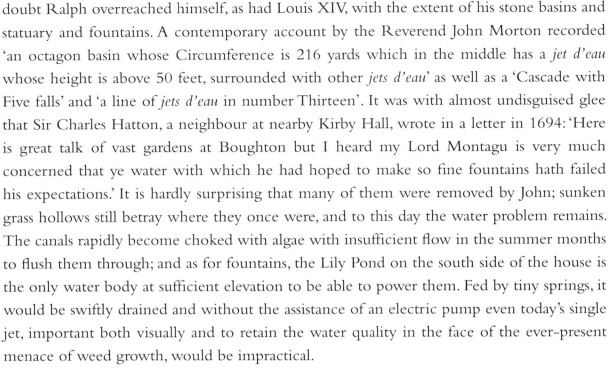

CLOCKWISE FROM ABOVE: Winter aconite, snowdrops and the spring snowflake, *Leucojum vernum,* (opposite top) carpet the ground underneath trees in the woodland adjacent to Orpheus

doubt Ralph overreached himself, as had Louis XIV, with the extent of his stone basins and statuary and fountains. A contemporary account by the Reverend John Morton recorded 'an octagon basin whose Circumference is 216 yards which in the middle has a *jet d'eau* whose height is above 50 feet, surrounded with other *jets d'eau*' as well as a 'Cascade with Five falls' and 'a line of *jets d'eau* in number Thirteen'. It was with almost undisguised glee that Sir Charles Hatton, a neighbour at nearby Kirby Hall, wrote in a letter in 1694: 'Here is great talk of vast gardens at Boughton but I heard my Lord Montagu is very much concerned that ye water with which he had hoped to make so fine fountains hath failed his expectations.' It is hardly surprising that many of them were removed by John; sunken grass hollows still betray where they once were, and to this day the water problem remains. The canals rapidly become choked with algae with insufficient flow in the summer months to flush them through; and as for fountains, the Lily Pond on the south side of the house is the only water body at sufficient elevation to be able to power them. Fed by tiny springs, it would be swiftly drained and without the assistance of an electric pump even today's single jet, important both visually and to retain the water quality in the face of the ever-present menace of weed growth, would be impractical.

Restoration of any landscape is a painstakingly slow progress, even with all the technology and machinery at our disposal, which makes the achievement of hundreds of labourers with carts and horses in the late seventeenth century all the more awesome. Boughton is particularly challenging because of its scale. The formal designed section covers some 100 acres, and that does not count the 450 acres of parkland beyond, embraced by the original fifteenth-century Deer Park, nor the thirty-three miles of avenues whose tentacles stretch far into the countryside. The sense of achievement that follows naturally from the number-crunching – three miles of nineteenth-century fencing replaced, two miles of lime avenues replanted, 70,000 cubic metres of silt dug and transported, one-and-a-half miles of six-foot-high canal-side boarding installed – is soon dissipated by reflection on all that remains to be done. Left for another generation are the *bosquet* compartments into which the Wilderness woodland was divided, or the intricate web of smaller canals and islands (now a wildlife-friendly swamp), and especially the two miles of ha-ha walls – part brick, part stone – that remain concealed for the most part beneath centuries of leaf mould.

Big transformations are, however, still possible. In 2014 one of the most important features of all, the *Grand Etang* lake closest to the house, was dug and relined and refilled for the first time in over 200 years. With just over an acre of water it provides the magical reflections of the north front so typical of great French châteaux, as well as a breathtaking 70-foot high fountain.

With so much to restore it might seem self-indulgent to have embarked on anything new, but my wife and I agree with those who feel strongly that the spirit of a great country house is enhanced by the sense that generation after generation has added something of their own time. Thus it was that six years ago the landscape artist, Kim Wilkie, came into our lives. We met first at a gardens conference in Edinburgh when he was one of several eminent speakers whose lectures Lance Goffort-Hall, our relatively recently appointed head gardener, and I attended. The form and scale of shapes, such as the grass terraces he had crafted as part of the restoration at Heveningham in Suffolk, immediately attracted our attention, as did his ingenuity at camouflaging the presence of the M25 beside Great Fosters in Surrey. At that time we weren't at all sure what we wanted, and there was even a notion, since superseded, of trying to find an elegant way to diminish the visual intrusion and noise of lorries rumbling along on the A43.

Kim came to Boughton a few months later and I have a photograph of him standing on top of the then unrestored Mount at what I remember as the 'Eureka!' moment. It seemed to arrive remarkably swiftly. Suddenly, given all the sensitivities about intruding into a designed landscape, it became apparent that there was really only one location to be considered, a flat area that had been a parterre in the 1715 plan but was open ground thirty years later and which then became the sacrifice area for dumping the silt from the lake restoration in 1975. Surely English Heritage wouldn't object if something was added there? Surely they couldn't object, said Kim, if we go down not up – and thus the notion of 'Orpheus', one of the most remarkable additions to English landscape in recent years, was conceived.

I make it sound simple. Of course it wasn't; and Kim's extraordinary talents lay in then developing the detail of his nugget of an idea so that it could find a relationship with the surrounding landscape. It achieves this almost subliminally, so that not every visitor is conscious of it, extending a quarter of a mile with a broad swathe past the house itself to the discrete plateau where tennis court and swimming pool are concealed. He gave it an intellectual coherence both in relation to what is there today but also with what might be deduced as the historical antecedents, the taste for a structure on mathematical foundations for the whole site, which Ralph and John must surely have had.

Thus the extraordinarily sensitive concept of a great sunken pool, mimicking the form of the nearby Mount and dropping the same seven metres below the canal water level as it rises above it, and thus managing somehow to be in sympathy with all that has been conceived before and yet entirely novel. Alongside and integral to Kim's vision is the adjacent stone rill, which follows a 'golden' spiral and originates from a small pool capped with a steel cube at the heart of a series of golden sections, rectangular spaces expanding to echo that on the top of the Mount as well as others that lead back to the Lily Pond and beyond.

OVERLEAF: The gentle descent to the tranquil space at the bottom of Orpheus. Despite its seven metre depth Orpheus harnesses a mirror-like reflection of distant trees

I see Orpheus being enjoyed by people in all sorts of different ways: solitary figures musing, gaggles of people laughing and testing the acoustics. For me there is nothing like the gentle rambling descent into this tranquil space that offers one of the most comfortable and comforting feelings of being at Boughton, but which is also capable, when filled with sound from the occasional concert held there, of creating a quite different sense of magic. I think we are only at the beginning of living with and exploring Orpheus.

Without Kim, of course, nothing could have happened but, without a host of other people too, the delivery would have been painful in the extreme. It would be boring to rehearse details of planning and construction processes that were challenging at times, but from all corners, whether from within the estate, in particular Vido Trkulja and his father Jo who have had a hand in most things in the park, or from the local firm of Barton Plant, or Rob Orford and his brilliant team at Miles Waterscapes, or Brian Dix doing the archaeology, answers were found. To all of them and many more go our lasting thanks.

There will be nothing quite like Orpheus ever again, but the taste and courage for adding here and there have continued. Most recently, to commemorate our thirtieth wedding

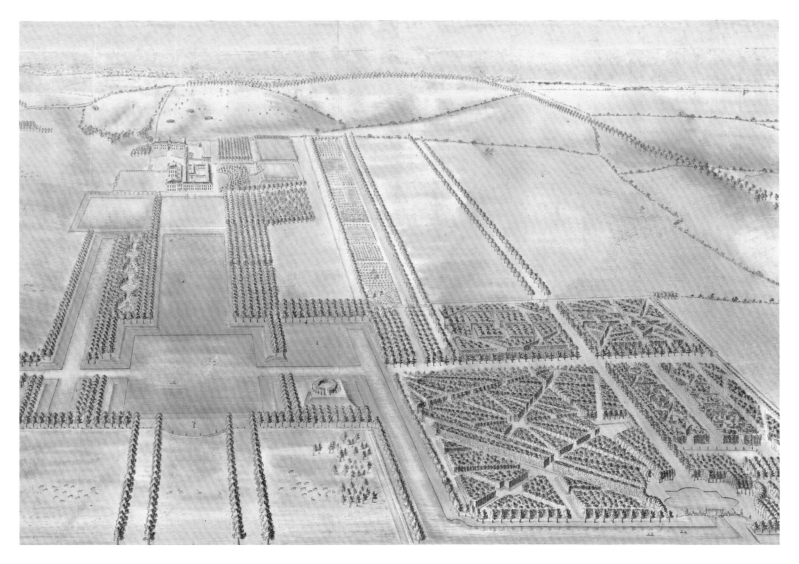

ABOVE: A 1729 bird's-eye view of Boughton showing the geometric layout of the garden

OPPOSITE ABOVE: A steel cube at the heart of a series of golden sections etched out in a stone rill reside above Orpheus

OPPOSITE BELOW: The view from the top of the Mount where Kim stood when he had his Eureka moment of inspiration about Orpheus

anniversary my wife commissioned *Life Force*, a magical piece by Angela Connor, which has found a happy space near to the Lily Pond. And closer still to the house there are quiet corners that tend to get forgotten about, such as the Fish Courtyard and the large walled garden, also a legacy of the late seventeenth century, flower gardens and herbaceous borders, all of which contribute to the atmosphere. Roses and wisteria tumble down the walls, syringa bushes scent the pathways. And then there is the Dower House garden, a legacy of one of the most remarkable residents of the complex, Sir David Scott and his wife the well-known gardener, Valerie Finnis, with its maze of pathways and special plants. So Boughton is not one but many gardens, which thrive as much as they ever have thanks to Lance Goffort-Hall, the head gardener, and the wonderfully dedicated, painstaking and knowledgeable team who work with him.

TOP: Mature limes line the north side of the Mount

ABOVE: A pair of swans in residence on the *Grand Etang*

OPPOSITE: The character of Orpheus changes in all weather and seasons

OVERLEAF: The vibrant viridian green of the Mount and Orpheus in midsummer

Eaton Hall

Eccleston, Cheshire

The Duchess of Westminster

WHEN I LOOK back on my early years living at Eaton Hall, I must confess that I was considerably more preoccupied by making a house and garden that would feel right for us and our young family than worrying too much about the illustrious ghosts of previous generations. Their legacy is formidable but there is a healthy Grosvenor tradition of freedom to let the estate respond to the spirit of its time from one generation to the next. To that end, every possible architectural movement has been championed in a succession of houses built on the very same site since William Samwell's neoclassical masterpiece commissioned by Sir Thomas Grosvenor in 1675.

The topographically perfect site had been chosen. The ground slopes gently down from the house to the River Dee, a river held sacred by both ancient Britons and Romans, who operated one of their most important military bases from Chester five miles to the north. It is also positioned to keep in view the romantic ruin of Beeston Castle seven miles to the east. Despite each generation thinking nothing of razing their houses to the ground, they did not seem inclined to tamper with the wonderful underlying garden geometry of axes, sightlines and vistas laid down in the seventeenth century. We still approach the house along the Belgrave avenue and enter the forecourt via the Golden Gates erected in the 1680s by the Davies brothers of Wrexham.

These wrought-iron masterpieces with their gilded tops remain in their original position, albeit added to by Alfred Waterhouse when he remodelled the house in the 1870s.

A monumental stone plinth topped by an equestrian statue of Hugh Lupus, the eleventh-century Marching Lord from whom the Grosvenors are descended, takes centre stage as you arrive. This impressive bronze was commissioned by the First Duke from the Victorian symbolist painter and sculptor G.F. Watts and became the incongruous centrepiece for a large collection of Nissen huts erected when the house was requisitioned during the war

OPPOSITE: Looking across a meadow of oxeye daisies and meadow cranesbill, *Geranium pratense* to the Golden Gates erected by the Davies brothers of Wrexham in the 1680s

and used as a Royal Naval Cadet College. These remained in situ until the 1960s when Eaton reverted back to the family.

Eaton is a complicated and multi-layered place and this forecourt, known as the Hugh Lupus Flat, is characteristic of the rest of the garden where strata of additions have accrued. It was plain to me from the start that the entire garden needed a cohesive master plan sympathetic to the place and reflecting an understanding of its history.

Eaton had been a centre of horticultural excellence in the nineteenth century and pre-war era when John Webb, William Nesfield, Edwin Lutyens and Detmar Blow all had varying degrees of involvement. There had once been a team of fifty-six gardeners, under a head gardener and his two superintendents. So the responsibility of bringing the garden into the twentieth century and beyond was daunting. With over fifty acres of garden to tackle and a significantly diminished workforce I decided to seek professional help.

During the building of the Hall we lived in a cottage in the grounds. We used the architects Percy Thomas Partnership, with Sir Hugh Casson as consultant architect. John Stefanidis masterminded the hugely successful and elegant transformation of the interior, and Arabella Lennox-Boyd advised on the gardens. We had regular meetings throughout the building of the house when the complete team was included, so that interior and exterior grew in

BELOW: Arabella Lennox-Boyd's masterplan for the garden at Eaton Hall

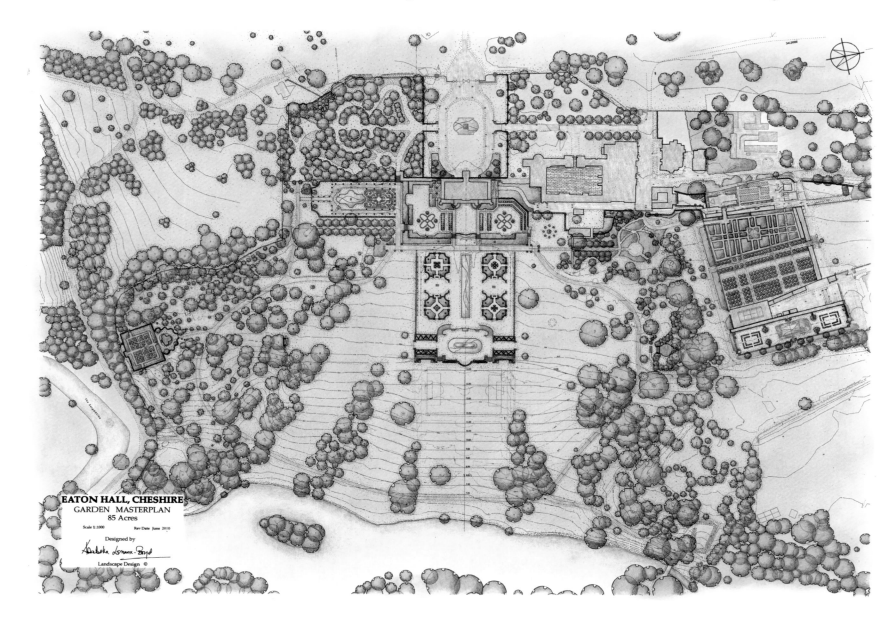

EATON HALL, CHESHIRE
GARDEN MASTERPLAN
85 Acres

Scale 1:1000   Rev Date June 2010

Designed by

Arabella Lennox-Boyd

Landscape Design ©

harmony. This proved to be very productive. As well as being efficient and enlightening my memory of all those meetings is that they were enormous fun. I think it would be fair to say that in the garden I was the steer but Arabella was the leading light. She recommended that we put a fifteen-year plan in progress. This was the beginning of a close collaboration and the garden at Eaton is one of several projects she and I have worked on together. Looking back it is astonishing to see how much we have accomplished and how few compromises we have made along the way.

We were constrained by the elements in the garden that are Grade I or II listed, but opted to see them all as integral to the estate's history and think laterally about how to soften or incorporate the disparate statuary, water and garden buildings. Both Arabella and I were concerned that the Waterhouse clock tower attached to the west end of the chapel – which is 175 feet high and visible from two miles away – would be out of scale with the house and would not relate to it. Arabella dealt with this by planting wings of clipped limes on the sides and jutting out from the house.

This clever planting has tempered its bearing on the garden. Instead of focusing on the tower your eye is drawn to the woodland gardens that lead off from the wings of the terrace. The quatrefoil turf plats in the foreground also distract the eye and decorate the large grass area without being too fussy. Planting on the top terrace was difficult because there are remains of underground rooms from Waterhouse's monumental Victorian Gothic mansion, of which our current house covers a mere fraction. Many factors had to be thought through, including drainage and making sure that trees were not planted on underground masonry.

The house had to relate to the existing Waterhouse terraces, the Park surrounding them and the landscape beyond. It was important to keep a sense of flow as the gardens descend from the east-facing façade to the river and the unspoilt patchwork landscape behind it. Arabella's solution to create a harmonious transition between formality and scale was to plant silver-leaved pear trees. These provide a thread that cleverly links the two upper terraces. They act as a motif which succeeds in softening the rigidity of the architecture and creating a winter structure with their clipped shapes. Another ploy for softening the enormous number of terrace walls, balustrades and flights of steps was to surround them with very deep borders. Once again, Arabella's sense of scale was invaluable here.

Eaton was a difficult garden to conceive as there were so many elements to be taken into account, such as the historical aspect, the intimidating size of existing features that could not be changed, and the different styles of previous gardens and planting. We also wanted gardens we could sit in or walk through and enjoy the scent and colour. We wanted some smaller informal areas and gardens for different seasons and colour, and of course a vegetable garden in which to grow my favourite fruit and organically grown vegetables.

We now have a charming paved terrace enclosed by roses and scented plants. My Aunt Sally (wife of the Fourth Duke of Westminster) had made a rose garden below the top terrace where there had previously been gardens by Nesfield and Blow. I also love roses and liked the idea of four gardens individually displaying pink, white, crimson and yellow roses. These were flanked by beautifully made upright trellis pillars joined by swags of rope festooned with rose 'New Dawn' and rose 'Felicité et Perpetue'.

I was keen to have an organic kitchen garden for the family, but obviously on a smaller scale than in the past. Eaton's walled garden had once been home to greenhouses that needed six miles of hot water piping. We were never going to return to the days recounted by a visitor in 1884: when he 'asked the young fellow the number of glasshouses, he endeavoured in vain to reckon them on his fingers'. 'Black Alicante' and 'Madresfield Court' grapes had houses all to themselves; a stephanotis and gardenia house (growing flowers specifically for buttonholes); orchid houses; two pineapple houses; melon and cucumber stoves; and a camellia house, the only extant remnant of this glass colony. Built in 1852, when it was described as a 'noble glass corridor of 400 feet in length', it is made of cast iron with copper sashes and glass reaching to its base. The windows, louvres and ceiling lights were all restored. This improved the air circulation and therefore reduced the botrytis which was blighting the collection of rare camellias.

Over the years temples and follies, steps and statues, ponds and paths all needed attention. Restoration continues but the balance of decay versus attention has been redressed. Early on we renovated John Douglas's 1872 Dutch Tea House, where I often retreated with the children when they were young, and I now do the same with my grandchildren. The garden it overlooks had been redesigned in turn by Lutyens and Mallows at a time when 25,000 tulips were bedded out each autumn. Later, in the 1980s, it became a herb garden. Arabella's new twenty-first century arrangement is less time-consuming but still scented and beautiful.

Her choice of plants keeps the garden interesting throughout the year, but spring is especially remarkable with avenues of cherry blossom and *Malus hupehensis* and a broadening collection of magnolias, dogwoods, rhododendrons and other unusual shrubs and trees. Mowing is one of Arabella's bêtes noires, so a considerable amount of lawn is gradually becoming long grass filled with camassias and cranesbills, which get cut down in late summer before the drifts of autumn crocuses appear.

It was quite an undertaking to bring this garden back to life, and our charity open days give it a sense of purpose outside our own enjoyment. Visitors walk across the remains of a road in the park built by the Romans and through gardens that have come and gone according to the fluctuating fashions of their time. The Mannerist garden was long grassed

ABOVE: A view over the rose gardens towards the River Dee. The clipped silver pears, *Pyrus salicifolia* 'Pendula', unify the terraces near the house and the lower garden.

OPPOSITE: The White Rose Garden with the Waterhouse clock tower and Eaton Hall behind

RIGHT: The trellis rose pillars are festooned with a mixture of roses 'New Dawn' and 'Felicité et Perpetue'

OPPOSITE ABOVE: Climbing and shrub 'Iceberg' roses are planted with lavender and silver-leaved *Artemisia ludoviciana* 'Valerie Finnis' in the White Rose Garden

OPPOSITE BELOW: In the Yellow Rose garden *Sambucus racemosa* 'Plumosa Aurea', *Thalictrum flavum* subsp. *glaucum*, *Campanula lactiflora* 'Prichard's Variety', *Miscanthus sinensis* 'Variegatus' and *Alstroemeria aurea* 'Lutea' gather around rose The Pilgrim

BELOW: The pond at the centre of the broadwalk has a statue of *The Lioness and Lesser Kudu* by Jonathan Kenworthy

over by 1822 (possibly on the advice of Capability Brown) when an article about Eaton describes a beautiful verdure fifty-acre lawn sweeping from the east front of the house to the recently enlarged River Dee. We have recovered the south-facing Dragon Fountain garden where Nesfield's elaborate Italianate parterre was recreated from photographs, the Lutyens gates have been repaired, an automatic irrigation system has been installed, and the two elements that have fascinated every generation of Grosvenors – water and statuary – have been restored.

Facing the house are two nineteenth-century life-size statues attributed to Westmacott. They depict Odo Bishop of Bayeux and the half-brother of William the Conqueror, in whose reign the Grosvenors came to England, and Joan of Eaton, who on her marriage to Raufe Grosvenor in 1443 brought this fascinating estate to the family. I am proud to be part of it and proud to have had the opportunity to bring the garden and landscape back to life, for it was more or less abandoned and unloved when we moved in.

I am now looking forward to completing the renovation of all the borders and shrubberies, which after so many years need a thorough overhaul. Gardening is an endless but rewarding task.

LEFT: The Hot Border is filled with a mixture of perennials and grasses, including bee balm *Monarda didyma*, *Crocosmia* 'Lucifer', *Lilium* 'Golden Splendour' and *Anthemis tinctoria* 'E.C. Buxton'

BELOW: Overlooking the walled kitchen garden with the Camellia House at the far end beyond the orchard

BOTTOM LEFT: A mixed border of lilies and herbaceous plants stretches the length of the south-facing wall in the kitchen garden

The Lake with a boat mooring edged
with meadowsweet and purple
loosetrife *Lythrum salicaria*

St Paul's Walden Bury

ST PAUL'S WALDEN, HERTFORDSHIRE

❧

Sir Simon Bowes Lyon

EDWARD GILBERT LAID out our garden at St Paul's Walden Bury from 1725 to 1730 on magnificent lines that are still retained today. It has always been in the same family. Fifty years after Gilbert it was the home of his granddaughter the unfortunate Ninth Countess of Strathmore, a keen botanist and gardener. Later in the twentieth century the house and garden had happier associations as the birthplace and playground of my aunt, the late Queen Elizabeth The Queen Mother. Today my wife Caroline and I live here, with various members of our family nearby.

The garden is an example of the French *patte d'oie* or 'goosefoot' design, with long avenues and rides lined with beech hedges stretching out from a focal point.

One of the characteristics of the garden is the importance placed on the element of surprise, so the approach is rather modest. From the gates, past a kitchen garden, the drive goes uphill, used by walkers or horse riders before turning to less public use. It passes a fine eighteenth-century lead group, a statue of Charity and her children, up to the Victorian front door. On this side the house and exterior court was designed by the architect Arthur Castings. To the east an expanse of lawn leads to a long lime avenue, part of the classical geometric layout of the early eighteenth century. Continuing around we come to the original eighteenth-century house, probably dating from the 1720s. On either side are hexagonal wings with a 1767 date. Nikolaus Pevsner attributed this front to Robert Adam. The house looks out to a lawn on the north side and here you are at the convergence of the original classical *patte d'oie* with three *allées* radiating out into woodland or statues or fields leading to the church. On either side of this concave-shaped lawn are pleached-lime-lined gravel paths.

We have here a basic paradigm: classicism, visual movement, rhythm, nature and then back to classicism. The garden is always dynamic; there is movement from a past interpretation to the future, from one season to the next.

OPPOSITE: Looking down the main avenue to the north-facing façade of the house attributed to Robert Adam (also seen overleaf)

What does classicism mean here? It gives us discipline and stability in a changing landscape and world. It is a geometric structure and is invariable. The main north–north–east to south–south–west axis consists of a broad *allée* to the north leading to a statue of Hercules flanked by two side *allées* that form a *patte d'oie* with a wider avenue to the south. On the east side the avenue extends upwards for three quarters of a mile. This intersects at its western end with another lime avenue running north–south, almost parallel with the main avenue, to a pavilion referred to as the 'Organ House'. This octagonal folly has the date 1735 cut into one of the bricks and is purely decorative. On the west a narrow *allée* leads to a lead statue of *Samson and the Philistine*.

The western side *allée* of the *patte d'oie* leads to a statue of Diana where it continues at an angle to join the main avenue at the statue of Hercules. The eastern side *allée* is aligned on the twelfth-century church half a mile distant. These three *allées* and the lime avenue are crossed by three further *allées* all lined with beech, the longest leading from a temple in the style of Wyatt (which came from Copped Hall in Essex) to a temple by William Chambers at the furthest end of the large pond.

Visual movement in the garden comes from design with a free hand in three dimensions without instruments. For example the north lawn with pleached limes is concave, whereas the main *allée* is concave only with its fall and rise, its widening and narrowing, but convex from beech hedge to beech hedge. It is spatially dynamic and rhythmic.

Rhythm is also felt in the curves of the many serpentine paths that run in the spaces between the *allées*. There is consistency blending with nature. Nature refers on the one hand to our human behaviour, on the other to our local landscape or woodland, to the wildlife and their tracks that become our paths. There should thus be no boundary or limitation. All *allées* should lead out onto the surrounding countryside. Some of our woodland glades are derived from the idea of forest clearings from which paths created by flocks or herds of animals lead outwards. Chaos is avoided by the discipline imposed by the basic geometric structure.

The time dimension gives the garden its maturity. We want to feel what has gone before and retain previous ideas and taste and equally imagine the future, but change is unavoidable. We have lost most of the fine trees that had reached their prime in the 1950s through disease or storm. We have softened or removed garden boundaries so we look outwards into the countryside or inwards to the main house that becomes an ornament in the entire scheme.

The garden was already mature when it was described in 1740 in a long poem by the nephew of its creator Edward Gilbert, and the core features of that garden remain today. The estate then was small, so that the avenue to the east had to avoid crossing neighbouring land. By the 1770s the house was the home of Mary Eleanor Bowes, who married the Earl of Strathmore, John Lyon. The Countess of Strathmore was a keen amateur botanist and gardener whose books remain in the house. She commissioned the explorer William Paterson to collect plants in South Africa and arranged gatherings in the house for well-known flower painters of her day. She was notorious for having been involved in some unwise romantic liaisons after the death of her husband, inspiring Thackeray's novel *Barry Lyndon* and compounding her problems by writing a book entitled *My Confessions*. Coaxed into marriage after clandestine meetings at the statue of *The Running Footman* in the garden by Stoney Bowes (who had adopted her maiden name and from whom the expression 'stoney broke' is derived) their attachment was doomed. There is a charming memorial to her dog Tirsi with a poem inscribed below the urn near the Copped Hall temple.

The walled kitchen garden and Garden House with its Gothic windows date from this time, and many trees were planted from about 1790 to 1805. In Victorian times up to 1880 little garden development took place apart from the planting of a few exotic trees. In 1881 the house was the home of Lord and Lady Glamis, later Fourteenth Earl of Strathmore. In 1888 they replaced the southern two-storey Georgian wing with the present work of Castings, together with the ancillary retaining walls: they also planted up a three-acre field on the north-west part of the garden. The next change came when my parents, their youngest son David and his wife Rachel came to live here in 1931. My father was an active and knowledgeable gardener, subsequently President of the Royal Horticultural Society; he restored all the *allées* and replanted the hornbeam hedges, many by then about 200 years old, with beech. The formal glade with terraces, used as an outdoor theatre (known to us as *The Running Footman*) was restored in collaboration with our family friend Sir Geoffrey Jellicoe.

ABOVE AND OPPOSITE: At the summit of the broad *allée* to the north a statue of Hercules stands on a plinth

OVERLEAF: The three *allées* that form a *patte d'oie*. These are crossed by further *allées* giving vistas in myriad directions

More domestic design and planting were undertaken around the tennis court to the west of the house and farmyard. The war years set all this back, but in the 1950s the *allées* were mown again, and starting in 1953 the north–south beech avenue on the east side of the formal layout was replanted with lime. My father enclosed the garden with a high chain-link fence intended to keep out animals. This really was his only mistake and it was never successful. In 1961, on his death, control passed on to my wife Caroline and myself .

Much has changed in fifty years. The chain-link fence rusted away and with it the boundary to the garden that now merges into the woods and the surrounding landscape. A greater emphasis on wildflowers has increased the profusion of naturalised daffodils, fritillaries, orchids and much else, ending with an abundance of devil's-bit scabious in the autumn. We have extended areas that can grow rhododendron and calcifuge plants. The geometric design was completed with the planting of limes and *Aesculus indica* on the east side. The original walnut avenue to the south now has Lucombe's oak *Quercus* x *hispanica* 'Lucombeana' and *Juglans nigra*, the black walnut. There are two individual small gardens also designed, or 'suggested', by Sir Geoffrey Jellicoe, and many other garden ideas that do not intrude on the classicism of the primary design. The main loss to the garden has been the fine specimen trees: those that were at their height in the 1950s and those lost to the elm disease of 1974–6, the three devastating storms between 1987 and 1992, and more recently the horse chestnut diseases. However, the standard of upkeep has been maintained, with particular attention to beech hedges in the formal layout.

To the classicism should be added three other themes found in the wider garden here.

We do the picturesque in the 'manner' of Capability Brown. Neither the garden nor the house was important enough for Capability Brown's personal attention in the eighteenth century. His 'style' exists in the landscaping of the Dell Park on the east side of the garden, with carefully placed trees providing a setting for the church. Separated from the main geometric design by woodland we have a view of the classical Stagenhoe mansion, which from the south also has carefully planted trees and water in the middle distance and 'natural trees' in the parkland. Within this landscape is another picturesque creation, a large pond, with islands and exotic trees. This is a completely different concept to the classicism with The Bury as its focal point, and we keep the two apart.

Secondly, in the woodland to the west of the geometric design is the more recent planting of woodland shrubs including rhododendrons raised from seed brought back from expeditions, including some that Caroline and I have been on to the Himalayas and south-western China. This is an interesting part of the garden in April, May or June, separated from the bright area of daffodils around the main pond and the formal geometry (which is less prominent when the beech hedges are dropping their leaves).

Thirdly is the more domestic gardening around the farm buildings, and in other areas are small gardens which come and go. We are plantsmen, so exterior decoration or pure floristic effect comes from those particular plants we favour at the time. The garden has flowers through most of the year. Early spring sees the flowering of rhododendrons with *R.* 'Praecox', *Rhododendron* 'Cilipinese', *R. strigillosum*, 'Tessa' and *R. oreodoxa* in that order, along with early bulbs. Extensive plantings of the tall snowdrop species *Galanthus platyphyllus* or *G. elwesii* are followed by the double form of *G. nivalis*. Other early flowers include forms of *Camellia* x *williamsii* and *Mahonia bealei*. The roll call of plants continues from month to month; a spectacular plant of *Magnolia denudata* climbs next to the front door of the house, and large plants of osmanthus and *Ribes speciosum* are found around the ruined orangery. The early rose 'Canary Bird' makes a dazzling display with the southern wing of the house covered in wisteria and banksian rose. Rhododendron species and very large bushes of *Paeonia ludlowii* are found in the woodland, with good stands of *Lilium pyrenaicum* and *L. monadelphum*. Our soil determines what we do; most of the garden has boulder clay sufficiently impermeable to seal off the alkalinity of the underlying chalk. On the east side gravel overlays the chalk. To the north there are patches of bracken; here we plant *embothrium* and *kalmia*. We take the plants to the suitable soil conditions but need to mulch the woodland plants heavily where there is virtually no topsoil.

For wildflower displays we care for and encourage primrose, cowslip, anemone and snakeshead fritillary and orchids. All are plentiful and we are increasing the near-native *Iris xiphiodes*. Betony, *Stachys officinalis*, meadowsweet *Filipendula ulmaria* and fleabane *Pulicaria dysenterica* may be very common plants but they give a good show followed by devil's-bit scabious in September. Different cutting regimes favour a particular plant, and if other plants benefit it is a bonus.

A temple in the style of Wyatt that came from Copped Hall in Essex is at the apex of the cross *allée*. At the opposite end a temple by William Chambers is beside the pond

Folly Farm

Sulhamstead, Berkshire

❧

Mrs Jonathan Oppenheimer

M
Y HUSBAND WAS the one who first fell in love with Folly Farm. He grew up in a house designed by Herbert Baker in South Africa, and his immediate affinity with the atmosphere here was no doubt based on this association. Lutyens and Baker were both English architects of the same period and even worked for a few years in the same architectural offices during the 1880s when they would frequently go sketching in the country together. Later they famously partnered to create the most important buildings in New Delhi before their great and long friendship turned sour, a dispiriting chapter in Lutyens's life which he would later call his 'Bakerloo'.

It is fortunate that we thought the restoration project would only take a couple of years at most. It is also fortunate that despite instantly discerning its significance amongst Lutyens's *oeuvre*, we weren't daunted by the weight of its cultural and artistic importance. We began with a grim determination not to be defeated by Grade I restrictions. After many long hours of research and collaboration, this evolved into a sheer delight and passion with a project we realised was a lifetime privilege. I remember retiring in the early morning hours from yet another engrossing study of Folly's history when my neglected husband asked me somewhat sceptically if *all* of this research was necessary *just* for English Heritage. During the six years it has taken to thus revitalise the house and garden, not a day passes without some element of Lutyens's genius astonishing me.

Lutyens's final transformation of Folly Farm in 1912 was accomplished at the height of his acclaim as the most important country house architect of the period but, surprisingly, it also resulted in totally unique periods of much-needed family harmony for the Lutyens family. Folly has the rare distinction of being the only one of his houses in which he actually lived. Personal letters and family records attest that the troubled Lutyens family spent 'the happiest summer' of their lives here in 1916 as guests of their friend, Folly Farm's then owner, Antonie Merton. Even Lutyens's beloved 'Bumps' (Miss Jekyll) was enticed to spend some time at

OPPOSITE: An enfilade of Lutyens-designed steps and paths in stone and herringbone brick lead out from the sunken garden. The circular beds bulge with Dan Pearson's herbaceous planting of *Macleaya microcarpa* 'Spetchley Ruby', *Persicaria amplexicaulis* 'Dikke Floskes' and *Echinacea* x *purpurea* 'Tomato Soup' and 'Sombrero Salsa Red'

ABOVE: Looking across the grasses and dogwoods in Dan's Wind Garden to Folly Farm

BELOW: *Bergenia* 'Abendglut' and *Tulipa* 'Recreado'

Folly that summer. It was always our goal to restore the estate to its former glory while also creating a family home for ourselves. Like the Lutyenses, we are now revelling in the joy of summers at Folly and finding it harder and harder to tear ourselves away.

Training as a lawyer in America proved useful for the endless boxes of papers and specifications we had to wade through as we immersed ourselves in the undertaking. I can thankfully say that we had nothing but good relations with the team from English Heritage who saw that we were determined to be meticulous from the outset. Our overriding intention was to give the impression that the house and garden had been lovingly restored throughout its life, not all at once in a twenty-first-century monster blitz. We knew we would not be moving into the house immediately, so our first step was to convert one of the cottages on the property, which became our cosy and much-loved home for the duration of the project.

At the outset, we were faced with a somewhat dispiriting and tired garden. The original Jekyll planting had been absent for over eighty years. Water features and various original planting areas had been cemented in; crumbling bricks were sticking up out of paths; walls were collapsing. It had become a place where bubble wrap had slowly replaced broken glass in the glasshouses and sheds were roofed with rusty corrugated iron. Sick roses clung to sour soil and a high proportion of perennial weeds had entrenched themselves with an iron grip throughout. It has been a revelation to watch this garden come magically back to vibrant life as we have all worked together from east to west, taking one project at a time.

The project began at the top of the property with the restoration of the glasshouses back to their 1912 design (as well as their modernisation). It was our good fortune to salvage much of the original material and also to discover two doors, discarded amongst the dilapidated clutter of an old storage room, which retained the nameplate of the original builders from Edinburgh. The glasshouses have now become a place of solitude and a mandatory stop on any walk through the garden. My favourite room overflows with a profusion of assorted pelargoniums in a nod to our South African roots. At certain times of the year it bursts with colour and we all enjoy rubbing the backs of the leaves to puzzle over different scents.

Most of the hard landscaping in the garden is protected as strictly as the house. The ambitious affair of repairing and restoring these bones from the bottom up was tedious and painstaking at times but has long since proven its worth. We were greatly aided in this mission by the library of glass negatives in the *Country Life* archives where I was able to spend many fascinating and productive hours. These pictures allowed us, for example, to restore an important water feature which had previously been camouflaged by gravel. Our English builders were meticulous, and when they left it looked – somewhat to our dismay – as though they had never been there. They had achieved our goal of making it appear as if the estate had been lovingly maintained over its life without any interference from us. Such, we learned, can be the paradoxically ego-bruising nature of restoration work.

ABOVE: The Parterre Garden in spring with corners of the geometric layout picked out in magenta *Bergenia* 'Abendglut' and *Tulipa* 'Recreado'

PREVIOUS PAGE: The
Sunken Pool Garden in
July with a tapestry of
planting. *Stipa gigantea,
Macleaya microcarpa*
'Spetchley Ruby' and
Hemerocallis 'Stafford'
grow out of a carpet
of *Acaena inermis*
'Purpurea', surrounding
the central cruciform
island where *Eryngium*
x *agavifolium* and
kniphofia 'Safranvogel'
are planted with creeping
clover *Trifolium repens*
'Purpurascens'

Whenever I saw a team of these builders conscientiously repairing the paths or fountains in the formal gardens an image would come to mind, originally conveyed to me by an acquaintance who had once spoken to Lutyens's daughter. She recalled visiting Folly Farm with her father while he endlessly sifted through roof tiles for hours on end, selecting the sequence of textures and colours to seamlessly flow on the massive roof. There is a warp and weave to all of these exquisite roofscapes as there is to the repaired brickwork that flows through the garden like a carpet underfoot. The varying garden enclosures, of which there are many, provide a lesson in how space can control a sense of movement, almost like music. The sunken garden really does feel like a basso profundo octave lower than the adjacent parterre which, with its horizontal expanse of wide paths, is lighter and more lyrical.

Upon looking at the plans for the garden it becomes clear that Lutyens was having a lot of fun with shapes, symbols, symmetry – and particularly water. Within close proximity to the house there is a large dipping pool, a long rectangular pool, and an amusingly shaped circular pool with an island in the sunken garden. By mining his profound knowledge of horticulture, our landscape designer Dan Pearson has added another dimension and this layout is now enriched and enlivened in an inspired dialogue with the planting.

When faced with the difficult choice of a landscape designer, we were strongly guided by a few imperatives. Perhaps most importantly we knew we needed to find someone who would be able to sensitively introduce a twenty-first-century aesthetic into an iconic Arts and Crafts layout with a high ratio of hard landscaping. Early on we had decided not to follow slavishly any original Jekyll planting plans, primarily due to the unrealistic human resource demands which this would place on running the garden. In addition, we were not likely to be in residence when the original planting was at its best, which made it highly impractical.

Moreover the house sits in a quintessentially English landscape, at least to eyes more used to the veldt in South Africa. We love the rolling meadows, lush trees and the way the landscape in England stays so green and verdant all summer. My husband and I felt we also needed a designer who was completely at home with the English country garden aesthetic and who could incorporate the garden itself into the wider landscape. Finally, whoever we chose would also have to respect the rather zealous family belief in organic principles. My mother-in-law has had a great gardening influence on all of us. She is widely respected as something of a holistic gardening trailblazer both in her garden here, at Waltham Place where she collaborated with one of the pioneers of the new perennials movement Henk Gerritsen, and also in her garden in South Africa.

Meeting Dan Pearson was a watershed moment. When he came, he loved the garden and instinctively seemed to understand our vision for it. We moved from trepidation to enthusiasm knowing that we were in safe and sensitive hands. Dan is perceptive and thoughtful and has managed to weave together the ghosts of the garden's original creator as well as its many subsequent inhabitants. He has also tied in the various anomalies that we couldn't put our fingers on and overlaid the whole with his own style of planting, softening the edges, restoring the balance and making a family garden that we all love and relish spending time in.

As we began to examine the gardens in earnest, we felt that there was one border area of the formal garden which curiously seemed to peter out. We likened it to a 'weak chin'. From Lutyens's plans in the Berkeley Archives it was clear to me that he had originally designed

this area with strong framing landscaping which he had later removed in order to accom-modate the owners' need for a tennis court and croquet lawn. After subsequent owners removed these gaming areas, the space had been left empty and hanging. Dan added some gently cambered paths with a simple oak bench at the end of the vista which has corrected any sense of weakness and tethered the missing links. In this space, he has created a Wind Garden, a matrix of brick-edged planting beds with red-stemmed cornus rising from a carpet of black ophiopogon and columns of panicum and stipa grasses that sway in the wind. Now when we stand on the balcony of our bedroom overlooking the garden, it is over a sequence of gardens that clearly knit together as they were always intended to be.

Dan felt strongly that we needed to relate the wider landscape of the property more closely to the formal gardens nearer to the house. Originally, the two areas had little connection and the barrier between them had only increased over the 100 or so years of the garden's life. The new scheme has immeasurably widened the horizon of the garden. My husband and I had first developed a meandering drive as a creative solution to increasing amounts of builder traffic. Over time, we grew to appreciate the way it swept past the new lake, continuing through meadows and orchards while providing glimpses of the formal garden as it passed by on the way to the house. Eventually, it was incorporated with a few amendments as part of the formal design.

The pond was earmarked early on in the project, arising out of a widespread problem with standing water. My husband worked extensively with the team to position it naturally. Like many debates around the garden's restoration, this one raged fast and furious but ultimately

ABOVE: The Sunken Pool Garden

BELOW: *Eryngium agavifolium* and *Kniphofia* 'Safranvogel'

LEFT: *Aquilegia chrysantha* 'Yellow Queen' with *Sanguisorba officinalis* 'Red Thunder'

RIGHT: *Verbena bonariensis* with *Perovskia atriplicifolia* in the Parterre Garden

BELOW: Dark purple *Salvia* 'Caradonna' with mauve *Salvia verticillata* 'Purple Rain', *Eryngium eburneum* and *Thalictrum delavayi* in the Parterre Garden

In summer and autumn large oak planters are filled with *Hydrangea arborescens* and *Pelargonium tomentosum* above a wide border of *Hakonechloa macra* and *Asarum europaeum*. *Rhododendron luteum* and *Tulipa* 'Sapporo' fill the pots for spring

ABOVE: Grapevines are
trained up and over the
rectangular arbour

BELOW AND RIGHT: Wide plats of *Lavandula* 'Sawyer's'
bring pollinating insects into the Walled Garden
bordered by strips of *Catananche caerulea* with
Centaurea orientalis

wound up in a solution satisfactory to all. Dan also fashioned a 'stream' which appears to flow from an ancient spring in the pond. This expanse of still and flowing water has miraculously added not only a new dimension but also a wealth of wildlife to the landscape. The swallows which swoop over the pond feeding on insects in summer and nesting in the barns give the impression that this is how it has always been at Folly Farm. This effort has contributed to our growing list of bird, butterfly and moth species which our team takes pride in recording each year.

We had a clean slate for the restoration of the walled garden, which has now evolved into the heart of the garden. As productive as it is beautiful, as lovingly maintained as it would have been in previous centuries yet uncompromisingly modern, the walled garden is the setting for joyous lengthy family lunches under the vines which have been trained along the long pergola and where the volume of conversation vies with the hum of bees feasting on the haze of lavender which is laid out in a maze of raised beds.

Dan has an extraordinary capacity to go from the macro to the micro and at times his attention to detail can be every bit as exciting and revelatory to us all as Lutyens's ingenious dowels or door latches. Not a day passes without a scent or bloom to captivate one's attention. Our team has staged a succession of seasonal horticultural curiosities, from auriculas in spring to salvias in late summer on a long high table by the door which we all use most to go in and out of the walled garden. This has been such a success that we now do the same indoors; pots of ferns and orchids rise out of a bed of moss that is as rigorously cared for and rotated by the gardeners.

As all the family are keen cricketers, it did take some persuading to solve the inevitable question of the cricket net. Perhaps Dan secretly hoped we were just going to forget about it; however, when he realised that breakneck-speed balls were going to be roaring through his plantations of delicate Japanese maples, multi-stemmed amelanchiers and halesias, a net was promptly procured and a place found for it backed by a magnificent copper beech. This beech joins many other ancient trees which populate the garden like distinguished characters.

The design is worked with a careful restraint to leave some areas quite simple. A fatally leaking 1960s swimming-pool area has been transformed into a calm and quiet space. Enclosed by yew on three sides, it overlooks a meadow with a long seating platform backed by a simple line of salix echoing the old pollarded willows across the stream. A golden rain tree, *Koelreuteria paniculata*, has become the regular perch for a pair of wagtails who have adopted this space as their own. The architecture of the various barns and buildings are most often left to take centre stage as crisp blocks of sarcococca and a few fastigiate oaks and pears give just enough greenery for subtle direction. Hints of lusher planting are positioned in corners, beckoning you to explore.

Living at Folly Farm and delving into its fascinating origins and history have been something of a personal odyssey. During this time, we have come up with a theory about the original garden design which we would like eventually to commit to paper. We may have discovered the key to what Lutyens was thinking at the time of creating the last and most important transformation of Folly Farm in 1912. If we are correct, our immersion into the deeper symbolism and significance of this alluring and evocative place seems set to continue. In the end, it is our hope that the great man himself would approve of our loving restoration of the house and garden which for our family have now become a home.

OVERLEAF: The pond with its marginal boardwalk and planting is a mirror to the sky and surrounding trees

BELOW: A bridge across the willow-bordered stream

The Collaborative Urge

Hatch House

HARE HATCH, BERKSHIRE

Pierre Lagrange Esq

I N AUGUST 2009 Harry Henderson, who knew we were looking for a lodge close to the shoot at West Woodhay in Berkshire, called to alert me that Hatch House was going to come on the market. I had told him I was looking for a 'Beatrix Potter cottage-with-a-view' in the area we had fallen in love with amongst the downs that are a hidden gem within the triangle between Hungerford, Winchester and Newbury.

I was in Salzburg so we bought Hatch House without seeing it in the knowledge that there was nothing my wife Catherine could not do inside and the confidence that Tom Stuart-Smith (with whom I had by then collaborated on numerous projects) would wield his magic in the gardens.

A month later our first visit confirmed the potential, as well as highlighting that the place was a total mess with a host of planning and topographical limitations. There were a few trees, the leftovers of a dairy destroyed in a lightning fire and a listed barn that was potentially, and proved to be, a big obstacle as well as a wonderful feature in what was an old orchard.

The landscape was phenomenal. There is a massive 'Wow!' factor on arrival as the view overlooks West Woodhay estate and the downs in an undisturbed panoramic view to the west and south. The grit in the oyster consisted of a bridleway irritatingly close to the house and electricity poles bang in the middle of the most beautiful vista, an eyesore from nearly everywhere. Nevertheless we trusted we could find a solution to remove what was ugly and magnify what was beautiful, both inside our plot and in our surroundings.

The ten acres that came with the house are girded by a beautiful estate of thousands of acres so we had potential to 'borrow' the landscape beyond our confines, an English equivalent of an age-old Japanese landscaping practice.

I had developed a wonderfully efficient way of communicating with Tom, mostly by email, as we were both frequently busy in incompatible time zones. By this time we had developed a sort of shorthand, and between September 2009 and July 2010 exchanged nearly

OPPOSITE: The front door of Hatch House, a Beatrix Potter cottage with a view, is reached through a richly planted garden

PREVIOUS PAGE: Purple coneflower *Echinacea purpurea*

ABOVE: A birds-eye pencil sketch of Hatch and its surrounding fields by Tom Stuart-Smith

100 emails; sometimes one word long, either saying great or awful, sometimes a modern–day take on one of Humphrey Repton's Red Books!

I particularly enjoyed the poetry of Tom's descriptions, and his very diplomatic ability to convey disapproval of my crazier ideas. Indeed I had lots of ideas, and wanted to have nearly everything I'd had previously on estates ten times bigger than this small, albeit wonderful, plot. I was trying to ignore Tom's pleas for me not to try squashing everything in, but I'm not one to easily take no for answer. The tennis court was a particular issue as it was another potential eyesore within such a tight and sloping plot.

Tom knew how to stop me when I was losing sight of reality:

'My thinking about adding the brick was that if we have too much stone it could be too unvaried. I'm thinking that it remains essentially a farmhouse and it shouldn't appear too grand. A bit of a mix of paving will make it have more of an organic vernacular feel, as if the plan has grown in response to need rather than as a grand design. Beware the golf clubhouse.' Tom knew I would be irked at the idea of our gardens looking like that!

We were trying to figure out how and where to position the tennis court for quite a while. It was only very late that we found the perfect spot, but from the very first conversation we

LEFT: The north garden is designed as a room in itself with a grid of beds alternately furnished with softly contoured box hedges. The barn in the background has been restored as a dining room

had the basis for the front and back gardens, as witnessed in another extract from an early email:

'The garden to the north of the house: this could extend from the house to the old barn so that there is an attractive route between the two. Perhaps a terrace close to the new barn could be the best place to sit in the garden for shelter from the sun and views of the farmhouse. Topiary? Could be a sort of modern take on the cottage garden. York stone and brick paths, perhaps an old water tank or large water trough somewhere, sophisticated, charming.

'Garden south of the house: I agree about making a hole in the hedge – perhaps bridging this with a rustic fence, possibly Major Bower again – again it would be good to keep the rabbits and deer out. I think this garden could be kept as a meadow, perhaps made into a really good wildflower meadow with grass paths cut through it and scattered apple trees. These could perhaps be crabapples which hold on to their fruit until early in the new year. I imagine you would want an area of terracing and planting outside the house looking out on to the meadow. Do you want somewhere to play football? In which case I guess long grass and trees are more problematic – but it would make this area a bit bland – as at present.'

The reference to Major Bower makes me smile as we have used him since our very first project together when I had spied a beautiful duck house advertised in the back of a magazine. This fearsome military officer has built a wonderful business making natural-looking cleft-oak buildings and fences.

The 'hole in the hedge' was intended to give us a great vista into the neighbouring fields, and an uninterrupted view of the downs on the horizon, with a starting point of wildflower meadows organised in a geometric structure, making a subtle *clin d'oeil* to formal gardens. Tom did not forget to include our need to find room for family football games in an adjoining field. Lots of other fancy designers would have sneered at nasty goalposts, but instead he got in touch with the Major again who made us some beautiful ones, quite probably the most expensive in the land!

The gardens north of the house are perhaps the most impressive, where Tom planted a wonderful selection of plants he knew I loved; embarrassingly I don't know any of their names. I have to admit I OK'd them based on pictures sent electronically. Taking as a starting point the original idea of water troughs, Tom designed a series of corten steel water tanks, in that wonderful rusted colour that blends so well in autumnal tones and with the roof tiles and bricks in the garden. (Remember this is a garden primarily for the shooting season.) While I refused to have modern material or structures in previous gardens, the case Tom made for the Donald Judd–inspired water tanks was irresistible, as in the following quote from his email:

'What do you think about lighting? I am assuming you will need to get easily from the guest building and barn to the house. I wonder if you think it might be a good idea to uplight the corten tanks? I have a 1.5 m. high wall at home that I light with a very neat almost invisible striplight in the ground (it is about 5 cm. wide and has a baffle in front of it so you don't see the fitting) and the wall glows a warm orange at night. It's really rather beautiful. I think it could be very dramatic and could give enough light for you to see where you are. Together with some light at either end on the buildings it could be enough. I would imagine we would light the tanks all around so that they were like orange cubes! Do you think this sound too freaky?'

Tom always studies what use we are looking to have from a garden and I am always amazed to see how much he cares about that, not trying to impose a design but creating what would work for the use we would want.

In comparison to the drama and detail on this side the south-facing garden takes on a rather calm, contemplative nature; it is for sitting out in, sipping coffee on the terrace or watching the sunset. At the front the garden is used as a beautiful thoroughfare, linking the dairy with guest bedrooms, the yard with cars where shooting meets are held, and the barn that has been restored into a dining room.

We paid particular attention to finding the right material for the paths, wanting to avoid traditional York stone and gravel. I love what (and why) Tom suggested we use first:

'Two things for you. There are some stone setts outside the cabin. One smooth sample is one that Gavin has found that are being taken up from the route of the Paris–Roubaix cycle race across northern France to the Belgian border every year, so quite a nice backstory.'

I quickly replied this would indeed remind us of our motherland but also of the cold and wet climate we had no desire to go back to, so I sent him on another trail. I actually

OPPOSITE ABOVE: The design of the north garden is reminiscent of a kitchen garden, beds criss-crossed with paths of uneven stone set on edge and ornamental planting including *Veronicastrum virginicum* 'Fascination', *Echinacea purpurea* and *Euphorbia seguieriana* subsp. *niciciana* set amongst ornamental grasses such as *Hakonechloa macra*, popping *Allium sphaerocephalon* heads creating movement and liveliness

OPPOSITE BELOW: A series of corten steel water tanks reflect the crabapple trees

A meadow mix with wild carrot *Daucus carota* and ox-eye daisies surround the tennis court, which is cleverly disguised by staggered and terraced box and yew with cleft-oak railings instead of nets

ABOVE: An orchard of
ornamental crabapples
in plats of meadow grass
with mounds of beech
and far-reaching views
of the landscape of the
North Wessex Downs

wanted to have smaller York stone, looking for unity around the house, but yielded when I saw Tom's last suggestion of uneven stone strips, with a red tint, that would echo the corten troughs and the red brick of the various buildings.

The north garden is designed as a 'room' in itself, enclosed by clouds of box north and south, open to the yard and barn on the east and abutting the house in the west. The bed design is reminiscent of a kitchen garden, criss-crossed with paths, yet the planting is totally ornamental and aimed at giving pleasure to the walker and the watcher during the shooting season. It gives us endless joy walking through it as well as sitting within it on an oversized bench, inspired by one I saw ages ago at Waddesdon Manor, there awaiting an impromptu moment of reflection.

Tom's other *coup de théâtre* at Hatch House is the tennis court. Fearless of the engineering works we dug deeply, in more ways than one, to build Tom's design for an enclosed room on the sloping area of land. The tennis court was eventually to be positioned in what is a very peaceful area at the south of the house whose vista could not be disturbed. A seemingly impossible task, but the clever use of staggered and terraced box and yew cloud hedging misleads the viewer into thinking of it as a 'foreground' ornamental feature, in symmetry with the nuttery that frames the other side of the wildflower meadow. It is only upon walking fifty yards from the house that one realises there is a tennis court hidden there at all. A beautiful cleft-oak railing was made wide enough by the Major for viewers to sit and watch play at the sides and slightly taller at the ends to catch balls. It is a work of genius and a template that should be used for tennis courts everywhere. No need to compromise with hideous plastic mesh.

I will finish with what is perhaps the most important endorsement of what makes the gardens at Hatch House and Tom's work so exceptional. As Tom designed the gardens to meet my desires I might have a bit of a bias. However, my partner Roubi spends much more time than me at Hatch House, so I asked him what he found beautiful in the gardens. Roubi

described to me how the front garden looks in all seasons like a painting, with a wonderful architecture that you are subliminally aware of while walking through, and struck by from bedroom windows. All the plants of varied height, the different materials, the branches of the trees, dense bushes, flowing herbs and popping allium heads combine to create a movement and a liveliness.

The garden always looks at its peak. In so many gardens one awaits the right moment when bare soil will finally yield some long-awaited flowering, or where the patches where planting is needed are as noticeable as what is in flower. At Hatch House the garden is naturally beautiful throughout every season. It is not a simple achievement but a tribute to Tom's exceptional *savoir-faire* and empathetic talent, for both of which I am eternally grateful.

One of our main reasons to own a country house is to feel an osmosis between interior and exterior, somewhere for family life where you just open the windows on Saturday morning, kids can roam and grown-ups can read morning papers in a bucolic setting. No need to go to the ghastly inner-city sports clubs to keep the kids busy!

Tom had understood our needs from the first time we met when he came to discuss a much larger project we undertook at Woodperry in Oxfordshire. He also well observed the psychology of all characters involved, especially me, a client who self-avowedly possesses a combination of creativity and control freakiness, is very clear on his likes and dislikes.

Looking back, there was a lot of Marie Antoinette's *Petit Trianon* retreat in our brief, to create a *ferme ornée* where the farmland and animals were legitimate by their aesthetics as much as their function, multiplying the pleasures of the land for all in the family.

Integrity was a big word for Tom! It took me some time to see how important it was in the landscaping world. Integrity of design, planting and, as Tom wrote to me, 'A garden is not the Chelsea Flower Show!' I guess that was his answer to my impatient desire to see everything grown very quickly, and to see a garden as a collection of all the plants I like!

Farleigh House

FARLEIGH WALLOP, HAMPSHIRE

❧

The Countess of Portsmouth

OPPOSITE: A pair of
wrought–iron gates by
Richard Bent marks the
boundary between the
garden and the lake

FARLEIGH HOUSE HAS been in the Wallop family since the mid-fifteenth century, but from 1954 to 1983 it was let as a boys' prep school and there was no garden to speak of, just prefabs and games fields. When I married my husband in 1990, he had recently moved back into the main house with his children and he gave me the happy task of finding someone to help bring the gardens back to life. The landscape historian Johnny Phibbs laid out the bones, based on a 1720 plan of the grounds that was found in the Estate Office. I took lots of advice, helped by our then Estate Manager, Nicky Lomax, and we drew up a shortlist of possible garden designers; they all came here and we, in our turn, visited gardens they had made or restored. Two great local gardening ladies, Rosamund Wallinger of The Manor House at Upton Grey, and Victoria Wakefield of Bramdean House, both mentioned the same name – Georgia Langton. We went to see Georgia at Stavordale Priory, her extraordinary house and garden in Somerset, and I fell in love both with her and her garden. I asked her if she would design a new garden for us, and she said no! I remember going out of the room and almost weeping with disappointment. It turned out that she only meant not yet, and so, a year later, she began her designs for Farleigh.

Georgia spent some time inside and outside the house sitting and thinking – 'pensing', she calls it – absorbing a sense of the place and of us. Farleigh House has an octagonal tower, and a series of octagons appear in the first part of the garden she designed for us within the old three-acre walled garden, which she turned into three gardens surrounded by cloister-like gravel walks. With her natural sense of proportion and scale, she planned the paths to lie in perfect and pleasing relation to the high yew hedges that flank them. Her taste is faultless, but never dull, and I love her sense of drama.

When I married I knew very little about plants and gardening. I loved a good garden and felt a spiritual lift when in one, but could hardly tell a daffodil from a dianthus. Shortly

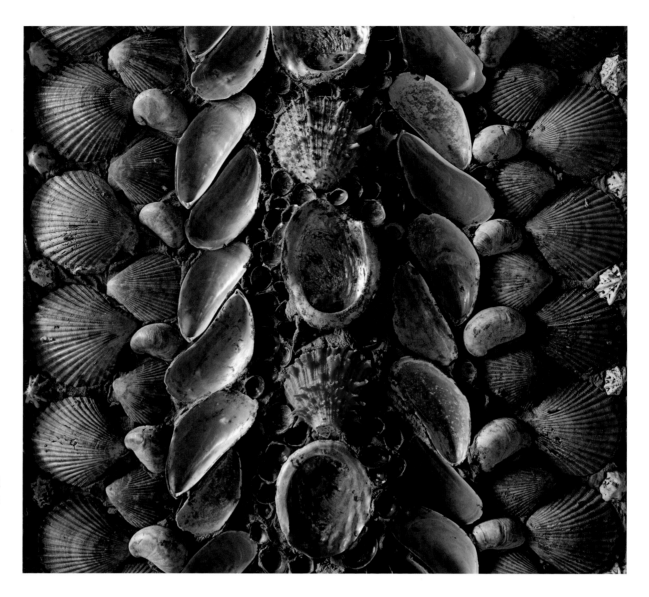

RIGHT: A detail of the shell patterns in the shell grotto by Jocelyn Hayden

BELOW: Diane Maclean's polished Indian granite apple in the orchard

after we started work, I set about, in a very informal way, trying to learn more. I did a course with Tom Moore with some friends, doing theory in the morning and practising on each other's gardens in the afternoon – pruning, propagating, plant association and so on. We all found ourselves in the same situation, having nice gardens and gardeners, but with insufficient knowledge and skill to be able properly to get involved or to ask for what we wanted. I also learned a lot from watching *Gardeners' World*, and from visiting other peoples' gardens.

Georgia has given us a garden that wraps elegantly around the house. It is laid out in quite a formal style, with vistas and *allées*, befitting the classical symmetry of the house, which was mainly built in 1731. Georgia's skilful balance between structure and effervescent planting is flawless; cleverly positioned evergreens, hedges and hard landscaping areas are all in harmony, and there are scented plants flowering somewhere all year round.

The formal part of the garden is about ten acres in all, including the ornamental potager, the formal rose garden and the wild rose garden. Four large vegetable beds divided by paths converge in an octagonal centre. There is a long herbaceous border leading down to the greenhouse, which visually dominates that end of the garden. The rectangular formal rose garden is quartered by gravel paths with four huge smoke bushes, *Cotinus coggygria*, one in each corner. Roses cascade in tiers of descending height underplanted with geraniums, alchemilla, catmint and lots of asters in the autumn. In the middle of this garden is an octagonal Coade stone fountain (copied from a picture I liked of one at Madresfield), cast

TOP: The knapped flint and stone façade of Farleigh House lit up by the setting sun with, above, the flag flying above the family crest

ABOVE LEFT: *Peonia mlokosewitschii*

BELOW LEFT: *Papaver orientale* 'Karine'

FAR LEFT: *Passiflora* x *exoniensis*

TOP: A wide herbaceous border leading up to the greenhouse in the walled kitchen garden with *Crambe cordifolia* behind Russell hybrid lupins 'Yellow Chandelier' and 'Noble Maiden', *Veronica austriaca* subsp *teucrium* and *Nepeta* x *faasenii*.

RIGHT: Philip Thomason's Coade stone fountain in the centre of the rose garden

in sections, with a mermaid sitting daintily upon a huge whale. The water spouts from the whale's blowhole. This statue, made by Philip Thomason, is a visual pun on our marriage. My nickname is Whale, while Quentin's family crest is a mermaid. Having seen the original Coade stone finials on top of the gate piers at the entrance to the walled garden, Georgia decided that all the urns, finials and pots in that part of the garden should be in Coade, and commissioned Philip Thomason to design them.

There is a wild rose garden, full of block-planted, single-flowering species roses, concealing the tennis court, with a small apple orchard underplanted with camassias. The rose hips in the autumn, huge, orange, black and red, are almost as dramatic as the flowers themselves. My favourite is a dark red arching *Rosa moyesii* 'Hillieri'. At the far end is a sculpture of a group of five, metre-wide, stainless steel seagulls by Diane Maclean. They dip and whirl above a large billowing box hedge that is pruned into waves with arching crests on the point of breaking. Originally the birds dipped and whirled above a froth of flowering smokebush, but when that grew too enormous — it now towers above the birds — we adapted the box instead.

At the entrance to the wild rose garden is a pair of beautiful wrought-iron gates by Richard Bent; antiques of the future I am assured. Richard has made all the wrought-iron gates, by hand, throughout the garden. We have five pairs of his gates, each more contemporary in design than the last, as we allowed ourselves to trust his skill and style. The final pair marks the boundary between the garden and the lake — stunning and monumental while still witty in style and for which he won a Blacksmiths' Company award.

There is a winding nut walk, where martagon lilies flower magically in June, which we have filled with gnarled tree stumps from the woods and planted with ferns and primroses. It is one of my favourite places in the garden. We have planted small areas of wildflower meadow at each end of the walk. The house sits on a hill, and at the back there is a rectangular lawn, sometimes used for croquet, bordered by hedges, beyond which the land falls away into a valley, with lovely distant views over parkland with groups of May trees. Between the hedges, a *patte d'oie* of *allées* leads the eye towards rides in the ancient Great Wood beyond. These refer back to the days when Farleigh House was a hunting lodge and riders would set out from the house after the deer in the wood. They are rather overgrown at the moment but in the longer term we hope these woodland rides will be cleared and reinstated.

Next Georgia put in a Serpentine Walk, a clever, low-maintenance, atmospheric link from one part of the garden to the next. It is a maze of sorts but with only one direction of travel, winding between yew hedges; the air is filled with the heady scent of unseen philadelphus wafting over, while *Rosa* 'Paul's Himalayan Musk' towers above in June. We have recently added a wonderful shell grotto, full of family references, by artist Jocelyn Hayden. She spent a year making beautiful pictures out of shells bought from a wholesaler in Penzance, to decorate an otherwise ugly entrance to a well. You pass what would seem to be the centre of the maze, where a curved bench is overhung by a cherry tree, guarded by topiary peacocks in a sea of violas; continue windingly along, and then emerge, blinking, into a bright, spare, contemporary Japanese pond garden, dominated by a white marble sculpture by Jessica Walters called *Hokusai's Boat*. Everything in this garden is green and white — green grass, green ivy screens, white bench, white roses, white statue in the pond, white *Nymphaea*

'Gladstoniana', white-stemmed silver birch. It is almost the last place to get the evening sun and I love sitting there tossing fish food to the giant koi carp that live there, watching them come to the surface in a feeding frenzy.

A Scot's pine walk leads from here to the new lake. Excavated in 2001 from open farmland on the south side of the garden, it covers about an acre and has an island, a little jetty and a dinghy and is planted with native marginals. The lake has given us enormous pleasure over the years, from admiring the writhing frogs and frogspawn at Easter, to the annual races every summer on home-made rafts, ending with an evening barbecue and music.

Every year we seem to have a new project. A cut-flower garden became a necessity when I found we were spending much too much on flowers for the house. There is a new woodland walk winding down to the lake, designed by our Head Gardener, Andrew Woolley, who is also taming the old apple orchard near the house, pruning the ancient twisted branches gradually over several years to re-establish strength and fruitfulness. We are lucky because Andrew has a degree in sculpture and it is he who is responsible for the brilliant topiary peacocks in the Serpentine Walk, and the waves under Diane Maclean's seagulls. In the orchard there is another sculpture by Diane Maclean of an outsized red apple, made from polished Indian granite.

In the greenhouse we have been helped by Lisa Rawley to assemble a collection of scented and tender plants to flower throughout the year. The greenhouse is used for propagating, as a place to look after houseplants, and a delightful place to visit. There is a ravishing espaliered peach, several huge brugmansias, brunfelsias, plumbago, scented geraniums, and mimosas. A gorgeous lipstick-pink *Passiflora* x *exoniensis* is an especial favourite. We have a constant battle against bugs and red spider mite who find the warm climate there as appealing as we do.

Now, more than twenty years later, the gardens have reached a settled maturity. Georgia has given me a totally undeserved reputation as a good gardener, and a summer career showing people around. The garden has made many thousands of pounds for charity from people visiting on open days and tours, and has greatly enriched the living inheritance of generations to come.

Editor's note: Since Lady Portsmouth wrote this piece, Farleigh House has passed to the next generation, and her stepson, Lord Lymington, has now taken charge of the gardens.

OPPOSITE: The pasture
where cattle graze in
the park

OVERLEAF: Georgia
Langton's ingeniously
designed yew maze

The Old Rectory

Naunton, Gloucestershire

Mrs Angela Cronk

'I THINK YOU WILL have to start from scratch' was Dan Pearson's conclusion after he had spent a couple of hours surveying our newly acquired garden. This pronouncement did not come as a complete surprise to me (although my initial request had been just for planting advice) but it certainly was to my husband, Michael. We had, after all, just purchased an old house that would require work, and a complete overhaul of the garden had not been on the cards. In truth, though, it was the only option.

When we moved here the garden was largely the creation of Nicholas Ridley MP. However the intervening owners had not lived here for much of the time and so the garden had become a shadow of its former self. The River Windrush seeped through a wall, waterlogging an ornamental sunken garden. The bog garden had dried up; a canal leaked into the cellar; walls had fallen down (and within weeks of exchanging contracts so did a pair of mature willows). It was a sad sight but I wrote to 'Mr Pearson' saying 'It could be magical' and indeed, twelve years later, it is.

In those very early days trying to figure out where to start was daunting and we knew that we were going to need help. The only person whose help I wanted, or sought, was Dan's. This was purely instinctive – we had never met – but I knew that his style of planting was what we wanted and what the garden needed. Without his guidance I am absolutely certain we would never have had the courage to undertake such a radical remaking.

I grew up in Ireland and my love of gardens and gardening came from my grandfather to whom I was very close. He was also a wonderful storyteller and we spent countless hours together in his garden. If and when it rained we would adjourn to the greenhouse where, as we pottered, he would tell me endless stories of 'long ago'. Looking back it was a quite idyllic introduction to gardening. When eventually I came to London, and then married, I knew someday I would have to have a garden but I also knew that it was not really a practical option while we were so committed with jobs, schools and

ABOVE: The edge of the timber stack in the woodstore

OPPOSITE: The unfurling fronds of the royal fern *Osmunda regalis* beside the pond with the east façade of The Old Rectory behind

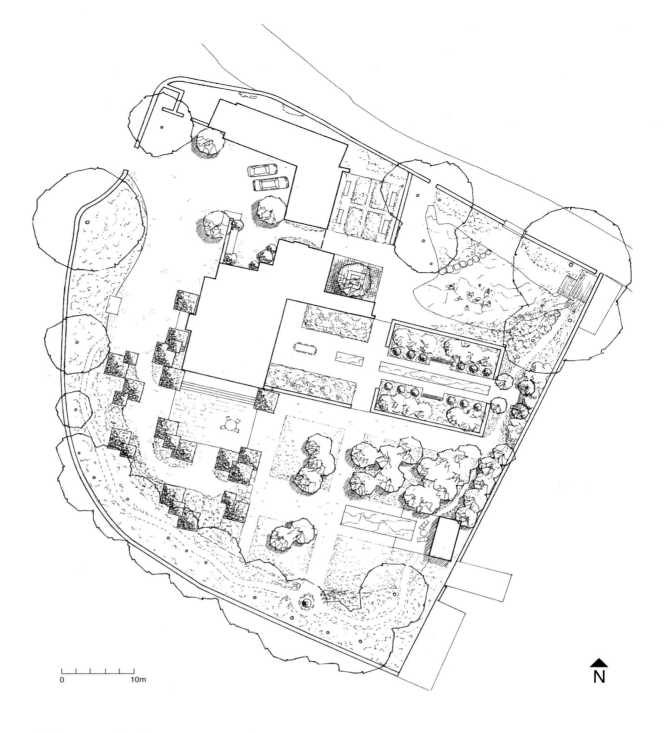

0 10m

N

ABOVE: Dan Pearson's masterplan for the garden

children's weekend city activities. The years passed but then in 2002 we found The Old Rectory.

We had wanted a large garden and some land but settled for just over an acre. So ours is not a particularly large garden but, in winter, it is a very cold one prone to hard frosts and, although bordered by a river and with water meadows beyond our back walls, it is on the dry side. It nestles at the end of a valley and has 'borrowed' views of sheep grazing on one side and of some lovely old Cotswold stone houses stretching away on the other. We get some beautiful morning hazes and, as the house is built on the compass points, sunlight from dawn until dusk; so plenty of what Padraig Pearse, the Irish poet, called 'slanting sun'. The Windrush borders the garden on its north side and a stunning 300-year-old beech tree stands by the entrance gate.

The scale of the work was enormous and inevitably took rather longer than we planned, most of the delay being weather-related. Steve Swatton and his team were with us for well over a year. His attention to detail matched that of Dan's and together they were a formidable combination. There were times when the ground was frozen solid and others when the place was like a quagmire, but each day brought its own excitement as the old disappeared and the new slowly but surely began to emerge. Smooth York stone, setts or riven stone were used to

ABOVE: Multi-stemmed
Snowy Mespilus,
Amelanchier lamarckii
on a corner of the south
terrace

suggest the 'feel' of a particular space. It is amazing how exciting the foundations of a wall or path can be as the bare bones of the hard landscape become visible.

Gradually the bog garden became a pond fed by the river. It was fascinating subsequently to discover from old plans that there had originally been a pond there with, according to the rector of the time, water snakes of 'wondrous length'. The sunken garden was dug out, membranes and liners put in to keep the river at bay, and the ground levelled to create a vegetable garden with four large raised beds. We replaced the canal with a longer, wider one enclosed by dry-stone walls with oak 'arrow slits' that offer tempting glimpses of the garden beyond. On the south side of the house a large and rather lacklustre lawned area was transformed by the creation of a terrace, three wild meadow areas and a swimming pool as discreet as we could manage. Dan had always resisted including a pool in his designs and he was not at all keen to begin with, but as he has actually swum in it I think he may have been converted! From a family point of view it has been a hugely successful element of the garden.

As the hard landscaping was coming to an end we began to make enquiries about possible gardeners. It was our great good fortune that Fergus Garrett at Great Dixter recommended Jacky Mills and her partner, Ian Mannall. They arrived in time for the initial planting and have been with us ever since.

Now that the garden has somewhat matured, it is easy to forget the scale of that planting – the shrubs, the trees and the thousands upon thousands of tiny pots that went in at the start. It is also easy to forget that, about two years later during the 2007 floods, the garden

ABOVE: The spring blossom of *Magnolia* x *loebneri* 'Merrill' and *Amelanchier lamarckii* are set within an asymmetrical grid of clipped box squares

was completely under water. Some damage was done by debris and by the contents of our log store floating in all directions; the pool cover rose with the flood waters like a magic carpet but, in the circumstances, the garden got off lightly (which is more than can be said for the dead fish which we were later to find in the pool). Such was the depth of the water that one neighbour, who was trying to help, forgot that there was a pond there at all and fell straight in!

Since then the garden has grown and matured beautifully. Each area is quite distinct, leads effortlessly to the next and creates a harmonious whole. We planned for year-round interest, scent and places to sit in both shade and sun. Each season has its own magic moments and we often have disagreements as to which time of year is best. It is impossible here to describe what is going on throughout the garden season by season but suffice to say there is always something at which to marvel.

Winter can be stunning when we have had a heavy frost. The canal freezes and the box balls that frame it provide a shimmering guard of honour ably supported on either side by a double row of *Hamamelis mollis*. As this is the view we have from our kitchen window we look out and admire it countless times a day. If there has been snow then the underlying symmetry and structure of the garden is highlighted and can be appreciated more than at any other time of year. Elsewhere cyclamen, snowdrops and aconites brighten winter days while on the terrace, large cubes of *Calamagrostis* x *acutiflora* 'Karl Foerster', which are left uncut until spring, weave a magic all their own as they waft to and fro against a backdrop of stately yews.

In spring the same canal garden then delights us as hundreds of 'White Triumphator' and 'Sapporo' tulips and *Brunnera* 'Langtrees' take over from the winter ferns and hellebores.

Then as summer approaches the cool white and pale-yellow summer palette begins its show with *Allium* 'Mount Everest', *Hemerocallis citrina*, *Phlox* 'David' and *Veronicastrum virginicum* 'Album'.

While all of this is going on at the far end of the garden the 'hot' borders near the house explode into a riot of reds, magenta and oranges with a plant list that goes from A to V!

In the meadows *Crocus tommasinianus* heralds the start of a six-month festival of surprises and colour which only ends when they are cut at the end of July. There can be few spaces in any garden that have so much packed in per square inch! It is such an exhilarating time as these meadows in spring and summer are a delight. They teem with wildlife – birds, insects, bees, butterflies and voles (which have been known to nest there). Less welcome, foxes and muntjac deer drop by at night-time.

The three meadows started life with an identical meadow mix, but by year two it became apparent that the area nearest the yew trees was both shady and damp and was going to need a rethink. Now it is quite different. Cyclamen thrive there as do narcissi including 'Actaea'. *Camassia leichtlinii*, *Tulipa sprengeri* and *Colchicum* 'The Giant' are recent successful additions.

Whenever I think of the garden, in my mind's eye, I see first the terrace with its three large beds of *Lavandula* x *intermedia* 'Impress Purple' absolutely teeming with bumble and myriad other bees and butterflies. The sight, scent and sound of these beds epitomise summer in the garden. Sitting there on a summer's evening, with a glass of wine, is heavenly.

I can easily picture the pond in its spring/summer colours of whites and yellows punctuated by leucojum, ligularia, mimulus, primulas and *Typha minima* among many others, with a dash of blue from *Iris* 'Gerald Derby' that provides a nesting place for our resident moorhens and the perfect backdrop for the *Nymphaea alba*. Kingfishers and herons are regular visitors here

ABOVE: *Clematis montana* 'Grandiflora' cascading over a wall. *Hamamelis* towers above *Allium* 'Mont Blanc', *Hemerocallis lilioasphodelus* and Welsh poppies, *Meconopsis cambrica* with plump box balls

LEFT: Marsh marigold, *Caltha palustris* and *Leucojum aestivum* with primroses around the pond in spring

RIGHT: The white-flowered *Anemone* x *hybrida* 'Honorine Jobert'

FAR RIGHT: Hart's Tongue fern, *Phyllitis scolopendrium*, emerging through a froth of sweet woodruff, *Galium odoratum*

too, the former never failing to thrill, and the latter to fascinate and irritate in equal measure. This is a favourite place to sit, listen to the river, watch the insect activity on the pond, wait for fish to surface, marvel at the *Rosa mulliganii* arching out over the Windrush from an old yew tree or wait for the sun to set.

Just beyond the pond lies our vegetable area: four raised oak beds, five large terracotta pots and several 'moveable' potato bags. From this relatively small space enough salad, vegetables and herbs are produced to keep us more than happy and we are spared the worry of a 'glut'. Given our frosts, a glut is probably too much to hope for from our *Ficus* 'Black Ischia,' but hope springs eternal! On the plus side our strawberry vine *Vitis* 'Fragola' (a present from Dan) often fruits happily.

It is not possible to think of our garden without imagining the autumn colour. Our giant beech may lead the way in terms of size but the *Hamamelis* x *intermedia* 'Jelena', *Cercidiphyllum japonicum*, *Amelanchier lamarckii*, *Euonymous* 'Red Cascade' and liquidambars produce a wonderful tapestry of browns, reds, golds and ambers.

These are but a few 'snapshots' of our young garden. It is, after all, a mere nine or so years old but it certainly 'punches above its weight'. It will be fascinating to see how it develops. We are certainly looking forward to the pleasures and challenges of the years to come.

Crockmore House

Henley-on-Thames, Oxfordshire

The Hon Mrs Julia Kirkham

I WAS VERY LUCKY to have met Christopher Bradley-Hole at Chelsea Flower Show in 1994, and on the strength of what we saw in his garden there employed his talents to create an oasis behind our mews house in Notting Hill. Christopher's acute attention to detail made us look no further when deciding on who would be the best person to interpret the site at Crockmore House when we moved here from France in 2000. The reward of finding the right landscape architect has been a blessing, as Christopher has created a paradise for us that even the children appreciate; they would miss the garden as much as the house if we ever had to move.

Christopher's interpretation and design composition show what can be achieved in the right hands in terms of anchoring a house to its site, giving it a sense of belonging to the landscape. I have learnt so much about the manipulation of space and intelligent composition from him. I now join Christopher's Chelsea planting team whenever he is lured back to create another unrivalled masterpiece there.

A subtle awareness of a great mind at work starts from the moment you come through the gates at Crockmore and register a bold arrangement of architectural yew hedges slightly offset on the diagonal either side of the front door. These cleverly act as a device that both subliminally ushers visitors to the parking area and discourages anyone from sticking their noses into your library windows! Christopher also configured a pair of concentric beech hedges on this side of the house that allude to a mysterious space behind, within which he planted a grove of multi-stemmed silver birch trees on the site of the original house before the current one was built in the late 1980s.

Our collaborative process started by standing in the garden and looking at the way the land fell away from the property. Christopher began drawing a series of curves. In his mind he had already visualised the terrace from the then-yet-to-be-built huge conservatory that would become the hub of the home, and the generous entertaining spaces it leads on to. His design

OPPOSITE: Edging the pool are various forms of fountain grasses including *Pennisetum villosum* and *P. alopecuroides* 'Hameln' backed by *Miscanthus* 'Ferner Osten'

surrounded these with a vast curved bank dropping down into the garden. He repeated the curves out as far as the fields, where a deer fence is concealed behind *Persicaria amplexicaulis* 'Firedance' and miscanthus grasses that seamlessly link the garden to the landscape beyond. Visitors to the garden always want to know the name of the persicaria as it works so well as a giant screening plant.

Beyond one area of the bank there were a few random apple trees. Christopher chose this area to reflect the concept 'Out of Chaos, Order' by arranging it into a series of eighteen large beds set out in a symmetrical grid. This is the heart of the garden. It gives me a great deal of pleasure to take visitors up to the top of the house so that they can see the effect the grid beds create from above: they read like a deliciously textured tapestry as the muted colours from the plantings converge.

Choosing the plants for the grid beds was left very much in Christopher's capable hands with me in attendance (plus very tiny baby) on the one sunny afternoon that he had free at that time, we spent a wonderful afternoon at Bury Court when it was still John Coke's nursery Green Farm Plants. I gravitated towards anything in the mauve, pink or blue spectrum. Christopher made the plant choices and these have sustained the garden well. *Knautia macedonica*, one of his trademark plants, punctuates the planting throughout, as does *Salvia* x *sylvestris* 'Mainacht'. There is a perfect balance with vast quantities of beautiful grasses, each with their own special qualities. *Calamagrostis* x *acutifora* 'Karl Foerster', *Miscanthus gracillimus*, *Stipa gigantea* and *Pennisetum alopecuroides* 'Hameln' are firm favourites. Every year clouds of *Aster* x *frikartii* 'Mönch' spill over the gravel pathways under the apple tree in the centre, and the odd *Dianthus carthusianorum* pokes its head through clouds of *Astrantia* 'Hadspen Blood' and *Persicaria amplexicaulis* 'Firedance'.

I know that the endless children and adults who have wandered among the plants must sometimes have felt like Alice in Wonderland, with *Eupatorium atropurpureum* towering above their heads and the ephemeral qualities of *Gaura lindheimeri* making gauzy veils through which to view the punchier plants like *Monarda* 'Garden View Scarlet' and *Echinacea* 'Fatal Attraction'. This area of the garden is an oasis, which works really well as a set piece where one can immerse oneself within wonderful grasses and perennials.

Fifteen years on it has only changed slightly from the original planting scheme. The ever-encroaching persicaria needs curtailing when it invades spaces where phlox and astrantia should be holding court. Fennel is also a thug, requiring serious editing from the grid beds and main border every year. My own love of late summer colours is reflected in one of the grid beds being filled with vibrant hot pink, magenta and mauve asters which I have brought back from visits to Orchard Dene Nurseries and Picton Gardens.

Connecting the grid beds with the enclosed raised vegetable beds was a wildflower meadow with pairs of medlars, Morello cherries, damson and quince threaded through. These trees suffered from my poor pruning and the meadow area, although a beautiful sea of marguerites and cowslips in early May, didn't work well when the grass had been cut in September at a time when most visitors come to the garden. Christopher and I had a discussion about the area and he felt it could become more of a *hortus conclusus* akin to one of his Chelsea Flower Show gardens which I had worked on. So last year I set about removing the wildflowers, returfing the areas of grass and lining them with a series of clipped yew

hedges. I have added six hornbeam cubes at intervals along the beech hedge that shelters the vegetable garden. This has been wonderful in terms of adding more structure to the garden and we now have a quiet contemplative space, a pause between the exuberance of the grid beds and the joyful cacophony of the vegetable garden with its clashing colours of dahlias and nasturtiums in late summer.

The grid beds are now bordered by two very peaceful spaces. As a bridge between the ebullience of the perennial planting and as a foreground to the beautiful pasture with its backdrop of mature oaks, beyond which you see Oxfordshire stretching to the far horizon from upstairs windows, Christopher conceived the idea for a very simple circular lawn. Intended to put one in mind of an ancient stone circle, this magical and meditative space was also an ingenious way of dealing with the slope of the land that angular terracing would have drawn attention to. There is a very simple distinction between the neatly mown grass within the circle and its ring of unmown grass suggestive of the fields beyond.

Also as part of the initial design a section of the terrace surrounding the conservatory was turned into a playground with climbing frame, swings and an amazing sandpit 'bakery' where our children whiled away many a happy hour. It wasn't long, however, before a swimming

LEFT: The open space of the circular lawn is separated from the circular beech enclosure, seen right, by an area of meadow grass

BELOW LEFT: The deer-proof fence is concealed by a mixture of *Miscanthus sinensis* 'Silberfeder' *Miscanthus gracillimus* and *Persicaria* x *fennica* 'Johanneswolke'

BELOW: The rich colours and textures of the grasses and perennials in late summer light

pool became more in demand so it was back to the drawing board with Christopher to plan a pool which would fit into the surrounding garden and from which you would look down over the mesmerising planting of the grid beds.

As it is close to the house the space needed to have an architectural impact in winter. Christopher chose black basalt from Italy as the stone for this area and arranged it in a series of contrasting textures, enormous wide open slabs around the pool juxtaposed by the precisely laid courses of the surrounding walls. Basalt chippings at the end of the pool give rise to a planting of foxtail fountain grass *Pennisetum villosum*, whose soft inflorescences are interspersed with upright *Verbena bonariensis* that has a luminous vibrancy when its clusters of well-spaced flowers catch the late afternoon sunlight. The combination of these two plants is something many visitors remark on, now happily replicated in many a garden. Alliums punctuate this space in late spring and their purple heads against the grey basalt are also beautiful. There is a pleasing simplicity to the stark masculine impact of this area.

When we moved to Crockmore with three small children from an apartment with a small terrace in France I had a desperate urge to contain them; even the patio areas seemed vast for toddlers to be left wandering around on. The area was enclosed by a low picket fence that was very suffocating to me but practical for containing young children. We then replaced the obtrusive picket fencing with marine-quality nautical wire that Christopher had used in the Chelsea garden. (It was actually one of the things that had brought him to our attention.) At last I felt I could breathe; we could see plants growing from the conservatory windows rather than be denied their therapeutic benefits. The final coming down of the fences happened late last year (when I was persuaded by a fresh pair of eyes to remove the heavy industrial grey barriers that had kept the pool area safe), and finally the nautical wire. I found this a very liberating experience; you now truly feel within the garden while sitting on the terrace, with *Sedum* 'Purple Emperor' and *S. telephium* 'Matrona' poking through by your feet. The beauty of being in this garden is that you can sit here at sunrise on a cold frosty morning surrounded by the monochrome tints of copper and bronze from the upstanding grasses and the seed heads of sedums, or in late afternoon sunshine as the sun glints through the grasses and they shimmer with an iridescent quality, all summer right through into the late autumn.

The design of this garden is simple yet strong, and demonstrates that a limited palette boldly planted with repetition is so relaxing to be in and live with. The fact that the garden Christopher designed remains so remarkably intact is testament to his design being right not just for the site but also for us as a family. Looking after it and sharing it with appreciative visitors on a visual and energetic level is an ongoing privilege.

PAGES 200-1: The garden as seen from above with a wide band of *Verbena bonariensis* growing through the *Pennisetum villosum* by the pool

RIGHT: The varying shapes and shades of ornamental grasses including *Calamagrostis* x *acutiflora* 'Karl Foerster', the giant oat *Stipa gigantea* and forms of *Miscanthus sinensis*

The Vineyard

Mrs Richard Griffiths

THE DAY MY husband Richard came to view The Vineyard I was grounded by blizzards at our home outside New York so had to rely on his description of a house with over an acre of garden overlooking Hurlingham Park in one direction. It sounded too good to be true. When he mentioned the separate gardener's cottage called The Coach House that was it. An offer went in before I'd even seen it, prompted I must confess by close friends who said if we didn't jump at it they certainly would!

Richard's spontaneous decision was not quite as impetuous as Lord Beaverbrook's when he bought The Vineyard in 1919. The story goes that one afternoon, irritated at none of the Hurlingham Club tennis courts being free, he spied one through The Vineyard's open gate and bought the property for £5,000. His granddaughter, Kirsty Smallwood, who we bought The Vineyard from in 1998, had made a lovely garden with borders full of all sorts of plants I didn't then have a clue about, nor how on earth I was going to maintain them as a novice gardener. My first thought was to get everything catalogued so that if I killed anything I knew what had to be replaced. Over two years Simon Johnson compiled our 'garden bible' and the 'daunting prospect' gradually shifted to 'joyful obsession'. We also commissioned an account of the house and garden from the architectural and landscape historian Ruth Guilding. Her research is the backbone of everything I know about the history of The Vineyard.

Parts of the cellar, ground floor and outbuildings are built on the foundations of a sixteenth-century Tudor monastery when Hurlingham was known as 'ffurnyngham ffyeld'. There was a plague pit and pest house a short distance away until 1665 when the Bishop of London, whose residence was at nearby Fulham Palace, records only ten houses between Fulham Town and the hamlet of Broomhouse. Unimaginable for what is now a rat run between terraced houses linking the New King's Road and Fulham Palace Road!

In the early eighteenth century this area was renowned for its market gardens: 'the great fruit and kitchen garden north of the thames . . . stocked with apples pears, cherries, plumbs

OPPOSITE: The exotic spires of the hardy *Yucca gloriosa* in flower with a haze of the dark-blue *Salvia guaranitica* 'Blue Enigma' behind

(sic) walnuts etc . . . raspberries, gooseberries, currants and all such fruits , shrubs and herbs, as will sustain the wet with the least injury'. If only wet were our problem today! After struggling to keep our garden alive through two dry summers we made the decision in 2007 to have our own water supply. Being so close to the Thames the water level is high at five metres so we drilled a borehole and went down through river terrace gravel and London clay to twelve metres. It is lovely to know that our little orchard and vegetable garden are continuing a local tradition that goes back over 300 years.

Charles Gray, whose father founded the famous Fulham Nursery on adjoining land that achieved an international reputation, took on the tenancy of The Vineyard in the early eighteenth century. He grew ornamental plants here for the horticultural trade that was then a new phenomenon. Christopher Gray was one of a group of professional nurserymen involved in the publication of *Catalogus Plantarum: A catalogue of Trees, Shrubs, Plants and Flowers both Exotic and Domestic which are propagated for sale in the gardens near London* (1730). The fame of the gardens of Fulham Palace may also have been an attraction to the Grays who purchased plants from Bishop Compton's famous collection at Fulham Palace. The *Magnolia grandiflora* Gray listed was from the first one to arrive in England from which all others in the country at that time were propagated. It would be nice to think that the two *M. grandiflora* we planted to camouflage the composting area are its descendants.

Mulching is a crucial activity with so many tree roots grasping nutrients from the soil so we purchased a large grinder and make satisfying mountains of delicious compost; only our rose trimmings and problem weeds now get removed in bags. The trees are a mixed but very necessary blessing for us and our many neighbours, but we have a marvellous tree surgeon whose annual visit aims to keep everybody happy. Whoever planted the magnificent beech tree, whose mast we use to cover the paths in the woodland garden, was not thinking of trees for small London gardens! The large trees in the garden include several limes, a large *Quercus ilex*, cut-leaved hornbeam, parrotia, liquidambar, ash and catalpa. That is just the big trees . . . My favourite is possibly the rusty-orange-trunked *Luma apiculata* in the east garden.

The nursery prospered until the end of the nineteenth century. The Grays had sold the house and nursery to the family of Dr William John Burchell, yet another extraordinary plantsman whose four-year voyage of exploration from 1811 yielded 63,000 natural history objects and specimens. His botanical collections and manuscripts went to Kew. Somehow The Vineyard survived the massive housing boom and was left as a rare survivor when most of the other old houses in the vicinity were pulled down to make way for rows of terraced housing in the 1880s. Maybe it was the garden that saved it from demolition. We have a few fragments of grotto-like flint work on an old wall with ivy-covered pillars that are believed to date from 1750. The garden went through various guises and inhabitants between then and Lord Beaverbrook's fateful wander down Hurlingham Road. Beaverbrook's friend and biographer A. J. P. Taylor considered The Vineyard 'the most delightful of Beaverbrook's main residences, the only one with real charm and character'. He built a covered loggia whose roof acted as a terrace where he supposedly slept outside on warm nights. Possibly sleeping off good dinners with Lloyd George or Winston Churchill, who used to come here to watch films projected onto the recessed cinema screen in his dining room.

Our move to The Vineyard after ten years on both the east and west coasts of America where I had battled with extreme temperatures in both our gardens was heaven: settling into such a historic house and enjoying the benign temperate climate. This acre of sandy loam is now divided into seven areas. We inherited good structural bones, but a lot of the beds required an overhaul so we put in fresh plants.

To a lot of passers-by who love to peer through our wrought-iron gates the south-facing front terrace garden looks much as it did when we arrived; the same wonderful plants with a Mediterranean feel, phlomis and fennel, sprawling sages, rosemary and cotton lavender all remain, occasionally renewed and spruced up with the injection of new ingredients. We now have lots of large tender salvias here and big pots either side of the front door with mounds of *Abelia* x *grandiflora* that flowers for months on end from late summer. These look lovely against the ochre-painted Regency façade and dark-green windows.

Sculptor and garden enthusiast Kenneth Topp helped us enormously. He planted a hazel copse, as suggested by Simon, which we now harvest for our plant supports, amongst the existing *Leucojum aestivum*, a giant 'snowdrop' that I love, and wild violets. It is a small area but transports your imagination to woodland walks. Many hours of exquisite pruning and gardening kept the garden flourishing before Kenneth set up his classic copper company Bronzino.

Inspired by a visit to Chelsea Flower Show we planted *Viburnum rhytidophyllum* as a canopy for a bed created out of cloud-pruned box. Kenneth started taking cuttings to provide a constant supply of fillers. There was no water feature in the garden so I asked Kenneth to design one that we could enjoy on a daily basis. It is hand-formed in the shape of a Mediterranean oil jar from copper which has been tin plated and set on a small brick plinth surrounded by large Scottish pebbles and water-tolerant plants such as mare's tail (which is contained). It cleverly masks the noise of traffic and marks a moment after we get out of the car to shed the bustle of the outside lighting and livens up what was a rather shady area walking towards the house.

The year 2007 was a momentous one for the garden. Bryan McIntyre arrived as a full-time gardener and he has transformed our lives. Over the past eight years the garden has become a real joy as we work together discovering new treasures and excitedly discussing where a new plant might be happy.

It was also the year I decided to move the greenhouse closer to the house. We had always had problems with the original one as it was tucked away in the north-east corner of the garden, shaded by trees and attached to a neighbour's house wall which was never popular. My lovely new Alitex greenhouse, painted green to match the house windows, has become the centrepiece of our kitchen courtyard with York stone paths recently replacing gravel and I can now potter around it, a stone's throw from the kitchen. *Rosa* 'Chevy Chase' with its stunning magenta flowers and deep-green leaves grows nearby.

Next up for revamping was the area around the old greenhouse which was being used as a vegetable garden, but urban pigeons were not helping. I was having some metal structures put up by Cotswold Decorative Ironworks and every time I asked them something they suggested I speak to Rupert Golby, so I got in touch with him. Rupert has done a whole lot

OVERLEAF: A north-facing border adjacent to Hurlingham Road is filled with male ferns *Dryopteris filix-mas* while phlomis, olearia, yuccas and salvias bask in the sun against the house across a lovely old York stone path

more than just revamp the vegetable garden, but his lovely list of additions there gives some indication of the changes happening elsewhere in the garden.

We have put in a new layout of York stone flagged and brick-herringboned paths centred upon a small dipping pool and enclosed by metalwork trellis, which replaced decaying timber-trellis work. Metal towers shelter timber benches and the tented canopy of a fruit cage protects crops from the ravages of urban birds.

This secret garden provides fruit, vegetables, herbs and flowers from its raised beds edged with York stone slabs while richly coloured rambler roses 'Bleu Magenta', purple-leaved grapevines and deep red honeysuckle *L. periclymenum* 'Red Gables' scale the walls and metal frames, complementing the rich variety of colour and texture found in the vegetables.

A timber pantiled potting shed has replaced the old greenhouse and partially conceals the gable end of the neighbouring house. This part of the garden, which for years had not felt particularly inviting, has been transformed into an echo of what this area was famed for. We now have gooseberries, figs and blackcurrants, lettuces, radishes and rhubarb as well as great bunches of picking roses in jewel-like colours – 'Chianti', 'Cardinal de Richelieu' and 'Charles de Mills' – that I fill the house with. The garden is peppered with roses and I particularly love them growing up through the old apple trees. This requires quite a lot of pruning but it adds to the extraordinary sensation that you are in a country garden and not in the middle of London. Possibly my favourite day in the year when I appreciate The Vineyard most is when I get back from Chelsea Flower Show, gloriously happy that my garden looks more natural and settled than anything else I saw that day. Poppies and peonies in the raised bed next to the croquet lawn look as plump and good as any getting medals a mile up the King's Road!

Richard and I travel a lot. We are sometimes away for what feels like weeks at a time, but I dream of what is going on in the garden and always look forward to coming home to find some wondrous surprise.

OPPOSITE: A wrought ironwork gate with a vine leaf design supported trailing tomatoes and now hosts a passion flower

ABOVE: A mixed border of roses and perennials is backed by swags of Rose 'Albéric Barbier' with Rose 'Gertrude Jekyll' on the corners underplanted with *nepeta*

RIGHT: An Ali Baba terracotta pot is halfway along the iris bed leading to an arbour festooned with rose Dublin Bay and rose Winchester Cathedral

FAR LEFT: The border in autumn with *Dahlia* 'Rip City' and *Aster novi-belgii* 'Red Robin' with a glimpse of the blue and white wendy house

LEFT: Herbaceous peony 'Monsieur Jules Elie'

LEFT: *Anemone hupehensis* var *japonica* 'Pamina' flowers through late summer and autumn

BELOW: *Abelia* x *grandifora* grows either side of the porch by the front door while *Salvia guaranitica* 'Blue Enigma' happily overwinters outside and euphorbias seed themselves at will in the lovely old York stone path

RIGHT: Dahlias extend the flowering season of the pots

Mount St John

FELIXKIRK, NORTH YORKSHIRE

Christopher Blundell Esq

WHEN WE CAME to look around Mount St John in the May before the Millennium there were three things that instantly really appealed to me and made me think that this was going to be really special: the terrace with its extraordinary panoramic view; the enclosed Yorkshire brick walled garden; and the completely hidden valley garden. I grew up in the very beautiful but much harsher landscape towards the Howarth area of Bradford near the Pennines, and my wife and I spent ten years near Skipton, the Gateway to the Dales. Here we are in the Hambleton Hills at Felixkirk on the edge of the Yorkshire moors at an elevation of 500 feet, halfway to the top of Sutton Bank, which is clearly visible to the west, but bizarrely we are in a microclimate that is much more benign than anywhere I have lived before, with a lot less rainfall.

There has been a settlement at Mount St John since medieval times. The bowl beneath the ha-ha of the Georgian house that was built in 1720 was the site of one of Yorkshire's many monastic centres. They must have chosen the site for the same thing that so appealed to us: the spectacular view stretches fifty miles southward across the Vale of York. Peppering our horizon are the twin spires of York Minster and a few power stations that have a certain romantic appeal from this distance! When Tom Stuart-Smith first came here in 2004 he compared the setting to the view of Rome from Tivoli. Very Tom! I doubt Hadrian witnessed quite the same weather coming towards him, for despite my theory that much of the worst weather goes over the top of us when it comes from Sutton Bank (as do the gliders that use the thermals on summer days), you can still time your watch by it when a weather front is coming.

We could have just sat and stared at this view that we will never tire of, but the house was crying out for a sensitively thought out garden to anchor it to the site and we needed a masterplan for the park and the trees that needed attention. I have been fortunate to work

OPPOSITE: Wide borders of perennials and ornamental grasses flank the terraces and croquet lawn in front of the house. *Eupatorium purpureum* is threaded throughout the garden's many areas, seen here in early summer with *Euphorbia palustris* and *Geranium* Rozanne

ABOVE: A pencil drawing by Tom Stuart-Smith with his original proposal for the garden around the house. The orchard was foregone in favour of more perennial planting as can be seen overleaf in this panoramic view that shows Sutton Bank in the distance

with some well-known garden designers, but Tom has been the only one who's got that wonderful creative design knowledge and, more importantly for me, being at the sharp end of it, plant knowledge. Tom clearly had a real enthusiasm for how the garden could sit within the overall landscape. We both thought that the immediate garden was obviously extremely important but then we had parkland beyond that, and the parkland led into the broader landscape. Tom seemed in great sympathy with the context, and I was keen to get a very natural link with the view beyond the garden. The nice thing about the view is that it is very much a reflection of the agricultural landscape and the diversity of agriculture in the Vale of York, particularly in the summer when it's a real patchwork quilt of arable land, pasture, woodland and a diverse mix of hedgerows. Tom reflected this in his design of the garden and took a lot of his cues from the dynamic shifts of form and colour; you can be overlooking the bright viridian greens of young wheat or barley, then a quilt of browns and ochres after harvest and ploughing. His ever-changing palette of plants in the garden cleverly reflects this.

Tom conjured one of his wonderful overviews, an artist's impression of how he envisaged the garden, and a decade on his imaginings have shifted from fantasy to horticultural reality. The plan set the context for the garden and was a wonderful tool for encouraging my wife and myself when all we had to show for a garden in those early days was hard landscaping construction and mud.

The garden was done in two phases. Levels needed changing and we made two generous terraces where there were three, giving a more expansive descent to the ha-ha that we pushed out so there is a seamless leap to the horizon. Yew divides more traditional beds that go with the Georgian façade from the contemporary garden that contains many thousands of perennials and grasses on a series of levels. Generous wall-backed borders and Tom's 'tumps' as he calls them, domes of beech, combine to make the whole composition look wonderful whether it's midwinter, spring or high summer. This part of the garden is almost better the worse the weather. In the middle of all this profuse planting is a quiet spot by a lily pond: a vestige of the seclusion one senses down in the valley garden.

You arrive at the house and have no idea that behind the yew hedge is a steep-sided ravine that has been utterly transformed in the last decade. Although still a work in progress, where there were muddy puddles with an inch of water there are now three descending pools, criss-crossed by stepping stones and weaving side paths bordered by appreciably tall planting that engulfs you. Some of the planting here is an echo of the planting above, the eupatorium and grasses, but the atmosphere couldn't be more different. One thing that differs from the top garden is the phenomenal jungle-like stands of gunnera.

The valley garden is a place of retreat and tranquillity. I like the fact that it is a very private area that looks in on itself more than out, except from the very bottom where Sutton Bank suddenly comes into view. It is a deceptive site as from Tom's viewing platform by the croquet lawn it seems steeply dramatic, yet when you are enveloped within it the scale changes utterly. The ponds have been recreated on the site of earlier monastic fishponds so we have stocked the lower pond with rainbow trout that resemble a swarming mass of piranhas at feeding time.

The valley garden is riddled with springs that were a mixed blessing during the development of the site. The fabric of the monastic ponds had long since vanished, but luckily we could puddle with clay from adjacent banks without damaging the magnificent grove of beech trees. The actual planting was a bit of a logistical nightmare initially, and thankfully Tom in his infinite wisdom planted lots of ground cover to hold back the soil erosion. It took five of us to do the planting and we ended up throwing the plants to each other because that was the easiest way to do it. To see the planting now coming to maturity you would never imagine the amount of work that was involved. We are making a nursery area at the top to bring on some interesting rhododendrons from Glendoick that we can then move to where they will thrive. I have a cascade in mind as where the steps go down already makes me think of an old riverbed; water would look wonderful pouring from the very top through the birch trees and banks of *Primula florindae* to the ponds.

Water is never going to be a problem at Mount St John; copious springs aside, there is an underground reservoir at the very top of the property that we are looking into reconnecting to the hydraulic rams in the field at the bottom. One of the Walkers, a fascinating family of engineers and inventors who lived here for 140 years from the start of the nineteenth century, was Chairman of the Thirsk Water Company with a legacy that Mount St John has free water in perpetuity. Liquid gold in the garden. Especially the walled garden.

My business life has been devoted to farming and food so I knew that bringing the walled garden back to life was going to be become an integral element of family life at Mount St John. However, even in our first years when we were only cultivating a quarter of the space there was still just too much food for us to get through. So we bit the bullet and decided

LEFT: *Kniphofia* 'Goldelse' and *Echinacea purpurea* are two of the dominant plants during this particular phase of the herbaceous planting that undergoes many variations of form and colour through the seasons

RIGHT: *Eremurus* 'Yellow Giant', *Anemanthele lessoniana* and *Eryngium* x *zabellii* 'Jos Eijking' with *Coreopsis verticillata*

to cultivate the whole space, edge the beds with beautiful stepover apples and pears that are underplanted with chives and supply a local Michelin-starred chef with our surplus. It has ended up being the impetus for a new chain of local inns, Provenance Inns, established in 2010, which now takes all our produce; the closest inn being the Carpenters Arms located on our doorstep in Felixkirk. Possibly the proudest moment for the gardeners here – well, for us all – was when we supplied the 2014 Tour de France dinner at the Royal Hall in Harrogate. We certainly showed the French what Yorkshire can produce! Mount St John tomatoes are something of a speciality. My favourite, warm from the vine, is 'Tomatoberry', a variety that looks like long trusses of strawberries. Surplus apples are taken over to the nearby monks at Ampleforth for cider. Having started with too much space, now we don't have enough, and a big polytunnel is the cut-and-come-again lettuce and salad leaves.

Adjacent to the walled garden, which we created out of a yew nursery, is another enclosed space that was a stallion paddock when we came here, with high walls and hedges so Diddycoy the famous Stanhope dressage stallion couldn't see any of the mares beyond. It is now a working cutting garden. With no stallion to keep in solitary confinement we commissioned a pair of gates from the Wren Man, a wonderful carpenter now in his eighties who trained with the Mouseman at Kilburn. The cutting garden also doesn't just supply the house any longer and we grow everything from spring bulbs to dahlias, some plants for drying in bunches or foliage such as the big bed of pollarded eucalyptus that is in constant demand. New varieties make their way here from things I spy when I have meetings at RHS gardens where I am a trustee.

I love the sensation of the different spaces, the continual awareness of the garden evolving and the scope for all the projects in the future. Tom has an idea for a belvedere on a spot at the edge of the ha-ha where clever tree thinning has opened up a whole new view over a different angle of the Vale of York. We have plans for a lake that will hopefully one day glint in the bottom of the valley. My wife and daughter have a thriving dressage business so there are always mares and foals 'animating the landscape', as Tom puts it, but with my practical agricultural hat on I like seeing our Aberdeen Angus cattle that manage the pasture so beautifully.

The garden and park work so well as it is the setting for the family's passions for horses and food, our love of the outdoors and Yorkshire. It is also a fabulous space for entertaining, with nothing better than big gatherings of friends on the terrace.

I think the fact that the garden does fit in a very sympathetic way with the landscape beyond is testimony to Tom's work and all the dedicated people who work here, making it such an invigorating place to marvel at and enjoy.

The English Country Garden, Updated Classicism

Wychwood Manor

BURFORD, OXFORDSHIRE

Mrs Alexander Wilmot-Sitwell

A QUEST OF TWO years led us here, to Wychwood, where our very precise criteria met finally with magnificent possibilities for both house and garden. Set between the Cotswold towns of Burford and Charlbury, Wychwood Manor sits slightly north of the remains of the Wychwood, in what John Piper describes as 'some of the best of the Oxfordshire landscape; open upland country under grass and corn . . . with ochre stone walls . . . and isolated clumps of sombre trees.' A big landscape, and we knew we would have to be bold about the garden and surrounding policies.

Having seen their work at Houghton Hall in Norfolk, Alex and I felt that Julian and Isabel Bannerman could give the garden the combination of robust structure and blowsy planting that we had so admired there and we hoped that they would help us connect the inner garden to the outer farmland despite the darkly encroaching thickets that grew all around the house. When we met them amid a city of builders' site huts, we all instantly agreed that what we most loved were the big panoramas of this topography, the trees, the spires and the broad sweeps that lay all around. However all that beauty was tantalisingly hidden, the house closely hedged in by mixed trees, rhododendrons and conifers in grant-aided plantations. The fact that the garden had a belt of acid clay running through it, that it welcomed calcifuge rhododendrons and magnolias, particularly excited Alex, whose family are knowledgeable about rare plants and trees. The previous owners and their head gardener Shirley, whom we were blessed to inherit, had lovingly tended the garden but had been happy to live with what we felt, with fresh eyes, gave a sense of confinement.

Alhough Alex initially recoiled at the prospect of removing a single tree, the Bannermans convinced us to open up to the broader landscape and the pastoral vistas, to see beyond the creepers and the shelterbelts. However he was seduced by miraculous machinery when he realised a tree spade could successfully move twenty-year-old trees around the fields and that we had scope for a colossal programme of sapling planting, the transformation of the garden got underway.

OPPOSITE: The vaulting Lime avenue flanked drive is crossed by an unlikely swathe of acid soil

PREVIOUS PAGE: An unhindered view on the south side of the house through a band of soft blue delphiniums rises to meet the woods beyond

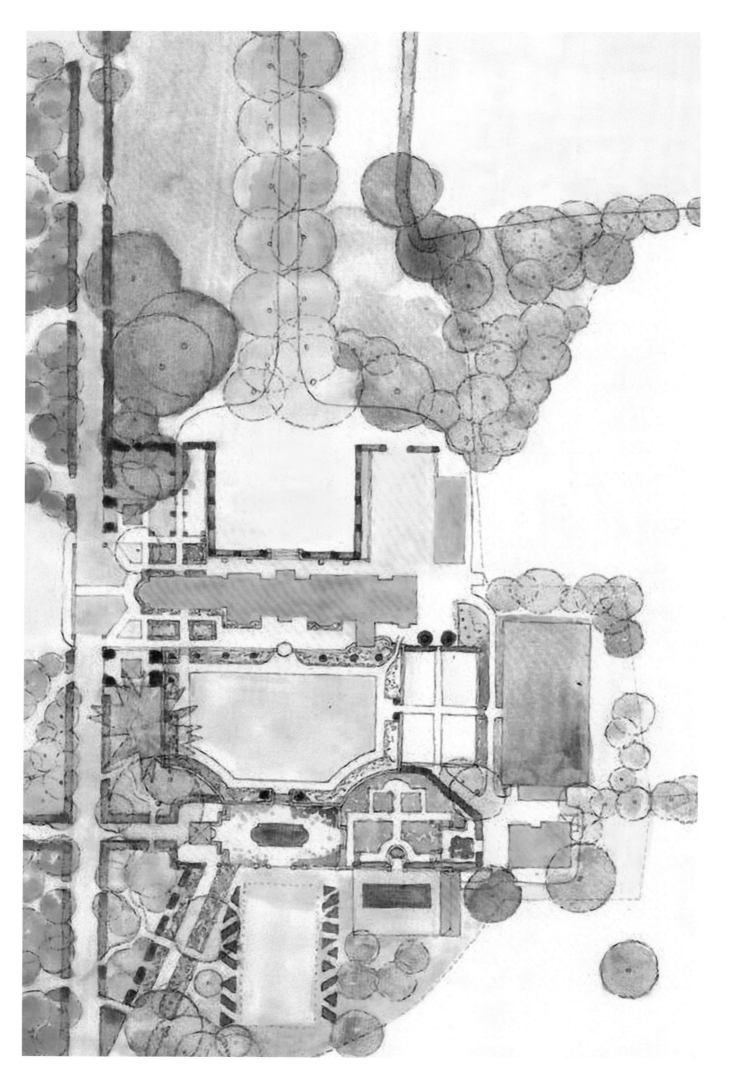

In 2006 the gabled 'Jacobethan' house, built in 1913, was being glamorised and extended, which meant the garden was being pulverised by builders and their machinery. The chief problem was that close to the west and east ends of the building, mixed plantations of native trees had been planted twenty years earlier. Left un-thinned these woodland belts had created scraggly dark squirrel playgrounds bang up to the house. A formal Arts and Crafts garden dropped away in stages to the south, but even here self-seeded ash and sycamore straddled the skyline, hiding a sodden and derelict tennis court. The Bannerman powers of persuasion showed that clearing these would reveal a dipping meadow, a pear orchard redolent of Samuel Palmer and the meadow rising to woods beyond, a glorious unhindered view that we now enjoy every day from every window on the south of the house.

The Bannermans brought on board Toti Gifford's landscaping arm of his extraordinary West Country circus and a lake was quickly nestled in the bottom of the meadow by diverting the gin-clear waters of the stream which runs along the hedgerow. The garden needed to connect to the landscape on all sides, but such unpicking had to be done stealthily to calm Alex's anxieties about the destruction and with a clear aim in mind. Shelter and protection, once gone, take a long time to re-establish. The plan envisioned a layered, lush, formal flower garden in the middle leading out from the house, and then the creation of radiating 'rides' to the sides created by judicious editing of the 1980s plantations. 'Goosefoot' triangles were created with the tree spade, keeping the best trees *in situ* and removing thinnings to provide material for planting parkland clumps in the meadows beyond. The result is a most satisfying transformation, emphasised by strong green lines of hornbeam hedges with the radiating avenues focused on specimen trees and the church spire that is now visible from the bay window of our new drawing room. Inside each triangle of thinned thicket we have added lilac, philadelphus and species roses in long grass that in spring is spangled with bulbs. These enclosures have a maze-like effect with cross views drawing you in a plethora of direc-tions; they are not laborious to maintain and help to make a transition from the tight visual intensity of the garden to broad open parkland. The park was created from a field of twelve acres that was given a sense of connection to the garden by the addition of a new ha-ha that is flanked by traditional iron park railing. The outlying copses were conjured from the more mature plantation trees we moved, mainly oak, lime, ash and pine, buttressed by a multitude of native whips and saplings.

At the heart of the garden, contemporary with the house, was a large dry-stone-walled enclosure, bordered with beds encompassing a level sward. We mirrored an existing curving wall with its matching pair that provided a backdrop to the swimming pool, immediately giving a sense of harmony. The Bannermans persuaded me that the addition of a wide hoggin path surrounding the central lawn would not only add light and texture to the garden but also allow for the lavish bowers of flowers I so desired to venture out of the confines of their beds and over the gravel. We all agreed there must also be plenty of structure, and scent. Every doorway, window or cross path would be dotted or crossed with plants like *Daphne odora*, sarcococca or philadelphus, making a trail of scent all around the garden. For structure within the deep borders, a dozen twelve-foot-high yew domes were planted as year-round sentinels peopling the garden. Grizzled on frosty days, fuzzy-coated when in new growth, they provide weight to the whole composition and a welcome sober note amongst the

OPPOSITE: A section of Isabel Bannerman's watercolour masterplan for the garden at Wychwood

Strong winter russet
lines of hornbeam hedges
with radiating avenues
focused on specimen
trees create a maze-
like effect of goose-foot
triangles, drawing you in
a plethora of directions

ABOVE: Characteristic
Bannerman green
oak doorways with a
Jacobean flavour are set
within the yew 'wing'
walls

exuberance of the floristry. Near the house my yen for glorious, generous borders full of erysimum, sweet rocket, irises and lupins, followed by poppies, delphiniums and shrub roses, was brilliantly interpreted by Isabel and Julian. The richly manured limestone soil is partly responsible for making this all achievable, but it is the mastery and brilliant cossetting of Shirley Emery and her team that make it look, and feel, so superb.

A handsome cedar of Lebanon presides on one side of a raised lawn, which again we had to free from a thicket of sycamore, with a sunken garden and lily pond lying below. Here we added a rill at the base of the recently completed gazebo. This is a fittingly 'golden afternoon' confection of green-oak columns and Cotswold stone roof, pitched steeply and splaying out at the bottom like those at Hidcote. It is the perfect place to have drinks in the evening and in its first summer of newly quarried stone and fresh oak it sometimes shone like a golden pavilion at sunset, but it is almost too quickly weathering to Cotswoldian silver. This presides over the long peony borders that start the year awash with hellebores then brim over with peonies followed by lilies in high summer. A few cleverly placed *Rosa rugosa* 'Roseraie de l'Haye' give height and structure, and their magenta blooms and hips look wonderful through a veil of *Verbena bonariensis* and the spider flower, *Cleome hassleriana*, right through to autumn. A sensational successive planting I would recommend to everybody, as these borders look wonderful from February until November. The geometry of these long double borders is also deeply satisfying, running downhill, on and out with a sturdy oak in the distance by the stream. Halfway down there is an opening leading to a different perspective of goosefoot triangles with a romantic tangle of rambling roses in the trees on one side and then more at the very end to the west, which are contrasted with a level 'football' pitch edged with yew cones as serried ranks of spectators on the other to the east.

The football pitch was always on the family wish list and this has become the perfect space for it quite close to the house. It provides a moment of calm (when a game isn't underway) before coming to the horticultural abundance in the swimming pool garden and the kitchen garden on the opposite side.

The terrace and the swimming pool garden both aim to be headily aromatic and hotly coloured for the hotter days of July and August. Made with slabs of old Cotswold paving that we found locally, the terrace is raised and well drained, allowing a *maquis* of French lavender, orange rock roses and magenta lychnis that luckily survive our perishing winters. Ramblers 'Adelaide d'Orleans' and 'Albertine' scramble through wisteria on the gabled elevation, but the new Georgian-esque drawing room is harnessed by the solid green of *Magnolia grandiflora* with violet roses 'Veilchenblau' and 'Rose Marie Viaud' between the windows. Yew 'wing walls' near the house with characteristic Bannerman green-oak doorways with a Jacobean flavour give an architectural framework. As you can imagine, the swimming pool is the bit of the garden enjoyed most by my three boys, who may as yet be unaware of the efforts we go to embellish this particular playground! Set in its warm arc of comfortable, high, dry-stone walls, it is filled with pots of agapanthus and a host of jolly July annuals and biennials including Californian poppies, calendula and shocking-pink salvias.

Over the wall, taking advantage of its warmth and enclosure, we have made a garden for vegetables and cut flowers. The corner that is now the centre of garden operations

BELOW: Roses 'Veilchenblau' and 'Rose Marie Viaud' grow between the windows of the new Georgian-esque drawing room, their colour picked up by rose 'Rhapsody in Blue' and *Erysimum* 'Bowles's Mauve' grown in the gravel with *Euphorbia characias* subsp. *wulfenii*

OPPOSITE TOP, BOTTOM AND BELOW: Every doorway window or cross path is dotted with plants like *Daphne odora*, sarcococca or philadelphus making a trail of scent all around the garden. Lavender and roses are a feature of the south-facing terrace.
ABOVE: *Hydrangea arborescens* 'Annabelle'

with greenhouse, potting shed and compost corner was yet another sycamore-choked copse with a dark back drive leading to the old coach house. Now it is a hive of energy, cultivation and delicious sustenance.

New projects bring new pleasures each year. Alex's longed-for acers and magnolias have been planted in the grassy glades where the vaulting lime-avenue-flanked drive is crossed by an unlikely swathe of acid soil. Piers and finials are added to gates and the parkland and boundary plantings get improved and modified. The business of releasing this garden and providing a reasoned structure to reveal previously hidden connections to the big upland landscape, while also creating the romantic garden I so yearned for, has been undertaken with patience, a gradual unpicking then putting pieces into place. The inner garden is now sheltered and settled, embowered in the broad sweep of the high wold like a 1930s railway poster of perfection.

OPPOSITE: Set in a warm arc of comfortable high dry-stone walls, the vegetable and cut flower garden and the swimming pool garden that hosts jolly July annuals such as love-in-a-mist, cosmos and Californian poppies *Eschscholzia californica*

THIS PAGE CLOCKWISE : Towering blue *Delphinium elatum* 'Galileo', rose 'Charles de Mills' and rose 'Comte de Chambord'

Stavordale Priory

CHARLTON MUSGROVE, SOMERSET

Michael Le Poer Trench

CAMERON AND I saw Stavordale for the first time in the early evening of 20th September 1992. The then owners David and Georgia Langton greeted us at the gate with the words 'You're late' (we had stopped for toasted teacakes at a Little Chef on the A303) and suggested that before viewing the house we look around the garden before it became too dark. I will never forget walking through a small doorway in a wall which, with the Priory buildings, encloses the cloister garden. Catching the last rays of an autumn setting sun, the sight stopped me in my tracks and literally brought a tear to my eye: I suppose it was love at first sight.

Stavordale is an Augustinian Priory founded in 1243 and majorly rebuilt in the early sixteenth century. After the Dissolution it became a farm and then at the end of the nineteenth century was converted into a gentleman's residence by T. E. Colcutt, who coincidentally also designed the Palace Theatre where *Les Misérables* ran for the first fifteen years of its life providing us with the means to purchase and maintain Stavordale. Photographs from the early part of the twentieth century show the Priory surrounded by traditional rose beds and *Thuja* hedges but after several years and changes of ownership the Langtons in 1979 inherited little of horticultural worth. Georgia set to work using her skills as a garden designer to create structure with clipped and fastigiate yew, box and various standards including Portugese laurels. The wasteland on the north side of the church became the quartered upper cloister and in the lower cloister gardens her mother, plantswoman Olive Taylor Smith, contributed in her own style. Georgia's inspired vision was in the process of maturing when we moved in. Without it we could never have developed the garden over the following twenty years into the magical place it has become.

It may have been love at first sight in 1992 but my relationship with the garden was not immediately the full-on passion that it is today. Working at the time as a professional theatre production photographer gave me little opportunity to develop much in the way of practical

LEFT AND OVERLEAF: Part of the Augustinian Priory at Stavordale founded in 1243. The two-metre deep quatrefoil pond surrounded by standard Portuguese laurels *Prunus lusitanica* and (overleaf) beautifully pruned soda bread loaves of box around pear trees *Pyrus communis*

or intellectual horticultural skills, but gradually the focus shifted from tripod to herbaceous border. I may now be getting confused between writing about the gardens at Stavordale and writing about my life since we arrived, but it appears that they have become one and the same. I even had a thought that a love of gardens and a love of Musical Theatre are connected – that wandering a well-planted border or wild garden backlit by the setting sun can elicit a similar response to that of repeated viewings of a well-crafted musical: a heightened emotional state. It makes you feel good. And just as the occasional visit to the West End or an NGS open day can create a warm internal glow, those with a greater knowledge of the medium will take even greater delight in a witty orchestration or an unexpected planting combination.

In the sense that I have no professional horticultural qualifications and that I am not paid for my work at Stavordale, I am an amateur gardener. However, although the *Concise Oxford English Dictionary* defines an amateur as 'someone who is considered inept at a particular activity', the eighteenth-century French and Italian (and therefore Latin) origin of the word is 'amare' – *to love*. And that's me: I love being in the garden, reading about gardening and plants, clicking on plants and putting them into my virtual wheelbarrow on specialist nursery websites, pruning, digging, making compost, mulching, Chelsea chopping and reluctantly detaching my secateurs from my belt and coming inside as the light fades on a midsummer evening.

These days, unless it's pouring with rain, I take a digital radio with me into the garden, also providing them for the gardeners. Luckily even the younger ones are prepared to listen to Classic FM. Jobs accomplished during cold or wet days may provide satisfaction but horticultural pursuit in the warmth of spring sunshine accompanied by Vivaldi and Mozart feels like pure pleasure. When I head to London and am asked where I have been to have such a healthy tanned complexion I am often not believed when I say 'Somerset'. There is also surprise at my filthy fingernails indicating I get down and dirty in the garden rather than directing others to do so for me. In fact I have to say 'My name is Michael and I'm a plantaholic'. Luckily for me this seems not to adversely affect my liver but does excite my senses and calm my soul.

Our first garden open day was in 2009 to raise money for the rebuilding of the local village hall. We opened solely for our village neighbours – about eighty people in total. Until then neither Cameron nor I felt that the garden was in a suitable state for public scrutiny as our work commitments had meant that various head gardeners had been left to manage our inheritence from the Langtons with limited input from us. The main credit for the transformation goes to friend and plantsman Sean Walter, owner of The Plant Specialist nursery in Buckinghamshire. As my interest in the garden increased Sean introduced me to the ideas, so fundamental to me now, of right plant right place, planting combinations and considering selections other than those available on a weekend visit to the local garden centre. Sean has never drawn up a formal planting scheme and planting combinations are constantly evolving as he continues to introduce me to his favourites and as I read, watch and absorb. He has been very patient with me, allowing me to discover and embrace various planting styles at my own pace. We also have disagreements – particularly over slightly invasive plants – as I believe that there are not enough hours in the day to control a plant that persistently

ABOVE: Topiary yew with a vigorous white rambling rose, 'Paul's Himalayan Musk'

wants to occupy considerably more space than that originally allotted to it, no matter how delightful the cultivar.

Visitors to the garden often comment on how 'natural' it looks which I find interesting because a truly natural garden would of course be overrun with bindweed and ground elder. I point out that keeping the balance between natural and neglected at Stavordale is an ever-present task. Of course it is the structure of the shaped yew and box inherited from Georgia that allows a more relaxed feeling in the planting and encourages this 'natural' reaction. Possibly it is this free and usually generous planting style that gives a sense of cohesion between the diverse garden areas. I am also aware that while newcomers to the garden see the wonder of it I have to stop myself just seeing the weeds. I imagine that this is the plight of many hands-on owners who need to be reminded to stop and smell the roses from time to time.

Although we give well deserved credit to Georgia for much of the structure that still defines the garden, we are also proud of the additions we made after moving in. An architectural fragment purchased locally inspired Cameron to commission the design of a grotto complete with a built-in provenance dating back to antiquity. Deciphering the mosaics on the lower level provides a challenge to visitors unsure of the date of the now overgrown folly. Even when it's explained that many but not all of the symbols reference Cameron's theatrical achievements there are a couple of obscure ones that are never guessed.

Concurrent to the construction of the grotto we decided to turn an existing circular pond of limited aesthetic appeal into one with a quatrefoil shape while still utilising the four standard *Prunus lusitanica* that Georgia had planted around it. In order to deter an ever-present heron from standing in the water and dining on the fish we decided to make the new pond two metres deep (and in the process coincidentally discovered that deep water remains cooler and therefore inhibits the growth of algae in the warmer summer months). The excavations for the new pond uncovered the buried bones of previous monastic inhabitants dating from the fourteenth and fifteenth centuries and we felt that these should be reinterred in a suitable location. The carpenters still working in the house kindly built a small coffin for the remains and our friend and then headmaster of nearby Downside Abbey school, Dom Anthony Such, agreed to perform a Mass for the dead in the Jesus Chapel attached to the main church building. For some reason he insisted on doing this on Hallowe'en so we insisted on scores of red and white tea lights to accompany the evening burial ceremony within the upper level of our newly constructed grotto.

We now open the gardens a handful of times each year to small garden groups. Although it is often suggested that I guide the groups my experience is that very quickly, even with small numbers, those at the back are soon chatting amongst themseves and following the group rather than actually experiencing the garden. So I send everyone off with a map of the main attractions and a rough idea of when refreshments will be served in the South Courtyard. I enjoy hearing over a cup of tea and housekeeper Lyn's renowned cakes and scones discussions of 'Did you see the elephant?', 'I loved the planting around the Granny Pond' and 'If you missed the grotto then you must pop in after tea'. I hope that, as individuals left to wander and discover the garden for themselves, the visitors are able to experience the garden in a way that not only suits their own horticultural interests but also allows them to

OVERLEAF LEFT: The cloister garden with its stone fountain in the centre is surrounded by the Priory buildings, also seen from above (overleaf below left)

OVERLEAF ABOVE RIGHT: The lake with mown paths leading through a meadow beyond

OVERLEAF BELOW RIGHT: Buster the Wheaten Terrier drinks from the quatrefoil pond in summer with its four Portuguese laurels underplanted with a ring of epimedium

RIGHT: The curvaceous
forms of the topiary are
offset by electric blue
Ceanothus concha, nepeta
and *Phlomis russeliana*
against the Priory walls

OPPOSITE ABOVE:
A view of the rill flanked
with striking vertical
leaves of *Iris pseudacorus*
'Variegata' and steps
covered in the trailing
bellflower *Campanula
poscharskyana*

OPPOSITE BELOW: A
detail of the beautiful
gate at the top of the rill

OVERLEAF: The same
view in winter, lit up
at night

briefly take ownership and enjoy more of a direct emotional connection with what they see.

Recently it occurred to me that one of the most notable yet subtle additions to the garden during our tenure has been the sound of water. The Hestercombe-inspired tiered rill, the fountain in the Upper Cloister (on a timer so that the trickling noise outside my bedroom window doesn't induce additional nocturnal bathroom visits – an innovation gratefully adopted by Alan Titchmarsh for his own garden), the Highgrove-inspired dish fountain in the so called lavender garden (right plant right place: lavender won't grow in the shade but I am keeping the name to bemuse visitors), the constant trickle through the wall of moss in the grotto and the stream connecting all the three lakes adds this extra dimension to the garden experience. Returning to the musical theatre analogy: a performer's ability to sing, dance and act is known as 'a triple threat'. Could a great garden be similarly equipped but this time with the talents of sight, smell and sound? Maybe that's why I am finding gardening photography so challenging: the camera can only capture one of those three senses.

Wyken Hall

SUFFOLK

❦

Carla Carlisle

I
N MY FAMILY I am known as the Duchess of Phoney-Baloney. The title stems from my tendency to swerve from the truth. As I was born on the banks of the Yazoo River in the heart of the Mississippi delta, you could say this moral flaw is embedded in my DNA. Where I come from our relaxed approach to honesty is called 'The Mississippi Truth'.

Nowhere is my honorary title more relevant than on these pages writing about the garden at Wyken. I am not a gardener. Certainly not in my husband's eyes. He is a true believer in the Church of the Holy Plantsman, which holds its services in Latin and adheres to the belief that the gardener who is not a plantsman is a horticultural sinner, whatever other redeeming goodness he or she may possess. I take a more forgiving stance and point out the importance of marriage in a garden.

The most obvious married garden is Sissinghurst and, with that garden as a template, I am Harold and my husband is Vita. I hold strong views on the design of a garden. I fuss over how things should be laid out, what you should see from one end to another, how it should relate to the house, the sanctity of materials. What matters to me above all, however, is how the garden makes you feel. I like a garden that makes you feel at home on this earth, cheers you up with its beauty and, a modest hope, enhances your will to live. I also like comfort in a garden. This means I prefer garden seats that say 'Come over here, take a load off' to sculptures that speak of antiquity and prosperity. Like my fellow southerner Nancy Lancaster, I also believe that white furniture looks like aspirin in the garden and, like her, I prefer moody blues, the shady tones that soothed us under the blazing sun of our hot birthplaces.

I was not always a horticultural fraud. Before I came to Wyken as a bride I had more confidence. In my left-wing youth out in California I planted rows of rosemary and lavender, although I had only seen pictures of Provence in the pages of *Gourmet* magazine. I grew tomatoes, a congenital passion in Southern women that met with disapproval by my comrades

OPPOSITE: Wyken is painted in copper red limewash close to the original Suffolk pink making the greens greener and the blues bluer

OVERLEAF: In the brooch garden, the L-shaped open veranda and five moody blue rocking chairs from Mississippi exude a sense of welcome. The quincunx of five interlocking box circles was inspired by Gertrude Jekyll's design for a herb garden at Knebworth

who saw it as evidence of bourgeois feminism. They were prophetic in their indictment. The better world I envisioned was one in which everyone grew tomatoes, kept a pot of basil in their kitchen window and possessed a beautiful wooden salad bowl. It was inevitable that I would end up in France where these tendencies toward individualism were not seen as a betrayal of the revolutionary struggle but fundamental requirements of a good life.

Despite my love of France and all things French, my years there were a horticultural low point. I loved the Tuileries but it is all trees, gravel, round ponds and Maillol sculptures. I lived near the Jardin des Plantes but all I remember is walking through the *allées* of plane trees, pruned every year with a brutality that never ceased to shock me. The only grand garden that I regularly visited was Vaux-le-Vicomte, created by Le Nôtre in 1661 for Louis XIV's finance minister Nicholas Fouquet. The ambition and grandeur of the chateau and garden triggered the king's jealousy and M. Fouquet ended up spending the rest of his life in prison, a sad ending that hovers like a cloud over the garden to this day.

The visits to Vaux-le-Vicomte did not provide me with any horticultural knowledge. It was like visiting the Grand Canyon and feeling stupefied by the sheer miracle of its existence. I only began to look and learn when I came to England. Long before I visited Sissinghurst I had read Quentin Bell's two-volume life of Virginia Woolf, as well as Vita Sackville-West's garden writings and *All Passion Spent,* so the garden had an immediate familiarity. What surprised me was the sense of intimacy. Somehow I realised that this was achieved by the 'rooms' and by the strict colour palettes. The overall sensation was a feeling that Colette describes as 'peaceful and exciting'. In one of those moments of gardening osmosis, I acquired an understanding of what a garden should try to be. An even greater influence was a visit a year later to Hidcote, the quintessential English garden created by Lawrence Johnson, an American. It was a *coup de foudre* and, although I was a novice, I could detect Johnson's influence on Vita Sackville-West. Again, separate areas divided by hedges and walls, on an intimate scale, with lavish planting created with a palette of brilliant and precise colours.

A garden scholar looking for signs of influence on Wyken would easily find the Hidcote clues. Blue gates. Brick paths. Holm oaks (Johnson bought his large from France; we bought ours young from Norfolk). The house at Hidcote, like Wyken, is not the focal point of the garden. Hidcote stands aside. Wyken, now painted in coppery red limewash that is closer to the original Suffolk pink, provides a foil for the planting, making the greens greener and the blues bluer. On one early visit to Hidcote I stood for a long while gazing into an avenue that connected the garden to the woods and fields beyond. Now there is a lime avenue at Wyken leading to the wood.

In the rabble-rousing sixties a poster from Paris *Mai '68* hung in my college rooms. It featured the Eiffel Tower with a banner across it emblazoned with the battle cry of anarchist Proudhon: 'All Property is Theft.' From the comfort zone of bourgeois feminism, let me rephrase that: 'All Gardeners are Thieves.' It is the most acceptable form of theft because you can't actually load up someone's white garden and transfer it to your own plot. The white garden you desire may be planted on acid soil at an altitude of 200 feet with a rainfall of twenty inches a year, but your plot may be alkaline with an altitude of 600 feet and thirty inches of rainfall a year. All you can steal are ideas and plant names.

We tried to create a mound à la Kim Wilkie but the llamas and lambs saw it as their playground and it is now a lump on the landscape. More successful is our quincunx, five inter-locking circles of brick inspired by Gertrude Jekyll's design for a herb garden at Knebworth which I found in a book. I persuaded my husband to sell the diamond brooch he'd given me for my fortieth birthday and use the proceeds to do away with the car park in front of the house. We now call it the brooch garden and it includes the quincunx, an L-shaped open veranda with five blue rocking chairs from Mississippi, topiary trees around the blue fountain and a curve of yew hedge that gives the illusion of being in a courtyard.

The rocking chairs – and the chickens, Norfolk Black turkeys, guinea fowl and peacocks who reign and range freely all through the garden – exude a sense of welcome. The two ha-has – we call them faux-ha-has because they are made without a stone wall – allow us to gaze out on our sheep, two llamas and Angelica, my Red Poll cow. Other American influences include a painted iron gate with cornstalks and morning glories made from the same mouldings as the famous cornstalk fencings and gate in New Orleans; Adirondack chairs with arms wide enough to hold a drink and a book; a dog kennel that looks like a small country church. All these give a sense that this is a marriage of two people from different lands who have brought out the best in this ancient plot. But I have to come clean. I may have pushed for the Red-Hot Border (Southerners believe that something a little 'vulgah' in the garden is like ice cream with cake: it cuts the sweetness) but Kenneth is the plantsman who filled it with flame-coloured crocosmias, startling orange geums, dazzling sulphur achillea and scarlet dahlias. He found the chocolate sunflowers, the lemon tropaeolums, the red and apricot evening primrose, *Oenothera* 'Sunset Boulevard'.

Another moment of truth. Long before we met, he had knocked a hole in the wall surrounding an orchard, pulled out the trees, laid the bricks and created a rose garden. The old French roses like 'Charles de Mills', 'Cardinal de Richelieu', 'Gloire de France', 'Souvenir du Dr Jamain' and 'Fantin Latour' preceded me. He is also a believer in free-grown bushes, tying them around supports if they are too unruly or training them up an oak trellis so that their flowering shoots fall down in cascades. There is no patch of bare earth in the rose garden at its peak. Nestling throughout are delphiums and amethyst alliums and *Stachys byzantina* (lamb's ears), all providing the elements of lavishness that a rose garden needs. My contribution? Two good seats, a sculpture of a barn owl almost hidden in the hornbeam hedge, a fountain that gently gurgles, a Gothic gate copied from Blickling and a trellis pergola, a miniature of the trellises on the terraces at Bodnant, the garden in North Wales created by my husband's grandfather.

Hanging in a passage in the house are photographs of that grandfather escorting the young Queen Elizabeth around the Chelsea Flower Show. He was president of the RHS for twenty-two years. His son, my husband's uncle, held the post for a further twenty-two. The Aberconway domination of the RHS might have been behind the decision to institute time limits and my husband was on the Council a mere ten years. When marrying into a family with such horticultural pedigree, however, it is probably a good idea to become an expert on paint colours and brick paths and, in moments of doubt, cultivate an intelligent silence.

In the same spirit of honesty, it is important to give credit to Arabella Lennox-Boyd. Before I arrived at Wyken, she spent a weekend here with her husband Mark. It was in the

OVERLEAF: Vibrant orange, red and yellow of *Achillea filipendulina* 'Gold Plate', geums, hemorocallis, crocosmias and rudbeckias are tempered by green foliage and the upright form of Irish yews in front of the house

early days of her career as garden designer and over Sunday lunch she pointed out to my husband that the area around the back of the house was 'a muddle'. A couple of weeks later a large envelope arrived containing a garden plan. It was a generous, imaginative and transforming present and my husband put it into place. The connecting rooms – the herb garden, the terrace garden and the knot garden – surround the house like a ruff on an Elizabethan lady. The planting has changed over the years but the structure is in place and now looks like it has been like this for centuries. Moreover, Arabella's plan provided the design integrity that enabled us to expand the garden with confidence.

It may sound like Duchess of P-B speaking now when I say that gardens age as their gardeners age (with the exception of Roy Strong). Increasingly I find myself looking for low-maintenance plants and ground cover. I've acquired a special fondness for plants that dislike disturbance, take time to settle down and are long-lived. I feel tender gratitude for herbaceous peonies, hostas, Japanese anemones, crocosmias, sedums and acanthus because they require little attention and they gently increase. I've always liked the serenity of swathes of planting, but now I like sweeps of green. Light green, dark green, blue-green. I like to think it's a sign that I want to spend more time being in the garden: sitting, reading, listening to the Proms on the Roberts radio, glass of wine on the arm of the chair. It is not a case of 'All Passion Spent' so much as 'Passion Fulfilled', realising that the whole point of the garden is the pleasure of being in it. There is nothing phoney-baloney about that.

BELOW: Low thymes and golden marjoram around a central sundial in the Herb Terrace. *Fremontodendron* 'California Glory' and *Solanum crispum* 'Glasnevin' flower against the house walls

OVERLEAF: Lily pads float on the sedge and rush-surrounded pond

Fonthill House

Fonthill Bishop, Wiltshire

❧

Lord Margadale

EVERY CENTURY SINCE 1522, when Sir John Mervyn bought Fonthill, a succession of impressive houses has been built on the estate. The demise of each of these magnificent edifices can be perceived as either a shame or a blessing depending on which period of architecture you prefer; they were pretty well all covered. The magnificent eighteenth-century Fonthill Splendens, Alderman Beckford's second attempt at commissioning a neo-Palladian English country house perhaps gets my vote as the greatest loss, but I am exceedingly happy that my great-grandfather, Hugh Morrison, chose the glorious south-facing site at Little Ridge to position his impressive Arts and Crafts house at the turn of the twentieth century, not least as it is a much better site for growing things. The foundations of our current house (commissioned by my grandfather in the 1970s) sit atop a fraction of Detmar Blow's colossal earlier creation that would tax even our exceedingly efficient horizon-changing woodchip boiler. Apart from a kitchen wing that my children and stepchildren populate animatedly over holidays and weekends the best indication of the scale of Blow's original layout can be gleaned in the garden. Most of his original garden walls remain; and as the house is built halfway down a greensand hillside, when I mention retaining walls think Renaissance Tuscan villa. Up a ladder pruning wisteria the gardeners probably think Isengard . . .

A survey done of the area around the house is bright pink with contour lines. The 'garden' covers twelve acres from the top of North Wood to the bottom of South Wood with a fall of over twenty metres if a crow flew north–south through the front door.

The setting is breathtaking. From my desk I look out towards Win Green and down a gently contoured valley dotted with mature trees and hawthorns to the lake created by Alderman Beckford, father of the notorious and extraordinary William. Much though I love having the lake in my sights so do a lot of other people, so we are lucky not to be down where the scant traces of all the previous houses are. The Fonthill Arch, possibly designed for

OPPOSITE: The South Lawn Garden is bordered by *Nepeta* 'Walker's Low' and *Rosa rugosa* 'Alba' with giant oat grass, euphorbias, campanulas and alliums

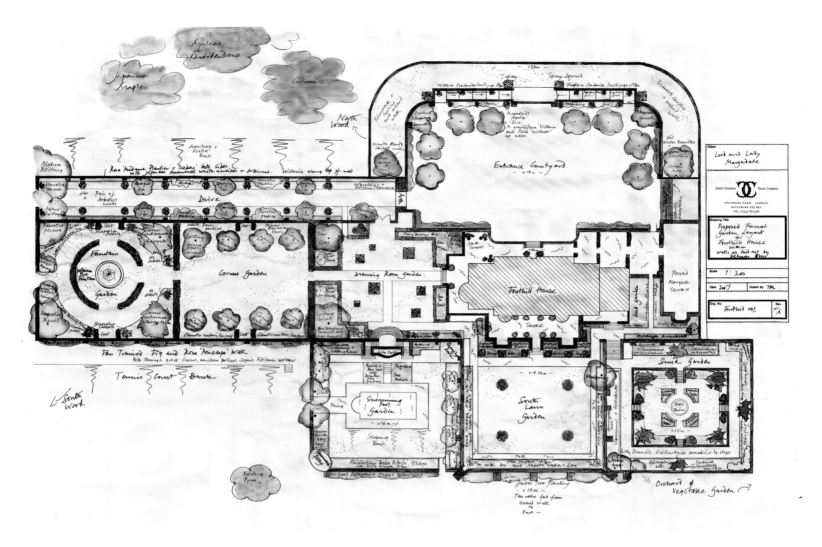

ABOVE: Tania Compton's plan of the garden

Lord Cottington by Inigo Jones, straddles a public road that historically went through the estate and may have prompted the reclusive William Beckford to build his ill-fated abbey in deep woodland to the west. The abbey site never formed part of my Morrison predecessor's estate. In 1829 James Morrison – 'The Napoleon of Shopkeepers', who made a fortune as a haberdasher and entrepreneur – rented The Pavilion, a wing of Fonthill Splendens that had survived the ravages of both fire and having been plundered as an unusual 'quarry' for Beckford and Wyatt in their building of the abbey. James Morrison subsequently bought The Pavilion with the eastern part of the estate that he gave to Alfred, his second son. Alfred Morrison and William Beckford were sons of phenomenally successful self-made men and, I imagine, had more in common than either would care to admit to; both amassed collections of art, ceramics and furniture that still send a *frisson* of excitement through auction houses across the globe today.

Our house is private, but during the shooting season I think my wife Amanda would disagree as a large amount of entertaining takes place here, so the garden needs a crisp structure that looks good through the winter. When we moved here in 2005 work was done on the house; however my 'shaving' view remained a wonky leylandii hedge that ill disguised fruit cages whose raggedy nets fell at all angles from wonky poles, and an ineffectual scarecrow clad in the gardener's old clothes. My grandmother was a serious gardener and was largely responsible for developing and maintaining the garden, especially the wonderful greensand banks where she grew a collection of her favourite acid-loving plants: rhododendrons, azaleas, camellias, cornus and acers. However, many of the plants in the main garden were woody and leggy and well beyond their sell-by date, and Amanda and I felt very strongly that a 'new broom' was needed.

Our friend Tania Compton's disparaging comments about the 'dwarf bedding dahlia-petunia combo' prompted me to lay down the gauntlet and ask her to come up with some plans. The brief was no extra gardeners, good evergreen outlines and a masterplan that could be implemented in-house from area to area on a yearly basis. We ended up installing phases one to four in one go the following year with the help of Mark Fane and his team from Crocus, but everything subsequently has been the work of the estate team. The garden's fortunes took a giant leap with the arrival in 2009 of Fonthill's new gardener Matthew Hutchinson, who heads a team with Sandra Baker and Chris Dinan.

My bathroom window now overlooks a trio of carefully orchestrated spaces separated by yew hedges whose scalloped shapes in the drawing room garden echo the shape that Detmar Blow devised for walls to soften the severity of too many right angles. Where possible we have kept the finest elements of the original garden. A magnificent lime tree has a wonderful year-round presence in the drawing room garden and the large *Acca selloviana* flowers, and occasionally fruits, against the south-facing wall. There is an exceptional mature *Cornus kousa*

ABOVE AND BELOW: A mixed planting of alliums 'Mont Blanc' and *A. stipitatum* 'Mount Everest' seen below along the drive with Rose 'Madame Plantier', loaves of box and young *Quercus ilex*

var. *chinensis* in the cornus garden where another seven specimens have been added, making a double row that will one day create an unforgettable explosion of blossom for June garden open days. Four types of banksian rose, from the double yellow to the single white, are being trained against the walls. This simple lawned space resides between the reds, purples and magenta pinks of the drawing room garden planting and the deep borders of the Fountain Garden. These are yellow and white with magnolias, irises and *Paeonia mlokosewitschii* in spring, but dusty pink in autumn when the fifty-metre ring of *Sedum* 'Herbstfreunde' matches the cascading heads of *Hydrangea paniculata* as they fade from white to red. Last year we installed a William Pye masterpiece that now resides within a yew circle at the centre of the Fountain Garden. It is the ultimate focal point: no one can resist its magnetic pull nor fail to be mesmerised by the reflection of the sky on its mirror-like surface. Our Fonthill fountain is similar to Bill's font in Salisbury Cathedral, strengthening another tie to the cathedral; all the stone in the garden is from the same seam of limestone in the local Chilmark quarry as that used for both the justifiably world-famous spire in Salisbury and Wyatt's less-resilient spire for Beckford's abbey!

TOP: Rose 'Isfahan'

ABOVE: *Baptisia australis*

The other element of the old garden we have kept is the 'ballroom' wisteria that has been trained along the top of the driveway wall. This immense veteran that had clothed the walls of the Little Ridge ballroom (whose dance-floor foundations still create drainage problems in this part of the garden) blocked the view from the drawing room's French windows. None of us held out great hopes for its survival when we witnessed the digger tear its shallow roots from the ground, but a severe cutback of its vast trunk followed by vigilant watering and it is once again snaking like a Chinese dragon along the length of the driveway wall.

The driveway creates a neat north–south divide in the garden. To the north the soil is leaf-mould-rich greensand, while to the south it is a mixed bag with patches of greensand amongst clay and then chalk banks leading down to the park. There is also a division in labour between the two sides, harmonious I hasten to add! Marie-Louise Agius, who grew up at Exbury, is masterminding the redevelopment of the North Wood that had been planted by my great-grandmother from the late 1920s and was being crowded out by sapling sweet chestnut. Following an inspirational trekking holiday in Bhutan, Amanda and I decided that this favourite daily dog-walking loop needed renovating and we took the bull by the horns. Marie-Louise's transformation is already magical and the incredible compilation of plants that she has added is now being catalogued alongside the earlier specimens that were never recorded at the time of planting. North Wood will be even more mesmerising in years to come.

We like to undertake a new garden project each year, and next on the agenda is the Sunk Garden. This suntrap sanctuary is incredibly evocative of how Fonthill must have been in my great-grandparents' day. There is a small lily pond in the centre of a harmonious composition of terraces, beds and paths. We are going to make sure we keep the atmosphere but lose the ground elder and bindweed that engulfed every bare inch. (I am convinced they are lurking in the very walls.) At present this is a sea of mud and plastic but before long it will be an unashamedly old-fashioned mix of scented shrubs and perennials. It will be a honeytrap for bees and a great place to sit with a bottle of wine. This is also one of the few inward-looking parts of the garden, as nearly everywhere else takes full advantage of the extraordinary views.

LEFT: Rose 'De Resht' in the Drawing Room Garden

CENTRE: *Cercis canadensis* 'Forest Pansy'

RIGHT: Rose 'Bleu Magenta'

TOP: Detmar Blow's bastion retaining wall in the Entrance Courtyard with topiary squirrels flanking the ascent to the North Wood

Writing this has made me realise just how much we have done in the past decade. I'm skipping over the new swimming pool garden whose *Philadelphus* 'Belle Etoile' hedge and banks of white dianthus and lavender smell incredible in summer, the fig walk, dubbed 'figs'n'roses' by me as *Rosa* 'Penelope' grows up the buttresses between our collection of fan-trained figs. The South Lawn garden now has a simple but effective year-round planting of box between single white *Rugosa* roses skirted by *Nepeta* 'Walker's Low'. Not to mention the greenhouses, the bulb banks. I know Tania would like more areas of meadow and wildflowers but I get terrible hayfever so I overrule her on most of the grass that she would like long. And the drive. Previously overgrown with an assortment of top-heavy diseased pyracanthas that distracted your eye from a sensational pair of Persian ironwoods, *Parrotia persica,* that frame the entrance to the drive, there is a new arrangement of clipped box and holm oaks and a succession on each side of white narcissi, then alliums, then roses… and finally what feels like a tunnel, as you drive through it, of Japanese anemones. We also found four multi-stemmed parrotias for the middle, making a foreground burst of scarlet and orange in autumn leading your eye to the original pair that have become stars of Instagram.

The view is the real star of the show here. North Wood has always been impressive with its magnificent rhododendron and azalea collection carpeted with bluebells, but we were almost too ashamed to open the rest of the garden when we moved here. Now we have more and more groups coming and I see the improving fortunes of the garden as symbolic of everything we are trying to do at Fonthill, keeping it vibrant and pumping on all cylinders. And, most importantly, it is now a delight to gaze across while I have my morning shave.

BELOW: *Veronica* 'Pink Damask' with *Nepeta* 'Walker's Low', growing in the South Lawn Border

BOTTOM: Lavender and nepeta with alliums and clipped Portuguese laurel, *Prunus lusitanica* 'Myrtifolia'

ABOVE: A pair of multi-stemmed *Cornus kousa* var. *chinensis* in the Cornus Garden with the North Wood behind

BELOW: William Pye's fountain is the focal point at the end of the main axis of the new garden

THIS PAGE: Bluebells, ferns and lily of the valley have naturalised under the soaring, twisted stems and canopies of the magnificent mature rhododendrons and azaleas in the North Wood.

LEFT: The white Rhododendron 'Polar Bear'

OVERLEAF LEFT: Bluebells and campion carpet the ground under *Rhododendron* x *mucronatum*

OVERLEAF RIGHT: A collage of *Cornus kousa* var. *chinensis* flowers including *Polystichum aculeatum, Hyacinthoides non-scripta*, the English bluebell, *Rhododendron* 'Delicatissimum', *Rhododendron luteum* and (centre) red campion *Silene dioica*

TOP LEFT: A spreading horse chestnut over the water at the beginning of the mile-long lake seen (right) at Fonthill

ABOVE: A pair of urns and an ancient beech tree mark one of the crossing points at the top of the lake

RIGHT: A group of red-stemmed willows, *Salix alba* 'Vitellino' are reflected through early morning mist on the lake

The Old Rectory

ALPHAMSTONE, ESSEX

Adrian Huggins Esq.

OPPOSITE: Hummocks of box, *Ruscus aculeatus* and *Euphorbia characias* subsp. *wulfenii* with soft shield ferns around the entrance to the house

ALPHAMSTONE IS A tiny village in rural north Essex on the border with Suffolk. Hilary, my constant source of comfort and sanity for forty-four years, found The Old Rectory in 1997, when there were doubts as to how smoothly our long-term home, Hong Kong, would revert to the People's Republic of China. Friends said we would never be accepted in an English country village for at least twenty years, but the inhabitants could not have been more warm and welcoming. We love it, the house, and the garden which has evolved from a shambolic and neglected wilderness with immeasurable help and guidance from Rupert Golby, who was introduced to us as 'one of the best plantsmen and garden designers in England'.

Although Hilary is an East Anglian, I was born in Uganda and then transported to the Far East at the age of two. I had no known connections with Suffolk or Essex, but Hilary's great-grandfather had been Mayor of Sudbury, her grandparents lived in Stoke-by-Clare, and her parents in Hadleigh, where Cedric Morris created extraordinarily sensuous botanical art at Benton End. A painting of his Suffolk pink farmhouse and garden, with red-hot pokers and silver mullein in the foreground, is a treasured possession.

We needed someone to look after our garden. We found Paul Gwynne. He had a degree in social philosophy and had had enough of commercial underwriting; he wanted to work outdoors. Enthusiastic, intelligent and articulate, he was the least experienced of those we interviewed, but Hilary said he was by far and away the most handsome. Paul and Amanda fitted into the village from the start. Both their children, Marley and Saffiya, were born at home in The Shieling. The village bee-keeper rang the church bells of St Barnabas to announce their arrival.

One of the secrets of the success of the garden is that Paul and Rupert get on so well.

Before Rupert arrived we had already started restoring The Old Rectory. Built in the 1830s, it had not seen a lick of paint or plaster since; all was disintegration and decay. But

Topiary yew cones surrounded by Sussex lavender *Lavandula* x *intermedia* line the curved path. Clematis 'Perle d'Azur' scrambles through rose 'Raubritter' by some steps

Hilary said it was a pretty house, we were in no hurry, and we could fix it. We found marvellous builders from the next village, Chris Harding-Payne and Les Weavers, both of whose ancestors had lived in the area for generations.

The house needed a garden to sit comfortably in. The rebuilding works had left harsh surfaces and stark angles and corners which called for toning down with living textures and colours. So we needed Rupert, whose greatest attributes when dealing with horticulturally-challenged enthusiasts, are patience, persistence, and an ability to gently put right our mistakes.

He designed a south-facing York stone terrace with seven Versailles planters in oak, holding clipped Portuguese laurels underplanted with Rosemary 'Severn Sea'. In addition, four double-cream-coloured Biot pots for tulips in the spring and agapanthus or *Salvia patens* in the summer. On one side of the front entrance he planted a young *Magnolia grandiflora*; on the other a vine, branching right and left. On the north side, five Japanese angelica trees, *Aralia elata*, amongst fronds of 'Solomon's Seal', box, ferns, and butcher's broom; on the corner, a hop which grows the height of the house every summer. On the east side a curved metal frame for climbing honeysuckle above sweet scented sarcococca. The builders are happy with all of this because little foliage touches the walls of the house; they hated the Virginia creeper which engulfed it before.

The property is blessed with several levels, sloping down from the road to the house and then falling away towards the pond and into the wood. In the shape of a triangular wedge, it was probably carved out in Roman times; there are signs of ancient quarrying, perhaps for sand or clay. There is farmland all around: grazing horses in the fields to the west and to the east, and rare-breed sheep in pasture to the north. We acquired a strip of wildflower meadow with patches of viper's bugloss, mignonette, storksbill, common centaury, wild thyme, and (most pleasing of all) bee orchids. Jonathan Tyler, a local botanical artist, painted one for us. Paul has added ox-eye daisies, lady's bedstraw, scabious, wild marjoram, basil, teasels, cranesbill, mallows, yellow rattle, and quaking grass.

Rupert's overall approach was to create a south-facing formal area, a walled garden on the west, an area of informal lawn between sloping winter and butterfly borders leading down to a pond, and, finally, an area of tamed wildness.

He designed semicircular terracing above the south facade: walls in Suffolk brick with York stone coping and paving between beds of Sussex lavender, interspersed with pointed yews. In the centre, on a brick plinth, sits an *Uruli*, used in India for cooking offerings to the temple deities and rice for worshippers and wedding guests. It came from Kochin in Kerala via Felixstowe. The birds love to bathe in it.

At the lower level herbaceous borders are divided by steps leading up to a metal-framed arbour supporting white roses, honeysuckle, clematis and white wisteria. Within the borders are ten iron obelisk frames which Rupert wanted left to rust, planted with *Rosa* 'Redleaf', perennial sweet pea, and climbing clematis. In the borders he planted strong repetitious clumps and waves of Himalayan indigo, Armenian cranesbill, pastel pink peonies, white mugwort, milky bellflowers, delphinium Cameliard, Japanese anemone, bronze fennel, Mediterranean sea holly, eastern galega and monkshood Bressingham Spire.

The walled garden has a lean-to greenhouse and potting shed. Tatam's Forge in Wake's Colne built a metal frame over the central well to carry kiwi, honeysuckle, grape 'Suffolk

BELOW AND OPPOSITE: Cheddar pinks, *Dianthus gratianopolitanus* and self-sowing *Erigeron karvinskianus* are dotted in paving pockets

Pink', and purple and white forms of the Cup and Saucer vine. Beside it stand two large rusty metal cockerels. Most of the herringbone brick pathways are edged with low clipped box; one, in front of the greenhouse, has a border of *Teucrium chamaedrys* (a treatment for gout and a component of Venetian treacle). The main path has three metal arch frames supporting gourds, inspired by the delightful gardens at Helmingham Hall.

On the granite setts of the stableblock stand two large Chinese rice wine jars. In one corner there is a craggy old Welsh millstone on a brick plinth: perfect for coffee in the morning, lunch if we need shade, and wine at any time.

Sloping down to the pond is the 'Bowl', where there was once a grass tennis court, framed by black mulberry trees. At the top are four 'Rambling Rector' roses, glorious in June. A chum from Cambridge days, Ben Crosland, plays bass guitar in a jazz band, Threeway, and wants to jam there one summer.

The Winter Border has evergreen plantings of holly, shrubby honeysuckle, and spurge laurel. There is a deciduous shrub layer of hazel, wintersweet, and table dogwood, and a groundcover planting of woodland strawberry, lesser periwinkle, sweet violets, snowdrops, cyclamen, lily of the valley, wood spurge, and stinking hellebore.

The Butterfly Border, in balanced contrast, catches the sunlight on the soft grey downy leaves and lilac flowers of *Buddleja Crispa*, and on Virginia raspberry, tridel berry, creeping blueblossom, Swany rose, blue globe thistles, giant scabious, thalictrums, clary sage, oregano, sedums, sweet rocket, honesty, and oxlips.

The pond was overgrown and empty when we arrived but we knew it had been there from an old map in the church, copied from one in the British Library by Joan Tyler, a talented local calligrapher, including the names of the local fields taken from the Parish Tithe Award Map of 1840. Keeping the pond free of weed remains a problem. I saw a man doing the job most effectively in Beth Chatto's Gardens, standing in a dinghy with a rake, and collecting the weed into a large basket hooked onto the stern. I found an old clinker-built tender which had been sitting in a barn near Gestingthorpe for twelve years. She has brushed up well and looks a gem on the water in the evening sunshine. In and around the pond are irises, kingcups, pulmonaria, hellebores, daphne mezereum, geranium phaeum, snakeshead fritillaries, and my favourite, summer snowflake.

Best of all, I love the Wood. There must be some airborne chemical or pheromone created in ancient woods which the human nose ingests in seconds and which soothes the brain more effectively than the very best Lebanese Red hashish or any pharmaceutical product yet invented.

To the existing alder, elder, oak, ash and chestnut, we have added hornbeam, black poplar, white willow, sweet chestnut, hawthorn, blackthorn, dogwood, ivy, holly, and hazel. On the ground, at different times of year, grow adoxa, bluebells, bugle, yellow archangel, red campion, cowslips, celandines, martagon lilies, dog's mercury, bellflowers, ragged robin, saxifrage, lady's smock, wild garlic, wood anemones, white dead-nettle, woodruff, wild foxgloves, pale primroses, and nodding violets.

When I turned fifty Hilary commissioned her god-daughter's brother, Alex Wenham, an aspiring stonemason, to create something special for the centre of the Wood. We chose a sculpted head of an ancient local leader, Alfoun, after whom some say Alphamstone was

named. He weighs three tons and wears a helmet with a wild boar crest over long–flowing locks and a large drooping moustache in the style of King Alfred of Winchester and Queen's Freddie Mercury. He is surrounded by butcher's broom. We scattered Hilary's father's ashes at his base. He guards the wood from potentially invasive spirits.

The Wood has three large natural root sculptures – driftwood imported from remote Canadian shorelines. They add an air of mystery to the wood's existing magic: one complex and multifaceted; another like some giant-beaked Inca bird-god; and the third conjures the image of a guardian to a pharoah's tomb.

A fundamental lesson we have had to learn is not to rail at whatever the wanton gods of Nature determine to kill for their sport. A storm brought down a giant chestnut from which hung a much-loved swing. But that has been replaced by a rustic summer house, surrounded by plantings of foxgloves, ferns, spindle, box, cotoneaster, cyclamen, honeysuckle, and sweet briar roses. The same fate befell the largest ash where King Alfoun stands now. Its large trunk was dragged out of the wood with ropes and chains behind a local Suffolk Punch. The oldest villager, Eddie Tuffin, had his hundredth birthday that week. He had left school at the age of twelve and ploughed the local fields behind these wonderful workhorses. Paul arranged for the Punch to be dressed in its Sunday best and walked down to his home to celebrate.

RIGHT: A wigwam of assorted sweet peas with a clambering edible squash

FAR RIGHT: Pollinators are attracted by borage, here with English marigold *Calendula officinalis* and annual clary sage *Salvia viridis* var. *comata*

ABOVE: A copse of mature alders make a soaring canopy in the woodland garden

OVERLEAF: A fern-lined rill feeds the pond bordered by hazels and flag irises. On the sloping bank near the house *Rosa* 'Rambling Rector' forms flowering hummocks in midsummer

When I met Barbara Saben, she was in her nineties. She visited regularly the grave of her husband in the village churchyard. He had lived in the The Old Rectory as a small boy, until 1910 when his father ceased to be Rector. One day in April she came for coffee. I expressed disappointment that it was raining.

'Don't ever talk like that about the rain', she said. 'I lived in Africa, where rain was considered a gift from God.'

'I was born in Africa.'

'Where?'

'Uganda'.

'I was there too.'

I had expected to meet a lady who would tell me all about The Old Rectory. Instead she talked of Africa. She was one of the first women members of Uganda's Legislative Council and a militant feminist voice on its Council for Women. It transpired that her brother was operated on as a child by a relation of mine in Rhodesia who was a surgeon before he became Prime Minister of Southern Rhodesia and then of the Federation of Rhodesia and Nyasaland. That extraordinary coincidence made me feel strangely connected to Alphamstone and to The Old Rectory in which her husband and his family lived over one hundred years ago. A colonial expatriate, I had never before felt any roots in England. Although my ashes will probably end up polluting the South China Seas, I will ask for a thimbleful to be sprinkled in the Wood in Alphamstone, beside King Alfoun.

E.M. Forster was right: 'Only connect'.

LEFT AND RIGHT: A pair of metalwork boxing hares have been placed in the long meadow grass

BELOW: A seat made from interlocking branches of driftwood built in situ encircles a tree in the woodland garden

Haseley Court

LITTLE HASELEY, OXFORDSHIRE

Mrs Desmond Heyward

OPPOSITE: The lovingly
tended box and yew
chess set with Haseley
Court behind

IN AD 1002, ETHELRED II gave the estate of Little Haseley to his chief minister Godwin, and by 1086 it was owned by William I's half-brother Bishop Odo of Bayeaux. In 1391 it was bought by the Barentyne family, and their descendants lived here until 1681. In 1543 the poet and antiquary John Leland was appointed Rector to Great Haseley church by Henry VIII and writes, 'at Little Haseley, Master Barentyne hath a right fair mansion and marvellous fair walkes topiari operis and orchards and pooles'. We know most of the previous owners of Haseley Court, which is fascinating.

The garden was created from a wilderness when Nancy Lancaster bought Haseley in 1954. Requisitioned during the war by the American Air Force, then used as a prisoner-of-war camp, only the large box and yew chess set and a few mature trees remained. Luckily the old gardener who lived in the next village had continued clipping the chess set, his 'Kings and Queens', some of which had been planted in 1850. Nancy totally fell in love with the house and garden and very quickly started the restoration of both. In 1963 – less than ten years later – Lanning Roper wrote: that few gardens made since the war had been as imaginative as Hasely.

We met Nancy in 1968 when we bought the adjoining farm that had been part of the original estate. She invited us for lunch soon after we moved in, and walking round the garden with her we were enchanted with its beauty as well as the sense of drama everywhere. It certainly never crossed our minds that we might live there one day. Even after forty years, I still remember that first glimpse of the garden that would become so much part of our lives.

When we bought Haseley in 1982 Nancy had moved to the Coach House with an arrangement that she keep the walled garden for her lifetime but we could still enjoy it, without having to weed it! We had twelve very happy years living across the courtyard from Nancy up to her death aged ninety-six in 1994. That gave us the opportunity to absorb

work in the rest of the garden until the walled garden reverted back and suddenly the garden doubled in size.

We have been asked many times if we felt daunted living next to her, but Nancy never once criticised anything that we had done and always emphasised that the house and garden were ours and we must make any changes that we wanted. I am sure that she winced many times.

As a child I had my own little patch in my parents' garden which I soon lost interest in when I could not eat the carrots within a day or two of sowing. My love of gardens started when I was a student at Winfield Place that had a beautiful garden with the formidable duo of Constance Spry and Sheila McQueen in charge! I so enjoyed it and learnt so much from them both about flowers and foliage combined on a grand scale. But I was not yet remotely interested in the how or why of gardening. That came when we had our first thirty-foot-square back garden in London, and a designer friend helped us transform a dull space with dreary plants into an oasis. Here we could sit and listen to the waterfall in the centre, but also have room for the children to zoom round on their scooters.

When we moved to the farmhouse in Little Haseley the same friend transformed a derelict two acres by bulldozing the entire area and creating a pond, a semicircle of limes, 'woodland', large grassy areas and two hills! Roses tumbled over the old stone walls and large borders were looked after by our gardener who knew I was not too good on the practicalities of it all. We were only there at weekends, and I did little hands-on gardening until we moved out of London and across the fields to Haseley. I knew I had to focus more, so I soon got stuck into the borders and have never looked back. I also learnt so much just by absorbing what Nancy was doing.

And I am still learning. We are so lucky to have an exceptional head gardener, Bryn Davies, at Haseley, who is so knowledgeable of every aspect of the garden and creates beautiful borders.

The garden is both formal and informal with a great deal of box and yew topiary, and large and small hedges which must all be clipped tightly. There is a large area of woodland, which looks wonderful in spring with a mass of flowers including blue and white *Anemone blanda*, fritillaries and cow parsley that looks ethereal in the dappled shade. An ever-spreading profusion of hundreds of martagon lilies appears in summer from the twenty bulbs I planted about fifteen years ago.

'The temple' sounds grand but it is a quiet resting place surrounded by petasites and balsam poplars which look and smell so distinctive in early spring. On one side of the woodland is an ornamental canal with gunnera at one end and a grotesque mask fountain with hostas at the other. The reflection of morning sunlight through the willows onto the canal is mysterious and beautiful. Herons devoured the carp and golden orfe two years ago, but I am hoping that they may have forgotten this is a favourite feeding ground so I can slowly restock. Maybe the voles will also fail to recall how delicious they found the swathes of hellebore buds they nibbled off in the nut walk last spring.

A hornbeam tunnel nearly 400 feet long forms two sides of the 'walled' garden; the other two are old walls. The tunnel is lined in spring with an abundance of naturalised bulbs, charming little *Iris reticulata*, scillas and puschkinia follow snowdrops and aconites,

OPPOSITE: The details of the topiary shapes take on abstract forms in early summer

BELOW: The spider's-web seat that was a favourite design of Nancy Lancaster sits under the spread branches of a venerable cedar of Lebanon

TOP: An arrow-shaped caryatid niche in a tall box hedge seen with rose 'Blairii no 2'

ABOVE: Rose 'Ghislane de Feligonde' trained up a trellis pyramid with *Delphinium* 'Darling Sue', *Campanula latifolia* 'Alba' and white foxgloves

RIGHT: *Cytisus battandieri* and rose 'Ferdinand Pichard' in front of the fig-clad Brew House

then hyancinths and crown imperials. It is a haven of cool shade on sweltering summer days.

Nancy's much-copied laburnum tunnel joins halfway down. It is an amazing sight in full bloom and she got the scale perfect at twelve feet high. I always had a problem with the dry, shady, weedy strip at the bottom of the yew hedge that runs parallel to the laburnum until I found a plant called *Trachystemon orientalis* which thrives in appalling conditions and looks good. Bryn has the awesome task of pruning these tunnels from scaffolding, and the arch at the top is now miraculously even all the way along.

The walled garden is divided into four quarters with a trellis arbour that is painted Confederate grey in the centre. Nancy, whose mother Lizzie was one of the famous Langhorne sisters, kept her strong Virginian roots to the end. This is a favourite place to sit when it is covered in roses and clematis.

One quarter has white, cream, pale-yellow, silver and blue plants. Rose 'Ghislaine de Feligonde' twists around trellis pyramids also in Confederate grey. Plants that everyone wants to know the name of here are *Aster schreberi*, *Gillenia trifoliata* and the snow-white corncockle *Agrostemma githago* 'Ocean Pearl' that waves gently in the wind. I love *Crambe cordifolia* which is so pretty with its clouds of flowers, sadly for such a short time.

We go for a vibrant combination of crimsons, pinks and other strong dark colours with just a little blue in another square, including a superb dark-red lupin which I bought years ago for ten pence as a seedling in a yogurt pot from the church fête: propagated and passed around many times, but still with no name. There are peonies, purple iris, sweet william, several salvias and inky-blue monkshoods in abundance. Dark dahlias and dusky pink and bronze sunflowers 'Claret' and 'Velvet Queen', *Cosmos* 'Versailles Tetra' and 'Rubenza' all last well into autumn. Evil-looking *dracunculus* grow up through hostas under an old quince tree and the fatally poisonous *ricinus* makes a striking companion for *Rosa rugosa* 'Roseraie de l'Haye'. It's not all roses in an English country garden.

But in June the walled garden is heady and romantic with roses lining the central paths, old-fashioned favourites with intoxicating scent and evocative names: 'Ferdinand Pichard', 'Souvenir de la Malmaison', 'Baron Girod de L'Ain', 'Souvenir du Dr Jamain', 'Fantin Latour' and 'Königin von Dänemark'. I love the delightful Chapeau de Napoleon moss rose *Rosa* x *centifola* 'Cristata', and there are two *Rosa virginiana* which Nancy planted many years ago. These are combined with delphiniums, salvias, campanulas and foxgloves, predominantly 'Suttons Apricot' (which is a delightful soft pink) and white ones as we weed out the dark pink.

The wonderful old walls are the perfect background for climbers that also scramble through apple trees and any shrubs and lilacs that look boring in late summer. The scent in spring and summer in the walled garden is almost overwhelming in early evening, with viburnums, roses, jasmine, lilies, nicotiana and brugnansii in pots.

Another square has vegetables, flowers and fruit radiating out from a central mulberry tree. In summer sweet peas and beans are overtaken by clematis and cobaea clambering up hazel pyramids. Large pots contain several lathyrus species including the wondrous electric blue 'Tutankhamun', apricot and yellow *Lathyrus belinensis*, yellow and acid-green *L. chloranthus* and a very pretty muted one called *L.* 'Hotham Red'. For late summer we

In June the walled garden is heady and romantic with roses such as 'Président de Sèze' and 'Maréchal Davoust' with foxgloves and delphiniums

LEFT: One of two tunnels of arched hornbeam that form living walls in the walled garden

The canal, seen here above and below in both directions, brings shafts of light and reflection into the shady woodland garden at Haseley

have a small-flowered red dahlia called 'Ragged Robin' and a very prolific one with a terrible name, 'Twinings After Eight', that has fantastic dark coppery leaves and pretty single translucent white flowers which glow at dusk. To follow on from the sweet peas ornamental squashes and gourds climb up the pyramids and are fun with extraordinary colours and shapes. There are four big groups of cardoons towards the middle, making a bold statement, as well as a dainty little red and black spotted poppy called 'Ladybird'!

The final quarter is an intricate pattern of box hedges with a large cartwheel of green and yellow box in the middle inspired by a Roman mosaic pavement at the cathedral in Torcello. The outer borders here are wonderful well into autumn, with large ornamental grasses, many different varieties of euphorbia and hybrid musk roses – such as 'Buff Beauty' and 'Moonlight' – that have a second flush of flowers, with asters such as *A. turbinellus*, *A.* 'Helen Picton' and *A.* 'Little Carlow'. *Thermopsis villosa* with its sulphur-yellow flowers looks so good here and I love its American name 'Blue-Ridge Buckbean': very appropriate for a garden created by a Virginian!

We have had to replace two avenues since we have been here. The first was the avenue of balsam poplars in the drive that were dying due to squirrel and storm damage and honey fungus. We replanted with balsam poplars because that first morning when you are aware of their scent wafting across the garden means spring is definitely here, but it was a mistake; they too succumbed, so the avenue is now planted with silver birch in groups of three. The bark looks so attractive in winter. A majestic avenue of horse chestnuts planted in the early 1950s leading away from the front of the house had been ring-barked by cattle, and several blew down in the great storm of 1987. We took the rest out – having consulted Nancy – and in 1989 replanted with limes. When we had finished David Hicks came to see it and, waving his hand in an expansive gesture, said that we must double the length of the avenue into our field on the other side of a small road. Of course he was quite right and we planted the second half. I'm so pleased that he lived to see it growing well and now, after twenty-five years, it stretches impressively away into the distance.

We do not keep the house and garden as a memorial to Nancy; we change things often. Her original design is very much in place not because we feel that we have to preserve it but because we love what she created. Most importantly Haseley is a very loved and lived-in garden. It gives Desmond and myself incalculable pleasure to see our seven grandchildren playing under the venerable *Cedrus atlantica* 'Glauca', having as much fun and in the same spot as their parents did, with a view out over the fields towards the Chilterns. How lucky we were to find it.

OPPOSITE: The topiary chess set as seen from an upstairs window overlooking the Oxfordshire countryside in summer

Garden Designers at Home

Trematon Castle

SALTASH, CORNWALL

≈

Isabel Bannerman

TREMATON CASTLE MAY be the ultimate expression of my and Julian's compulsion to take on bedraggled houses and gardens, usually in the wrong place, but crammed with the right things: charm, mystery, possibilities, dissipated grandeur, lost domains. Where did this infatuation with the palimpsest of architecture and the pentimento of fallen landscape originate? Obviously it was many things, and very different for each of us, but maybe the seed was sown in the 1970s, the dingy days of the 'three-day week', the pop group Slade and soccer hooligans, when those in authority seemed hell-bent on bulldozing town and country. For the romantically minded it was hard not to be affected by the destruction and negative attitude to forlorn and neglected places like Painshill or Stowe. Julian always had an affinity with plants, soil, stone, trees, with the epic outdoors and I, barely more than a London teenager when we met, took some teaching, but I had a childhood love of the chalky downs, elm trees and treehouse building, a fixation with old clothes, objects and houses. Somehow we found a way of making a living through these passions, and poured our energies into finding stranded bits of architecture and making places sing again.

History is here in spadefuls, but the trouble with Trematon Castle, it might be said, is that being such a magical world in itself it could not be improved by gardening. The bailey walls dip and skirt round a basin levelled off in the centre to create the flat space upon which the pared-down Regency villa sits, like a creamy pat of butter, commanding a view across the Tamar and Lynher estuaries 300-odd feet below. An embattled gatehouse straddles the sunken drive. The motte rears up inconceivably sheer to the shell keep 100 feet above, pinned to earth by two monumental *Quercus ilex* which cast a deep Italianate shade over its southern lower slopes, and bisected by the colossal bailey wall, in the very bottom of which is punctured the tiny door of the 'sally port', back door to the castle. Thick with moss and lichen, toothy, jagged, glistening wet in places, the walls are populated with jackdaws and polypody ferns singular to Trematon, all things that are magical about Cornwall. The 'garden' mostly slumbered under the lush lapping leaves of winter heliotrope, a pernicious Victorian introduction which, having had free rein for many decades, rampaged through the flower beds, lawns, shrubberies, and up two sides of the Mount, blotting out the ancient English wild flora which had embroidered these vertiginous heights since the days of the Black Prince.

There were few borders: a shallow apology for a bed round the croquet lawn, and beds either side of a path leading to a deeply mysterious and enticing tunnel passing under the bailey wall and out into what was barely an orchard, more a handful of very elderly apples, branches be-furred with rippling blue lichen. Beside this a neat vegetable patch hard against the high back wall of a long-gone glasshouse, and next to it a little white wooden green-house. However, in the great curve of the curtain wall that embraced the gravelled entrance side of the house there were the remains of a border, reputedly set out by Norah Lindsay in the 1930s. Possible remains of those glory days were several magnolias, one with a punchy pink outer and pure winter inner petal which might be *M.* 'Pickard's Ruby'. There was a handsome *Cornus capitata* grown into a small tree, and a chunky wisteria, the flowering tendrils of which trailed, just as one would wish, 100 foot along the ramparts. South- and east-facing, but sheltered by the house, this was the place to garden with flowering plants, where they could be enjoyed from the house without any competition from the panorama on the other side.

We arrived in January 2012. Grey skies, grey granite, grey shaley soil, bitter and wet. There were no snowdrops and no aconites to cheer the soul, but a great mound of *Sarcoccoa confusa* in the 'border' greeted us with its welcoming scent of sugar and spice. The thin soil turned out to be surprisingly limey, as the castle has collapsed in on itself over the centuries and the 'garden' is really a well of lime mortar and rubble. It was 'goodbye' to any fantasies of blue hydrangeas. Camellias, planted by our predecessors along with a host of rare rhododendrons, acers, *Paulownia tomentosa*, *Davidia involucrata* and a grove of wonderful tree ferns, blazed along the drive, marvellously brazen in the winter gloom. We cut armfuls of chick-fluffy chick-yellow *Acacia pravissima* for the house. To keep our spirits up we planted snowdrops and aconites in the green and magnolias in huge holes, big bold colourful Jury hybrids such as 'Apollo', 'Atlas' and 'Vulcan' and, for their delicacy and mysterious scent in June, many *Magnolia sieboldii* and *M. wilsonii*. At Easter the 'Kanzan' cherry flowered, heartening and ravishing but for the purple leaves which, to us, always seem to be at war with everything else that is happening in spring. Julian dedicated himself to knocking out the winter heliotrope, spot-spraying it again and again. He climbed like a mountain goat up and down the Mount's near-vertical slopes, the ramparts and the woods down to the creek, and the abandoned double-walled garden knitted through with ash, sycamore and brambles.

The spring revealed that the motte and the woodland were awash with wild daffodils, bluebells, campion, unfurling ferns, but the lack of so many things; not so much showy or rarefied plants, but no pheasant's eye, no fritillaries. The lack of old friends made us hanker. No summer came, only a deluge, when everything melted to a mush under weeks of unremitting rain. Only the encouragement of our neighbour Alice Boyd kept us going because she would turn up with big smiles and armfuls of unbelievably special daffodils or buckets of *Scilla liliohyacinthus* bulbs. With the help of Mike, a trainee gardener, we began to dig out the petasites on the Mount and the banks, and to dig out other things, the shrubs that always survive decades of being ignored, like *Viburnum rhytidophillum*. The cyclamen, that had been under a huge and venerable beech tree on the bank beside the lawn before it had split open a decade earlier, had to be crated up and reserved while the bank was divested of a thick tapestry of heliotrope, ground elder and bramble. More positively we began to dig dustbin-sized holes, wrenching out boulders and putting back clods of manure and fresh soil, into which we tenderly planted a huge number of rambling roses: 'Wedding Day', 'The Garland', 'Rambling Rector', 'Cedric Morris' and 'Cooperi' to clothe the ramparts. Along the drive went all the philadelphus we could lay our hands on, including cultivars new to us such as 'Starbright', 'Snowbelle' and 'Snow Velvet'. We needed the smell of *Viburnum carlesii* and *V.* x *carlecephalum*, of *Ribes odoratum* and of all those stormy-coloured lilacs. We missed the sacristy smell of the incense rose *Rosa primula* and the aptly eglantine-leaf-smelling *Rosa* 'La Belle Distuinguée'. A big Rock's tree peony had come with us in a giant pot, and tree peonies seem to like Cornwall. We made a small start, with cottagey beds down by the tunnel, using scented annuals, *Nicotiana sylvestris* and *N. suaveolens*, *Matthiola incana*, *Lupinus arboreus* and *Coronilla valentina* subsp. *glauca* 'Citrina'. We planted the shoulder-high walls with *Daphne* x *transatlantica* 'Eternal Fragrance', with 'Mrs Sinkins' pinks and with trailing rosemary. This 'cove' faces south and is encircled by banks so it is hot and sheltered, capturing scents that are then drawn through the tunnel in a gravy trail out the other side. On a bench here we sit sometimes and enjoy the fruity bubblegum scent of *Philadelphus* 'Mexican Jewel'. But it turned out that the bottom of 'smelly path' was a sump for the endless rain, and everything began to rot off. There was nothing to be done but deal with the drainage and bring the levels up. The following spring we replanted, adding *Bupleurum fruticosum*, *Azara microphylla*, *Carpenteria californica* 'Ladhams variety', *Crinum* x *powellii* in pink, and many *Echium pininiana* grown from seed.

On the bank opposite, having taken out a lot of ancient sludge-coloured hydrangeas, we rather perversely replanted with hydrangeas 'Annabelle' and 'Limelight' only mixed with the big philadelphus cultivars and with our favourite *Ribes odoratum*, the clove currant, which smells of hot cross buns at Easter time. This being Cornwall – too wet, if not too acid – we are nervous about growing roses, but are hoping that rugosas and Scotch briar roses will love it. We planted the ragingly scented *Rosa spinosissima* 'William III', *R. rugosa* 'Roseraie de l'Hay' and 'Blanc Double de Coubert', and *Rosa moyseii* 'Geranium' for a burst of single 'war-of-the roses' red. Mixed in on this bank are *Euphorbia characias* subsp. *wulfenii* which flow down from a planting of the same with sarcococca in the gravel above.

As the season soaked on we made lists of what was missing: the freshness of flower and scent, old favourites, plants which need not compete with the ancient architecture and the aching estuary light, but which would complement them and somehow introduce a note of husbandry. There was need of a garden and we hankered for summer abundance, albeit nothing too complicated. But with very limited depth of very poor soil and potential archaeology everywhere beneath the ground, to create a proper border would entail building up on top of the existing level. We did this by bringing in tons of topsoil and manure in small trailer loads, the only transport that would fit through the lanes and the entrance gate, which then had to be moved around and 'sculpted' to make a workable double border on the

OPPOSITE: White, pink, shocking pink and purple conjuring something of the illuminated manuscript in the Norah Border. The shell keep is partially hidden by the two enormous holm oaks. *Salvia involucrate* 'Bethelii' and *Deutzia* x *hybrida* 'Mont Rose', with fennel in the foreground

ABOVE TOP LEFT AND RIGHT AND BOTTOM LEFT: *Lilium regale* lilies are planted with abandon along the Norah Border and at the front of the house

ABOVE RIGHT: Meadow has replaced lawn in many areas

OVERLEAF: Bailey walls surround the flat space upon which the Regency villa sits. *Echium pininiana* are massed under ancient holm oaks

curving bank in front of the house. Julian had visions of a level path halfway up, lengthwise through the middle of a double border, along which he dreamt of strolling on imagined summer evenings, lost in a jungle of flowers. But in the continuing rain all we seemed to be making was a mess.

But in the autumn things were brighter and drier, the pernicious weeds were on the wane, and the beds puffed up like duvets with tons of council compost and the farm manure. We had reduced the amount of close-mown grass, opting for 'meadow' and the chance to plant bulbs by the many thousand. We planted camassias *C. esculenta* and *C. leichtlinii* and narcissi *N.* 'Actaea' and *Narcissus poeticus* var. *recurvus* all through the orchard, the drive, and up the Mount. On the terrace we filled big terracotta pots with stripy tulips and wallflowers for the following spring. We had discussed taking out the Kanzan cherry by the house but instead we raised the crown of it so that you could see the gentle mounded lawn beneath and planted crocus and autumn crocus, scillas and *Tulipa sylvestris*, snowdrops, aconites, fritillaries and added back the cyclamen we had gleaned from the bank on the other side of the house. We planted anything that would bring pleasure to the view from the kitchen window. It was just as well as it turned out to be a long winter.

Only in the second January did we treat ourselves to really planning the big herbaceous and shrub planting. After a summer of drizzle and no plants it was hard not to go berserk when it came to planning the 'Norah Border'. Whatever we did had to be manageable with little labour, and we have learnt over the years to manage the lack of labour by putting in a lot of weeding work in the spring, followed by deep mulching and by planting densely. Bulbs such as alliums and lilies can come through the dense planting, but some areas are left free for annuals or biennials that add spice. Early in our second spring we drew out a trapezoidal path around the croquet lawn with boards and flinty yellow gravel – an anathema to some as it is not local to Cornwall, but, since the sources of pretty local riverbed gravel have all gone, and almost the only option being crushed granite, we broke the rules and chose a flinty gravel from east Devon which bounces light around the garden. This bright gravel path has given form to the whole area and had the remarkable effect of making the lawn look much bigger. We created another trick of scale by placing a pair of green-oak cannons that we had made pointing out to sea and framing the tidal reaches below.

Beside the path beneath the terrace waves of 'Mrs Sinkins' pinks, Bonica roses and *Matthiola incana* 'Pillow Talk' spill out, jostling with *Agapanthus* 'Back in Black' and the saturated pink *Nerine* 'Isabel' in groups of thirty or forty. Singing on throughout November the nerines echo the mounds of *Pelargonium* 'Pink Capricorn' flowering in big terracotta pots on the terrace. These pots have helped boost the floweriness on this side of the house without compromising the bigger picture. All the planting here has to achieve this balance between joyfulness and submission to the view that is framed by gatehouse and ramparts. One day these will foam in June with rambling roses and, on the bank beneath them, a sort of *maquis* of cistus including *Cistus* x *dansereaui* , *C.* x *d* 'Decumbens', *C.* x *hybridus*, *Cistus* x *argenteus* and *C.* 'Peggy Sammons'. *Lavendula stoechas* and *Rosmarinus* 'Severn Sea' is clipped into low blue-green mounds and already scents the air all about the terrace. Cornwall is good for scent, being warm and wet, and when the sun does appear aromatic plants exude their turpentine tang. Into this subtle mix we could not resist adding some shimmering blues, *Iris pallida* 'Argentea Variegata' and *Agapanthus* 'Northern Star'. Blue seems to speak to the sky and the estuary in a way that is very calming, and it complements the vibrant pinks which we have used a lot as a much-needed counterpoint to the granite, slate and the iridescent moss.

The great double Norah Border to the west of the house has been a huge source of pleasure and surprise. The castle walls provided a terrific back curtain to a plan which consists of a deep back border under the wall, a grass path through the middle and grass ramps enclosing a central sloping bed about four metres deep at its widest. Opposite the front door we made a shallow flight of steps from green oak leading to a big green-oak vermiculated obelisk. The borders needed solid dark punctuation in winter and summer. Six clipped yews in 'onion' shapes a metre high are planted in the front sections, while ranged across the back bed are eight tall columns of yew over which red *Tropaeolum speciosum* already romps. These and the mature magnolias, dogwood and eucryphia are a foil and scaffold for the energies of the new herbaceous planting. A secondary level of evergreen 'body' is provided by 'Miss Jessop's Upright' rosemary, *Erysimum* 'Bowles's Mauve', *Daphne odora* 'Aureomarginata' and *Sarcoccoca hookeriana* var. *humilis* to be clipped like loose box. All this stops it from completely falling apart in winter.

All the herbaceous planting was done with nine-centimetre or bare-rooted plants. Our biggest mistake was planting lots of achillea that expanded and flopped everywhere in our rich new soil, to no great visual effect. The asters also grew like rockets and fell over, but at least the show in September was radioactively magenta, mauve and lilac. Much more successful were the lupins, especially 'Masterpiece', which was the price and colour of a Rembrandt but drew gasps from everybody for weeks on end. Although some people resist them, especially in Cornwall, we think irises can work in a border, given enough space and good drainage. There are stands of *Iris* 'Braithwaite', 'Jane Phillips' and 'Sable' and their glaucous swordlike leaves contribute to the outline and definition of the border even in winter. *Gladiolus communis* subsp. *byzantinus*, which grow on the dual carriageway hereabouts, are massed at other key points.

The colour scheme developed itself somehow, nothing very clever, but pretty: white, pink, shocking pink, purple through shades of blue, with pale sulphurous yellows to intercede in plantings of *Thalictrum flavum* subsp. *glaucum* and *Scabiosa ochroleuca* and a single primrose-coloured hollyhock. Alcea, alliums and eremurus are great for fireworks in a border, and a particular success has been the branching cherry-pink *Alcea* 'Park Rondell'. There are more white rambling roses up the back wall, but also the cool grey-violet *Rosa* 'Veilchenblau' against the craggy stone. For shrub roses, afraid of the rain and balling brown buds, we chose bonny blowsy pink ones like 'Rose de Resht' and 'Charles de Mills', boudoir pinks also to be found in pools of peonies 'Monsieur Jules Elie', 'Madame Calot' and 'Karl Rosenfeld'. For height and upward thrust onopordum and artichokes. Threaded throughout, as a counter-point to the thick bursts of colour, is a veil or filigree layer of umbellifers. The best of these is *Selinum wallichianum*, along with earlier flowering *Cenalophium denudatum*, *Ammi majus* and *Crambe cordifolia*, pepped up by the acid greens of culinary fennel, giant *Ferula communis* and *Angelica archangelica*. Reliable border stalwarts keep the thing going, such as *Campanula* 'Loddon Anna' and *Lupinus* 'Flame Red'. Never be afraid of red; it somehow works in a large composition. *Dahlia coccinea,* given to us by Mary Keen, zings things up for months. Later in the summer a wave of papal purple rises up in in the form of *Astilbe* 'Purpurlanze' with *Phlox* 'Blue Paradise' and 'Eva Cullum' and *Salvia buchananii*. These brassy blasts of colour are tempered and the shadows lightened by the calmer woody green and white areas. The very middle near the obelisk and steps is cooler, with *Cardiocrinum giganteum* amid *Hydrangea* 'Limelight' and 'Iceberg' roses, fronted with white agapanthus, and hundreds of deliciously scented *Gladioulus murielae* also given to us by Mary Keen, and white crinums.

It is not complex or rarefied planting, but even in its infancy it has perhaps conjured something of the illuminated manuscript, Bocaccio or *The Romance of the Rose*. The planting also heightens a pre-Raphaelite mood about the castle, recalling the bold days of the Black Prince.

RIGHT: Pots of exotics such as the Asiatic lily 'Orange Art', banana and Chusan palm trees with vivid orange furniture around the Indian-style pool house

OPPOSITE: The motte rears up to the shell keep

The Old Rectory

DUNTISBOURNE ROUS, GLOUCESTERSHIRE

Mary Keen

WHEN WE HAD to move from a brick Berkshire rectory with Venetian windows, where the garden had taken sixteen years to make, I could not bear to think of living in a cold stone house in the Cotswolds. By the time we left Berkshire the orchard grass was painted in spring with *Crocus tommasinianus, Rosa* 'Madame Isaac Pereire' had covered all the iron arches and we could swim in an inky pool looking out over a wooded valley. There was a walled kitchen garden, a sea-blue trellis arbour with a fig tree and *Tulipa clusiana* flourished in a hot dry bed under the greenhouse.

The new Old Rectory was surrounded by dark conifers and laurel. Virginia creeper clung to the house and the garden contained formal rose beds, quite a lot of heather and a giant thuya hedge screening the view of a wood. The place felt claustrophobic, flower -free and not *at all* like home. The lane that led down the valley of the little River Dunt was beautiful and so was the church of St Michael over the garden wall, but the house needed eighteen months of work and in the garden there were enough stones to build walls from the ones that we dug from the ground. We inherited an orchard of five Samuel Palmer apple trees, a large copper beech, a horse chestnut and a Norway maple as well as a collection of little sheds and buildings with stone roofs and moss-covered tiles. Outside what had once been a privy there was a bed of lily of the valley and some dark-red tree peonies, *P. delavayii,* lurked under the orchard wall. The writer Katharine Mansfield's sister, Jean Renshaw, had lived here twenty years before the people who sold us the house and locals said she loved the garden, but it took years for the place to grab me.

Today, it is hard to remember what hard work it was and how much I resented the change. There is now no time of year when I cannot bear to be outside – except perhaps in late November and most of December, when sodden rags of plants cling to borders, or lie in heaps on beds and paths. Sometimes people ask, 'When shall I come to your garden? When is it at its best?' For me, apart from those days at the low point of the year, the garden is never *not* best.

OPPOSITE: The strong verticals of the house and beech tree beyond are echoed in the clipped columns of yew. A large scented *Viburnum* x *burkwoodii* 'Park Farm Hybrid' and seedling *Euphorbia characias* subsp. *wulfenii* flower in spring

ABOVE: Groups
of terracotta pots
congregate outside the
porch, which is filled
with scented-leaved
pelargoniums

At the beginning, nearly a quarter of a century ago, I found it hard to see where to start. It was the tidiest and pokiest of plots. There seemed to be nowhere to make a garden. Landscapers had paved over old bricks with regular square slabs. There was a swimming pool of Hockney blue where I wanted flowers. Privacy seemed impossible, nor were there any views out to the Cotswold landscape that surrounds us. No secrets, no mystery, no surprises. What I make for clients tends to be about display, but we needed to create somewhere that was a place to live. Clients have more labour than the five days' help a fortnight that we can afford, and our lives are busy, but I have always minded more about the atmosphere of a place than high horticultural tidiness, although we do work through the winter which is vital for keeping on top of things.

The garden wakes up with the New Year. Every day something happens. Snowdrops whiten, aconites uncurl from their ruffs of green and streaks of shocking pink appear among the leaves of *Cyclamen coum*. Narcissi nose through the orchard grass, and if you peer you can see thin strands of crocus as soon as Christmas is over. After twenty-two years, the *C. tommasinianus* that I loved so much in the old Berkshire orchard are beyond my dreams. They have seeded everywhere. There is a whole bank of 'S. Arnott' snowdrops grown from a handful given to me by Ruth Birchall of Cotswold Farm, and colonies of other named snowdrops sprawl over beds and in grass. Round-petalled hellebores – no stars, no doubles – are out for my birthday in February, and the scent from a huge bush of sarcococca greets us as we go in and out of the back door. The bowl of grassy slopes that we call the dell is full of snowdrops, followed by sky-blue patches of *Anemone blanda*. Those that naturalise are the plants I love best. Snowdrops making a milky way, *Cyclamen coum* seeding crazily into the hot south slope of the lawn and *Cyclamen repandum* hiding under the yew hedge. On the tiny lawn with clipped pillars of yew, under the topiary cake stands that we shaped from lumps of yew, we have grown a mixture of small flowers in the grass. *Crocus vernus* and *Tulipa turkestanica* already seed themselves, but what I really want to see is *Anemone pavonina* spreading everywhere.

In March there are more winter flowers and wild narcissi. I collect what Alan Street of Avon Bulbs calls the 'Old Ladies'. These gentle daffodils are a far cry from 'King Alfred'. In April the orchard is full of fritillaries and the potted auriculas begin to flower in the shed that was once a privy. May brings the bright fresh green of new leaves, blackthorn in the hedges, blossom in the dell, lilies of the valley under the larder and tulips like hundreds and thousands among deep purple honesty. There are irises, old unfrilly sorts in the gooseberry garden, and orange eremurus. In June the list lengthens. This is the month that spells 'garden' to most people and when groups want to visit. Americans only come when the roses are out. Why? July, August and September are packed with dahlias and blazing colours. The gooseberry garden turns orange and blue. October is for Michaelmas daisies, hips and berries in the dell and lingering annuals until shocking-pink nerines and the scent of *Viburnum farreri* start. Just saying the names of these flowers makes my heart leap with excitement. But if all that went I would still dream about the deep green underpinning of the garden, the rounded box hedges, the swelling topiary, the ancient apple trees, the view of the valley, the peace of the place.

Although the garden is just under two acres and fairly intensive, we grow vegetables as well as flowers, propagate all our own plants, run a greenhouse and the auricula collection is demanding, it is never too much. If it were, I would change it, or open less frequently. Summer groups often find me hot and bothered with a broom and secateurs as people arrive. Dead-heading is critical, so is sweeping the spaces. But in the evening when the visitors are gone, I love how fresh it looks. The plants can surge about as much as they like, but the paths need to be clear, stones swept and edges cut. The rest I aim to make as natural-looking as possible. Our lawn is mostly moss and daisies, which dismays some visitors.

In the summer garden things are high, wild and plentiful. Here four unmatched beds are divided by paths that form a St Andrew's cross, pinned centrally by a large copper pot. Four fastigiate box bushes, *Buxus* 'Graham Blandy', mark the middle circle; they are over six foot tall and slim and need minimal clipping and tying. The shrubs in the beds are a couple of silvery *Rhamnus alaternus* 'Argenteovariegata', a large *Ligustrum quihoui, Elaeagnus* 'Quicksilver', *Buddleja* 'Dartmoor' and roses 'Cerise Bouquet', 'Madame Isaac Péreire', 'La Reine Victoria' and 'Constance Spry'. Between these permanent fixtures there are waves

ABOVE: Groups of topiary yew, clipped box and rosemary outside the Old Schoolhouse and greenhouse

LEFT: The various irregular and curving forms of the solid evergreens are a backdrop to emerging leaves in spring

RIGHT: Shadows cast by the keyhole entrance to the summer garden from the terrace and sun on the inflorescences of *Euphorbia characias* subsp. *wulfenii*

of background colour from May to October. We have a good dark form of honesty with purple-tinged leaves that seeds itself freely, and I am trying to replace it with the perennial, blue-er form of lunaria grown from seed collected in Corfu. We let it run right through the beds to underpin a mixture of tulips in scarlet, pink, crimson, purple and a few in palest yellow. No white. And I prefer the lily-flowered shape, although we do usually have 'Couleur Cardinale' and 'Queen of the Night.' I like the colours mixed, not in separate parks-type groups. There is also a good blue comfrey, *Symphytum* x *uplandicum*, that holds its own in May. As the tulips fade, we pull them out. Peonies, giant fennel, several forms of *Iris sibirica* follow and the great silver onopordon start to grow, backed by *Allium* 'Purple Sensation' and brilliant opium poppies throughout the beds. By June the crambe is foaming with giant yellow scabious, *Cephalaria gigantea* and *Thalictrum rochebrunianum*. I like enormous plants and the sensation of being surrounded by their huge shapes. We use a lot of half hardies and a few annuals: salvias, penstemons, verbenas and cosmos and plenty of dahlias, especially a single crimson *D. coccinea* that grows six foot in a season. The plants change from year to year. We do as much standing and appraising as we do gardening. Sometimes I think that eyes are the best tools of all.

I use plants differently, in other places in the garden. The hellebore beds outside the kitchen window are welcome to self-seeding Welsh poppies, as the snowdrops fade. Here the colours are copper or yellowy, with apricot foxgloves, then repeated clumps of *Dahlia* 'David Howard'. It would never have worked at the brick Berkshire rectory, but yellow lights up grey stone at all times of year.

The gooseberry garden is for fruit and herbs among annuals and even brighter oranges with blood red, or singing yellow, as well as plenty of blue. Christopher Lloyd gave me a dahlia called 'Chimborazo' which looks terrific here. The church border in the kitchen garden is different again. It was once much more traditional with delphiniums and poppies and sweet williams in old-fashioned clumps. This has now been replaced with a Pictorial Meadow, the annual seed mix developed at Sheffield University. In 2013 I began adding perennials and grasses and this separate place is still an area that is being developed. The old-fashioned flowers are relegated to rows for picking in the kitchen garden. Ammi, cornflowers, sweet williams and sweet pea 'Matucana' provide bunches until midsummer and beyond. Zinnias, dahlias and chrysanthemums keep us going until hard frosts begin.

Because I am more interested in creating atmosphere than impressing gardeners this is not primarily a plantsman's garden but, like all of us, I cannot resist new plants. Gardens need to feel settled, but that is not the same as stagnant. The annual meadow has been an interesting experiment and the snowdrop and iris collections are growing. Some box has died. The battle with ground elder continues to be fought. On the gravel in front of the house plants are allowed to seed, especially giant silvery *Verbascum bombyciferum* and the single pale-yellow hollyhock *Alcea rugosa*. Trees have been pruned to let in more light, others have outgrown their places. The process of making a garden, the way it changes and develops, is thrilling, but what I love best, now that it has all started to mature, is the feeling of deep calm that the place produces. Last summer I came round a corner to find two visitors talking in whispers because, they said, they didn't want to break the spell of the place. That was the biggest compliment of all.

LEFT: Tulips including 'Flaming Jewel', 'Mickey Mouse' and 'Raspberry Ripple' with the taller 'Brown Sugar' and 'Dordogne' line the wall from the back door to the school house

ABOVE: Over the wall is a lovely view of the twelfth-century St Michael's Church. Clematis 'Frances Rivis' scrambles through *Kerria japonica* 'Pleniflora'

OVERLEAF LEFT: The old privy is home to a collection of auriculas

OVERLEAF RIGHT CLOCKWISE FROM TOP LEFT: The greenhouse with *pelargoniums* 'Rollison's Unique' and 'Leslie William Burrows'. Seedling annuals *Abutilon* 'Patrick Synge' and *pelargonium* 'Leslie William Burrows'

ABOVE AND OPPOSITE:
The gooseberry garden
is planted with oranges,
yellows and blues
including sunflower
'Earth Walker', *Rudbeckia
fulgida* var. *deamii*, *Salvia
guaranitica* 'Blue Enigma'
and *Dahlia* 'Bishop's
Child'

RIGHT: The blue
pincushion flowers of
Succisa pratensis with
orange *Helenium* 'Sahin's
Early Flowerer'

Malplaquet House

STEPNEY, LONDON

Todd Longstaffe-Gowan & Tim Knox

ESCRIBED VARIOUSLY AS a 'tip' or a 'treasure house', and its unkempt garden a 'howling wilderness' or a 'welcome oasis', Malplaquet House is one of the metropolis's more unusual confections. For almost three centuries it has been an inconspicuous denizen of London's East End. Built by the bricklayer and speculator Thomas Andrews in 1741, Malplaquet House is one of a pair of surviving double-pile merchants' houses which replaced an even larger house, the 'Mansion House', at the heart of what was formerly known as Mile End Old Town. This district was in the eighteenth century famous for its nurseries, market gardens and public pleasure grounds. Malplaquet House, like other large houses in the Mile End Road, stood well back off the street and possessed a forecourt and a capacious back garden. What these looked like when they were first laid out is anyone's guess: the first account dates from 1794 when the 'excellent garden, inclosed with brick walls' is described as 'cloathed with fruit trees' and the house as 'suitable accommodation for a genteel family'.

For the first 150 years the house was inhabited and transformed by a host of colourful characters, including a well-heeled Sephardi widow, a retired surgeon and a raffish Jamaican-born slave owner. None, however, was as rich and improving as the brewer Harry Charrington, who from the mid-1780s modernised extensively the house and presumably its gardens. The family's Anchor Brewery lay only a few doors down the Mile End Road – its site is now mostly occupied by a retail park. To Charrington we owe the house's large Regency rooms, its four-floor rear extension, its doorcase embedded in a severe Soanian niche with a broad frieze of Greek Key pattern, and its handsome fenestration. With his death in 1833 things took a turn for the worse: Malplaquet House, like the social and physical character of the East End, went into rapid decline. The house was carved up into mean tenements, and in 1857 the original railings and gate piers were destroyed to raise shopfronts in the forecourt. From the mid-nineteenth century much of the house was given over to commercial use, and the last residents moved out in 1894.

OPPOSITE: An assortment of pots with regale lilies, *euphorbia*, ornamental grasses and *Geranium maderense* line the path to the front door of Malplaquet House

TOP: Malplaquet House in May 1998 as Todd and Tim found it

ABOVE: The house exposed after the shopfronts were blown down in a gale in December 1999

The house was completely hidden behind a crumbling row of shops when the Spitalfields Trust acquired it in 1997. It had been compulsorily purchased by Tower Hamlets Council who handed it over to the Trust – who in turn sold it to us the following year – on the condition that the house and its mirror image next door were restored and returned to single-family occupancy within three years.

The revitalisation of Malplaquet House has been a great adventure. It was our obsession. Its gentle improvement absorbed us entirely, and gave us years of pleasure and frustration in equal measure. Our aim was to make the place comfortably habitable and to keep as much of the ancient fabric as possible – not only because we had to, but because it was (and remains) so remarkably evocative. Few London dwellings of its size and age have changed so little over so long a time. Happily the house has not only proven to be a very genial place to live, but also a perfect receptacle for our extensive and ever-growing collections of paintings, drawings, sculpture, natural history, ethnography, decorative arts and other curiosities. The house and garden have, in fact, evolved into a single entity: a *kunst und wunderkammer*, or cabinet of curiosities.

A great part of the charm of Malplaquet House may be attributed to its gardens. Not that they are by any means distinguished or extensive; nor are they original. They are nonetheless an achievement insofar as they were recovered from oblivion. What is now an irrepressible tangle of climbing roses, jasmine, wisteria, honeysuckle, melianthus, olive and box was formerly a labyrinth of Victorian building extensions and dank cavernous cellars. These were demolished with the encouragement of Tower Hamlets Council so as to liberate the early building from its disfiguring additions and to restore the forecourt. This was, in our view, an enlightened decision, as there were not at the time any private front gardens in our stretch of the Mile End Road; as in so many high streets across London, these spaces had long ago been sacrificed for building.

We began our garden improvements immediately we took possession of the house in May 1998, hollowing out the shops from the line of the original house to the edge of the public footpath, until only their façades remained – like flimsy sets from a Wild West film – and turning the cellars into vast planters. What we began, Mother Nature completed: a violent gale in December 1999 blew down what was left of our shopfronts into a heap of bricks, mortar and glass in the Mile End Road. This *coup de théâtre* precipitated the building of the forecourt's garden defences – walls, piers and railings – and the planting in earnest of our little south-facing garden.

Although I have an informed interest in historic London gardens, the layout of our forecourt has no historic basis. I didn't wish to create a pastiche of an eighteenth-century town garden. The context of the road had changed so dramatically that it needed a modern response. The aims of the layout and planting were threefold: to insulate the house from the thundering traffic of the road; to create an environment that would be attractive and hospitable to birds and other urban wildlife; and to compose the space in such a manner that reflected the idiosyncratic character of our interiors and their collections.

Foremost in our minds was the treatment of the entrance from the road – the transition from the hurly-burly of the high street to the comparative calm of the garden. The gate is our

ABOVE AND BELOW:
Rose 'Kew Rambler' and *Jasminum officinale* make irrespressible tangles above the ivy-clad walls on the Mile End Road. The entrance gates were made by Andrew Renwick to an eighteenthth-century design

OPPOSITE ABOVE LEFT AND THIS PAGE ABOVE: Pots of succulents including *Agave americana* 'Variegata' and a stooled Paulownia that erupts annually in a fountain of leviathan leaves

OPPOSITE ABOVE RIGHT: A view of the garden at the back of the house from a downstairs window

LEFT: Australian tree ferns, *Dicksonia antarctica* and climbers such as *Actinidia arguta, Clematis armandii, Solanum jasminoides* 'Album' and *Muehlenbeckia complexa* create an urban jungle in which to eat outside

RIGHT: A sheep skull poised on top of a bamboo cane with *Lilium regale* in the background

window on the world; and through this opening in our otherwise densely planted boundary, curious passers-by can peer with impunity to catch a glimpse of a confusion of planting and building like no other in the Mile End Road. A screen of high wrought-iron railings set on dwarf walls with Portland stone copings encloses the south side of the garden. These are backed with hazel wattle panels. One enters the garden through a broad iron gate based on a mid-eighteenth-century design commissioned from the Sheffield-based blacksmith Andrew Renwick. Its elaborate overthrow bears a cipher and a grotesque *repoussé* mask modelled by the sculptor Christopher Hobbs. The gate is flanked by a pair of giant brick piers crowned with Portland stone capitals surmounted by composition stone eagles cast from a pair at Knightshayes Court in Devon. The whole length of the forecourt screen that adjoins the public road is heavily embowered with great masses and festoons of greenery.

To enter the garden is to leave behind the mundane world: its enclosure on three sides by high walls and its luxuriant planting intensify the sense of mystery and romance. Our little jungle is punctuated by two Chusan palms, planted symmetrically along the central path and which allude to our exotic pedigrees: Tim's African and Fijian upbringing and my own Central and South American and West Indian childhood. Other denizens include a few phillyreas, a hazel, some shrub roses, several myrtles (which are regularly pruned so as not to get too large), and a single asparagus which contrasts handsomely with a paulownia stool that erupts annually in a fountain of leviathan leaves. Every inch of the walls is, like the railings, covered with a dense blanket of *Vitis coignetiae*, trachelospermum, clematis and roses. Roses are a favourite, and we delight in their seasonal display which begins with the pale-yellow flush of *Rosa banksiae* var. 'Lutea', and is succeeded by clouds of 'Kew Rambler', 'Sander's White', 'Paul's Himalayan Musk' and, most ravishing of all, climbing 'Cécile Brunner', which offers up thousands of delicate blooms every May. The remainder of the front is given over to a chaotic array of broadleaf evergreen shrubs, drifts of hakonechloa, euphorbia, ferns, geraniums, acanthus and ivy. The dense evergreen planting attracts nesting wrens, blackbirds, robins, titmice and, most recently, a colony of greenfinches, which must be a first for the Mile End Road for some time.

The garden's greenery is relieved by a generous sprinkling of lapidary curiosities, most of which have been supplied by Darren Jones of Lichen Antiques. These include a clutch of inscribed meer stones (resembling pets' gravestones), a prickly French limestone memorial in the Gothic taste, an ancient weathered pinnacle from Gloucester Cathedral, and a pair of granite Nilotic slabs inscribed with bogus hieroglyphics surmounted by a pair of goggle-eyed early nineteenth-century carved stone Portuguese water dogs. The largest eye-catcher in the forecourt is the Marshfield War Memorial. This 3.2-metre-high obelisk, which is inscribed with the names of twenty-seven men who died in action during the two Wars, was removed from the High Street in the eponymous Cotswold market town in the early 1990s and has since been replaced with a gleaming granite cenotaph.

Our north-facing back garden is about the same size as the forecourt. It had originally been over thirty metres long, and boasted a terrace, orchard and summerhouse; these had all, however, long vanished before we arrived. We found the area covered with decaying Victorian sheds and marshalling yards. These were demolished and much of the ground ceded to a local housing association as part of the rescue package struck between the Council

OVERLEAF: A pair of Chusan palms *Trachycarpus fortunei* either side of the path to the house and *Melianthus major* allude to the overseas childhoods of Tim Knox and Todd Longstaffe-Gowan

and the Spitalfields Trust. The patch we are left with is rather small, and surrounded by imposing but very desirable four-metre-high brick walls. The latter are now covered with a mat of climbing roses, wisteria, kiwi vine and maidenhair vine (*Muehlenbeckia complexa*) and the ground is colonised by a grove of *Dicksonia antarctica* and *Cyathea australis*. It was my first flirtation with these majestic vegetables, and I am grateful to Lyndon Osborn – one of the metropolis's foremost purveyors of tree ferns and unusual plants to the pterido-curious – for introducing me to them. Their evergreen canopy brightens up the garden and emits a soft green glow that permeates the ground-floor and basement apartments of the house. Indeed so atmospheric is our primeval garden that I half expect to hear the tramp of a giant iguanodon or the whir of a hideous flying lizard when I open the back garden door.

Here too, like the forecourt, we have recycled former building materials, including paving slabs, bricks and cobbles. Eye-catching embellishments are also much in evidence, including a bed of giant clam shells, fragments of Indian stone carvings, wall-mounted red-deer and reindeer skulls and antlers, and a life-size terracotta statue of the Dead Christ, made in the late nineteenth century by Mayer and Company of Munich. Propped against the north wall, and emerging from a fog of British ground ferns, is a 'lithargolite' allegorical relief by the Regency sculptor George James Bubb. The figure was one of a procession that animated a frieze depicting 'The Origins and Progress of Music' atop the former Italian Opera House in Haymarket. The back door of the house that gives access to the garden is sheltered by an arcaded porch, which was described in 1807 as the 'varanda'. It harbours an outdoor water closet studded with yet more molluscs and a plastic black baby doll's head (the gift of an artist friend). We use this loo year-round, regardless of the weather.

Malplaquet is like every garden a work in progress. As I write we have only just taken receipt of a monster stone capital and part of a fluted column from 212 Piccadilly, rescued by the Georgian Group. It now forms a memorial to Tiger, our late lamented miniature sausage dog. And we're poised to commission a new front path in black and white marble (as described in the house's sale particulars of 1781), stone steps, iron handrails to the steps and landing, and lined-out stucco facing to the basement storey. What is certain is that as long as we live at Malplaquet House the gardens will retain their romantic charm and studied decrepitude. One gets a great deal of pleasure living in a ruin emerging from vegetal chaos; and, judging by the comments of some passers-by, our little oasis goes a long way to enhancing the character of one of East London's busier streets.

Gresgarth Hall

CATON, LANCASHIRE

❧

Lady Lennox-Boyd

S A CHILD I grew up in rather idyllic circumstances an hour or so from Rome at an elevation of 600 metres with nothing between our house and the Apennines. There was neither electricity nor running water and bats roosted behind pictures. My mother was preoccupied with the family farm and I was free to wander the countryside with my friends from the village.

It was here that my love of nature began, for although the climate was inhospitable the wildflowers were out of this world. If anyone had told me then I would one day swap the Apennines for the Pennines, for a Victorian Gothic house that sits in a frost pocket at the bottom of a hill but still exposed to the north-west wind, I would have thought they were mad. But this is the place I now call home. It is where I want to be more than anywhere else; it is where the hours melt by when I am in my greenhouse full of seedlings. The garden at Gresgarth surprises a lot of people who come here expecting some sort of hybrid of a formal Italian and an English garden. It is a garden rooted in its Lancashire soil that has developed without any masterplan; it is the crucible within which I indulge my passion for collecting and growing plants, especially those from seed.

Being in a place where you could actually grow plants in a domestic situation was extraordinary to me when I moved to England in the 1970s. My eldest daughter Dominique and I lived in a wonderful house in St John's Wood with a huge garden. Life was much slower in those days, and I remember being able to fall asleep in my garden to the sound of cricket games at Lord's. I loved being out of doors, but in order to stay where we were living I needed to work. I had a gardener once a month, who was the first person to suggest I should be a garden designer. I had become a member of the Royal Horticultural Society, went to all the shows and was reading lots of books. I couldn't believe that normal conversation here amongst girlfriends centred round plants and gardens. Suddenly the whole thing fell into place and from drawing ideas on the backs of envelopes I set up a secretary (who was also an

OPPOSITE: The Artle Beck runs through the garden at Gresgarth Hall, seen here with the blossom of *Prunus* 'Shirotae' echoed on both sides of the river

ABOVE: Topiary and roses fill the stepped terraces between the house and Artle Beck with rose 'Rambling Rector' covering the octagonal gazebo

opera singer) on the top floor of the house and learnt on the job with the lovely Malaysian assistant I also took on. It was a lot of fun.

Mark came into my life in 1974. He was a barrister hoping to stand for Parliament and we both shared a love of design. He got the seat for Morecambe in 1978 and our Lancashire life began in earnest. I was gloriously happy in the little cottage we rented in the village where Mark canvassed. We looked in vain for a little farmstead with lots of outbuildings when a friend suggested we go and look at Gresgarth. I was non-committal even about renting it, but within a month Mark had bought it. I went along with his plan in a bit of a daze, as I was expecting our daughter Patricia.

The garden was very depressing. Because the house had been rented it hadn't been gardened for a long time. There were thickets of ponticum rhododrendron and sycamore everywhere, no views and a suffocating airlessness around the house. The hill (which is now opened up and peppered with cornus, was then thick with saplings right down to the water, so we slowly started clearing and I discovered the odd jewel such as a large handkerchief tree *Davidia involucrata*. I worked out that there had been a garden across the river that had been overrun by all the evergreens.

I knew nothing about the climate, and over-zealous clearing exposed the whole garden to the west wind that I hadn't accounted for at all. I had no idea about the damage that wind can do, or the damage that bad drainage can do, or how the short days also affect the growth of things, so within one season of planting up a collection of rhododendrons I had enthusiastically bought up from Cornwall they were all looking very unhappy.

Our great friend and northern horticultural ally Hugh Cavendish came over from Holker and suggested that I turn my attention to the hill on the south side of the garden. His lifelong knowledge of the area led him to observe that it turned against the west wind and that the bit of wood there would be very protected. I hadn't even thought about it. So I wandered around there disturbing the woodcock and gradually started opening it up. I took out all the beech, bar a few, kept the oaks and started planting my collection of magnolias, rhododendrons and many other taxa. I learnt as I went along, and have since added all sorts of other things too.

Thirty-five years on I have reached the stage where I'm having to take things out. My very first magnolias came up with me in the car from Wyevale in Herefordshire. We had been staying with Mark's cousin, the wonderful late plantsman George Clive, who said that we should stop off en route as they had some particularly good magnolias in the nursery. The area I planted them in is now thick with magnolias. The other day I stopped to register how huge and extraordinary they have become. And to think I nearly heeded Sir Peter Smithers's solemn advice when he came to stay in the early days that I should stick to alders and birches, that it would be impossible to grow magnolias satisfactorily at Gresgarth! I think there must be about 300 scattered around the garden. The one that I single out as being truly stunning is *Magnolia* 'Kew's Surprise'. I heeded Sir Peter's recommendation for the birches and get immense pleasure in autumn and winter from the textures and colours of their leaves and bark. Like so many other plants in the garden they also remind me of wonderful trips to observe plants in the wild or garden visits with the IDS.

I like hearing other people's views on the garden. A friend recently suggested that I fell the yews that flank the entrance to the house in order to get a better sense of the setting. I was interested and realised that maybe I should have been more daring but have now come to the conclusion that yews give a sense of history and scale. I will be planting rambling rose through them and maybe reshaping some of them in order to catch glimpses of the large oaks behind.

I now select trees and fell ones that are crowded and I seem to have come full circle at Gresgarth, first clearing then planting, and back to clearing again. I am keener on opening up views and I don't really find it as painful as I thought I would. That said, I have a mammoth planting spree forecast for this winter as I need to make space for new seedlings.

While all the early work was going on in the woods I had to turn my attention to the garden around the house. With narrow little terraces you could barely tiptoe around and from which the ground fell away sharply, the house felt rather off balance and there was nowhere to sit down comfortably, in sun or shade. I also had to connect the house to the small lake, then shaped as a comma, but I knew that I wanted the lake to feel like the result of the river flooding into the little valley. I copied the Lutyens steps at Great Dixter with their central octagons of grass that are so clever at getting you down a steep drop without being too heavy in hard materials, and made a lower terrace that runs to the water's edge. So that the paving isn't too harsh, and in order to create a sensation that the house rises out of a mass of planting, I made generous beds along the walls and at the edges of the terraces. The steps

OVERLEAF: *Rhododendron augustinii* and other mauve and pale pink rhodendrons such as 'Blue Tit' and 'Caerhays Lavender' are threaded through the woodland garden with pale pink *Prunus* 'Accolade' and white *Rhododendron williamsianum*

and terraces were the only thing I plotted down on paper.

Although Gresgarth is firmly designed in my head I don't want it to feel that way. It has a certain wildness about it; the Lancashire landscape, the geology and the river that roars through it call for a reasonably untamed atmosphere. Gresgarth means 'the place of the boar', and if you stand beside our stone copy of the original Roman Calydonian Boar you can hear the sound of the Artle Beck breaking over a weir at the back of the house. The noise of water is a constant and soothing feature throughout the garden. The river also seems to be a magnet for frost that descends towards it and gets miraculously carried away in its flow. I have realised that if you have anything overhanging the water the frost gets trapped, so keeping the banks clear in winter is essential. There is one part of the garden we cannot protect with a shelterbelt and the frost wreaks havoc on anything delicate in its path; I learnt my lesson with some lovely embothriums. I also opened up a gap in the wall at the bottom of the kitchen garden, replacing it with a gate to allow the frost to escape.

The kitchen garden is heaven but it was choked with mare's tail which we got very excited about when we arrived, mistaking it for asparagus. Despite years of double digging

BELOW: *Magnolia campbellii*, and *M. x loebneri* 'Leonard Messel' with *augustinii* rhododendrons in the woodland garden

RIGHT: *Lilium martagon* 'Black Prince'

FAR RIGHT: The purple-throated white foxglove, *Digitalis purpurea* 'Pam's Choice'

BELOW: A pair of spreading *Cornus kousa* var. *chinensis* in long grass with dome-pruned rambling rose 'Francis E Lester' and 'Polyantha Grandiflora'

and the diligent attention of my fabulous gardening team led by David and Sue, those two still grow together! The whole garden is like a lush weed factory. I honestly have never known a garden like it.

The gardeners have their greenhouse and I have a smaller one, my horticultural version of Virginia Woolf's *A Room of One's Own*. I also have my own potting shed and holding area and I look after them as I don't want the gardeners to feel that I'm taking them away from all the things they should be getting on with, so apart from watering when I am away this is firmly my domain. Growing and gardening is a sort of madness for me. But a very happy one.

I must have grown 1000 trees, and apart from selling them at the odd garden open day they all have to be given away otherwise I have to find room for them in the garden. This winter's resolution is to plant absolutely everything from my greenhouse and plunge beds and everything that is in a pot. It is not going to be easy as on top of a mania for propagating I also can't resist buying plants in nurseries or trying out new things. I am potty about Stewartias: I don't know why more people don't grow them.

I have a lot of cherries from Chris Lane. I find ornamental cherries really useful at concealing the dottiness of a collector's garden; they are 'edge of woodland' trees and you can plant them harmoniously *en masse*. Hamamelis, also from Chris Lane, don't do quite as well but I love all the colours together; you need the pale ones to set off the darker colours and some have a divine scent. I am also an inveterate collector of limes. It is fatal for me to go to plant study weekends. The Styracacae weekend, for example, ended up with me putting myself forward for a Lancastrian National Collection of Styrax. It will not be easy to compete with Hugh's Cumbrian collection at Holker as he's got a much better climate for them than me, but I can try!

So, from the Apennines to the Pennines. People often ask how much time I spend in our house in Lazio, where bats no longer roost behind paintings but where the wildflowers still burst abundantly to life in spring. Not much, is the answer. Springtime here at Gresgarth with the cherry blossom, the narcissi, sheets of fritillaries and primroses is every bit as wonderful. This Victorian Gothic house is as cosy as can be and I can honestly say that the two hours I spend wandering around the garden each time I return to Gresgarth having been away are far and away my happiest times.

OPPOSITE AND ABOVE: *Clematis* x *durandii* sets the tone of purples and reds in the herbaceous border in summer with large clumps of *Campanula lactiflora* 'Prichard's Variety'. Borders encased in scalloped yew hedges are filled with purples, blues and russets of *Clematis* x *durandii, Campanula lactiflora* 'Prichard's Variety' and *Sedum* 'Herbtsfreude' with shots of magenta and red

OVERLEAF: Gresgarth Hall seen from across the lake in midsummer with roses and perennials cascading down the terraces in front of the house

Rockcliffe

Upper Slaughter, Gloucestershire

Emma Keswick

OPPOSITE: Looking back towards Rockcliffe from the dovecote

WHEN ASKED FOR his next choice on 'Desert Island Discs' the late Lord Charteris, aged eighty-two, requested a waltz '…because I just have to dance every day'. I feel the same way about gardening.

My grandmother was a good plantswoman and head of the Scottish National Gardens Scheme, and my great-aunt features in this book's predecessor. Gardening is in my blood. I have always wanted to garden and I can vividly remember the first plants I grew, *Dahlia* 'Hi Dolly' and portulaca in a town house in Sydney in 1971, the year I married, aged twenty.

Since then I have never stopped gardening wherever I have lived (mostly between Hong Kong and Britain), and I have always been lucky to live in houses with gardens. During the years we spent in Asia we travelled often and my sponge bag always contained cuttings. My children tell mildly exaggerated tales of uncomfortable aeroplane journeys with twigs stuffed down their knickers. Some understandably shrivelled and died, but the cuttings that took and thrived brought immense satisfaction and a sense of provenance. I hesitate to admit that I continue this habit.

My husband Simon and I bought Rockcliffe in 1981. We then promptly returned to live once again in Hong Kong and it was another seven years before we finally unpacked our bags. Rockcliffe was very different then to what it is now. The house was smaller with no garden at all. To begin with I tried to garden from afar.

Rockcliffe was built in 1860 as the dower house to Eyford Park. It perches above a lake, rendering the back of the house pretty useless. The garden had to be on the front of the house, so we moved parking to the side, paced out a long lawn up to the field and built a ha-ha. The beautifully made dry-stone creation that curves in a semicircle the width the house and thence to the sides is the well-earned recipient of prizes.

I tried with less success to copy my parents-in-law's pretty old York paving path up through the garden. Unfortunately the builder could not believe that I really would like to

lay a new path with old York paving and took it upon himself to lay newly quarried stone. Disappointing both at the time and thirty years on as the stone, sawn and not hewn, is still ugly and *lethal* to walk on in winter.

When finally we returned home in 1990 I began to make a garden in earnest.

While our good friend the architect Nicholas Johnston added two small wings, a mansard roof and an orangery we moved into Batsford House for a year. I wish – when we returned to Rockcliffe – that I had planted all the wonderful trees I had been surrounded by in the arboretum at Batsford, but I didn't.

Despite understanding structure to be the most important element of a garden I had no master plan at that point beyond the terrace and the kitchen garden. Once the bones of a garden are in place, you can plant it up and light the touchpaper of nature. Then usually stand well back, leaving it to grow into a blowsy moll.

The terrace all around the house is old York paving with planting pockets, not too many but enough to soften the stone. A low wall covered in *Rosa* 'New Dawn', *Lonicera pericly-menum* 'Serotina', *L. p.* 'Belgica', *Clematis* 'Comtesse de Bouchard' and *C.* 'Niobe' surround it with a soft froth of white from *Centranthus ruber* 'Albus' at its base. We collect seed from this white valerian as well as foxgloves, sweet peas, martagon lilies, *Phacelia tanacetifolia* and *Malva moschata* f. *alba*, so in early autumn the orangery is full of drying and dying stalks.

OPPOSITE: A door at the end of wide borders separating the kitchen garden leads up between yew topiary birds to the dovecote

The main terrace on the south-east-facing side is wide. Originally it was planted up with an interweaving parterre of *Buxus sempervirens* but that got both *Cylindrocladium boxicola* and *Volutella buxi* so I resolutely removed all box from the terrace and around the edges of every border in the kitchen garden. I then planted *Lavandula* 'Sawyers', imagining the smell wafting in through my bedroom window (I always thought it would be fun to plant a 'Rambling Rector' under my window), but it never did well and last year, with the help of Rupert Golby, I replanted the terrace with large, bold yew shapes including four big obelisks. The interplanting of *Cistus* x *cyprius*, *Euphorbia characias* subsp. *wulfenii*, *Salvia candelabra,* purple sage, *Helleborus orientalis*, *Daphne odora* 'Aureomarginata', regale lilies, *Agapanthus campanu-latus* 'Northern Star', *Aster amellus* 'King George', *Salvia glutinosa*, *Bupleurum fruticosum* and *Rosa gallica* 'Versicolor', the lovely rosa mundi, has been so successful it merits that marathon listing. Wherever possible the shrubs are shaped into mounds, and smaller plants such as santolina and teucrium have their heads chopped off in early summer to form hummocks. The good strong evergreen planting keeps it in year-round shape. There is a pair of obelisks on the terrace that echoes the beech obelisks up the lawn. The terrace finally feels grounded to the house and I love looking out over it to the beech topiary, the ha-ha and the sheep in the park beyond.

We built a high dry-stone wall around the kitchen garden and made a gate into it that we copied from Snowshill, an Arts and Crafts garden twelve miles away that always reminds me of the heavenly sunny autumn day when I walked there from here. The kitchen garden is sadly in a frost pocket, but what to do? There was no other place to put it because of the contour of the land. It is productive and pretty, just late. We produce vegetables and flowers for picking all year, and in the greenhouses we strike all our own cuttings for the pots on the terrace that rise, like soufflés, throughout the summer. We also grow many plants for inside the house including a pelargonium that has been named 'Willa' after my mother, sister and daughter.

ABOVE: The fruit cage is topped by a decorative frieze and finials and bordered by wild strawberries. *Anthemis punctata* subsp. *cupaniana* and *Erysimum* 'Bowles Mauve'

RIGHT: Lollipop the dog amongst *Iris Germanica* 'Wild Swan', *Euphorbia characias* subsp. *wulfenii*, *Erysimum* 'Emm's Variety' *Geranium* x *magnificum* and *Erysimum* 'Bowles Mauve' with lupin 'Noble Maiden' beneath the espaliered fruit trees in the kitchen garden. English foxgloves sow themselves around the garden (left) into a border of *Iris sieboldii* 'Silver Edge' and (right) amongst rose 'William Lobb', peonies, violas and *Phuopsis stylosa*

I look out of my bedroom window first thing every morning and I walk around the garden five times a day. Somehow from this the next design step emerges, often unconsciously inspired by an element of something I saw in a garden the previous summer or many years before in Italy, France, Asia or maybe from a book or magazine. I believe most gardening ideas are triggered by a memory then refined and reproduced to suit the site. I have six large and beautiful *Cornus controversa* 'Variegata' around a rectangular pond that now hold hands across the water, having fallen in love with this tree when I went to Helen Dillon's Dublin garden in 1980. The avenue of large beech obelisks leading up to the ha-ha from the house narrows as they climb the lawn, making the perspective appear longer. This trick was noted at the Palazzo Corsini where an avenue of narrowing statues elongates a walled garden in the middle of Florence. Beech is indigenous to the Cotswolds, juvenile beech retains its leaves throughout the winter and, to me, there is no prettier colour than the rice-paddy green of young beech leaves.

We planted an orchard on a slope and planned for a dovecote to draw the eye to the top. I looked at designs of dovecotes and doocots for years while my topiary yew doves leading to the allotted spot 'grew up'. The final design was an amalgamation of the dovecote at Rousham, weathervanes on College Chapel at Eton and stone benches from The Gothic Cottage, Stourhead, with a band course copied from the one above the windows of the Old Toll House in Stow-on-the-Wold. One day we shall build a Gothic chicken house like the one I saw at Glin Castle over thirty years ago.

It is not so difficult to make an interesting summer garden but the English summer is short while spring, autumn and winter can be agonisingly long. Of course each season has achingly beautiful days, but strong design is essential for the winter garden. I love looking out at the snow-covered topiary birds that lead up through the orchard, or at the beech obelisks covered in frost. One of my god-daughters is writing a book in which these birds fly off on adventures at dusk and just make it back onto their perches by dawn!

I planted yew hedges enclosing individual gardens and have made chess-pawn yew topiary to unify the structure throughout the garden. Yew is a strong green; too much and it can be sad, so I have also planted lime and hornbeam hedges. All the hedges at Rockcliffe are underplanted with *Cyclamen hederifolium* that give such pleasure in the autumn. We built walls (note the 'we' in deference to the cost of the walls!), put in two canals and the rectangular pond overhung with *Cornus controversa* 'Variegata'.

I couldn't resist making the field we walk through to the stud part of the garden and planted it with trees that flower or have good autumn colour, preferably both, including *Prunus sargentii*, *Malus hupehensis*, *Prunus padus* 'Watereri', *Acer cappadocicum* and sweet gum *Liquidambar styraciflua*. These are underplanted with a spreading blanket of *Narcissus obvallaris*, the lovely Star of Bethlehem *Ornithogalum nutans*, ox-eye daisies and *Colchicum byzantium*. Grass paths are lined with *Buxus rotundifolia* that, so far and fingers crossed, is box-blight-resistant here. A new idea is that there will be explosions of *Rosa* 'Cerise Bouquet', but no sign of any explosion yet!

I have a wide herbaceous border, which my husband Simon says is dated. It has four mature Irish yews along it that I advertised for in the *Evesham Journal*. We bought them for £100 from someone altering his garden and they thrive in their new home. To take Simon's point (in this case!) I have added several *Rosa rugosa* 'Roseraie de l'Haye' and *Buddleia indica* for volume among the perennials. I plant in groups of at least eight plants and repeat down the border. When in doubt, think stout. *Aster amellus* 'King George', one of my favourite plants that I first saw at Pusey House a very long time ago, extends the flowering season with its dramatic electric-blue flowers that pick well. I also love lilies and plant *Lilium regale* in every border because they smell heavenly and reliably do their stuff from one year to the next if annually sprayed to deter lily beetle. We have huge pots of regale lilies on the terrace and grow *L. candidum*, *L.* 'Muscadet' and *L.* 'Conca d'Or' for inside and out. *Lilium martagon* is gradually naturalising under beech trees. This year we sowed 500 grams of our own seed.

My latest crush is agapanthus and now that so many are hardy I can't resist just a few more every year. Other favourite plants include *Viburnum* x *carlcephelum*, *Hoheria* 'Glory Of Almwch', *Syringa* 'Sensation' and *S.* 'Maud Notcutt', *Garrya elliptica* when it is pruned close along a wall, tree peonies, *Paeonia emodi*, *P.* 'Buckeye Belle' and roses galore. There are so many plants I love, and increasingly we try to give them the right conditions in which to thrive. I want them to look bludgeoning! But there are also many failures. I have a basket that is the dead-plant-label cemetery.

Happily I have achieved my goal of being able to pick a posy from the garden on any day of the year. As I write this on 6 January several snowdrops are out and a vase of *Daphne bholua* and *Lonicera fragrantissima* sits on my desk. Through the window I can see buds of *Helleborus orientalis* peeking through their leaves, which now need cutting off.

It is not easy gardening in the Cotswolds, particularly if you live at a place called Rockcliffe! Our topsoil is a couple of inches of Cotswold brash before we hit the cliff bit. We have a large compost area and use every bit of compost we make. We add mushroom compost and leaf mould to improve the condition of the soil. Cotswold brash is wonderfully free-draining, but if we have a lot of rain – as in 2012 – any goodness is leached out of the soil. We aim to feed everything in the garden. We are at a height of 550 feet so it can also be very cold. In severe weather we fleece plants, and a friend of one of my children reminds me of a time I got a gang of them out of their beds to wrap young cornus to protect their flowers from a late frost! At times like that I think of Kiftsgate, Hidcote, Daylesford and Abbotswood and take heart . . .

I haven't finished my garden and I never will, because the more I learn the more I realise there is to know. Gardening is a lifelong passion and I am never happier than when bottom up in the garden listening to BBC Radio 4. I have a very knowledgeable and experienced head gardener and two other gardeners who are master pruners. They are a good team and great fun to work with. My heart lifts as I prepare my gardening basket.

ABOVE: The Beauty Bush *kolkwitzia amabalis* is scattered through the shrubberies beside the beech pyramids, seen here with some of the yew topiary pawns

FAR RIGHT: Pyramids of beech line the lawn leading to the ha ha. The terrace is planted with a mixture of evergreens, roses and perennials, including, clockwise from top right, *rosa* x *gallica* 'Versicolor', *Phuopsis stylosa* and Cheddar Pinks, *Dianthus gratianopolitanus*

Southern Shade, a bronze
by Nigel Hall is positioned
atop the edge of the ha ha

Helmingham Hall

STOWMARKET, SUFFOLK

Xa Tollemache

I WAS A HORTICULTURALLY raw and totally ignorant young mother when we moved into Helmingham. In 1975 my father-in-law, John Tollemache, died aged only sixty-six so my husband, Tim, had to take up the reins sooner than any of us had expected. We found ourselves with a very young daughter, and a baby on the way, moving into the 'big house' and taking on all its responsibilities.

OPPOSITE: The approach to Helmingham Hall is lined by an avenue of oaks

Eventually I was overcome with a sense of shame. Not only did I not know the names of any plants that were growing in the garden, but I also didn't know the difference between an annual or a perennial, a rose or a peony. And what the heck was a 'half hardy'?!

Once I had managed to get a small grip on the house I marched out one day, spade in hand, and said to Roy Balaam (the head gardener), 'Teach me how to dig.' I was incredibly lucky to have Roy by my side. Still with us today, he started working in the gardens at only fourteen years old and rose fast to become head gardener at the age of twenty-three. With his unstinting patience, support and good humour I slowly began to get my head round what was growing around me and how to look after it.

Confidence crept in and tentatively I began to make changes within the garden. By 1978 I had created the parterre with its hedges of box and *Santolina incana*, the aromatic cotton lavender. I was still pretty clueless but I suppose there was a deep-seated creativity within me; and I was conscious that whatever I did in the garden needed to be architecturally sensitive to this red-bricked, moated, ancient house. Most importantly it also needed to look good when viewed from the upstairs bedrooms at all times of the year, and be as low maintenance as possible.

One feature that was sacrosanct was the wonderful border of hybrid musk roses that my mother-in-law had so successfully planted in 1963. That opened the door for me and broke down a few barriers.

Tim discovered some wonderful old plans of the garden showing how it had originally been laid out with considerably more borders. Taking this as a starting point we put in iron *allées* within the walled garden to divide the four large vegetable patches into the original eight. From the start we covered them in the sweet peas, runner beans and ornamental gourds that have become something of a Helmingham hallmark. At this stage I was constantly trying out new plant combinations, some of which worked and lots that didn't! However, in order of my priorities it was still young family first, then horses, with gardens in a firm third place.

In 1980 we thought of laying out a new garden on the east side of the house where there was just lawn. My design business had not yet kicked off and I needed professional help. It was an obvious choice to ask Mollie, Lady Salisbury to help design this garden. Helmingham had been built between 1490 and 1510 and the Old Palace at Hatfield dates from the same period. The gardens at Hatfield were an incredible source of inspiration and the knot, herb and rose gardens Mollie had created outside the Old Palace sat perfectly in their setting. I thought I could do the planting scheme within her suggested framework, but was constantly on the telephone asking her advice!

This creation led me further along the path towards my career. I started visiting gardens of the same period all over the country, staying in B&Bs wherever I happened to be at the end of the day. I read *The Education of a Gardener* by Russell Page and noted his wise words: 'The garden must curtsey to the house.'

Helmingham has taught me the invaluable lesson of scale and proportion, and everything I do here is on a generous scale. Even today when I go to a new site I am always conscious of the lessons I have learnt at home. There is no place for mean borders or steep and unfriendly steps!

In 1996 I thought about a career in garden design. Jill Fenwick taught me architectural drawing and I had the opportunity to design a few gardens for friends. Then the very brave and kind editor of the *Evening Standard* asked me to design a Main Avenue show garden for the Chelsea Flower Show in 1997. Of course I didn't have any idea of what it involved. I had a family conference, and my children told me that I was always telling them to take challenges in life and so I ought to practise what I preach. Suitably humbled, I accepted, which led to 363 sleepless nights with a thudding heart.

Amazingly it turned out well and the Gold Medal I won catapulted me on to an incredible platform from where to start my business. I still work from home with one invaluable and extremely efficient assistant and we now have anything from six to fourteen projects on the go at any time, each one providing a different challenge but nevertheless immensely exciting and rewarding.

Gertrude Jekyll said that the garden is a great teacher. She is right. Garden design is not just the most physically expressive of art forms; it is the only one that grapples with the notion of time and space. It might be said that the destination of our culture is reliant on our relationship with nature, and the ancient art of gardening establishes that relationship.

This brings me back to Helmingham and the creation of a special garden that dates back to 1510 and that had been lovingly cultivated with an astonishing continuity. At no time had the garden gone into a state of sad disrepair; every generation did their best. It is just lucky that I found my vocation and passion and have been a sensitive but sometimes impetuous steward of it.

BELOW: The east façade of Helmingham Hall with its drawstring entrance over the moat

I have slashed and trashed, pruned and trimmed, dug and planted, weeded, fed and nurtured. Recently I created a woodland garden in case future generations have neither the inclination, passion nor cash to keep up an expensive garden. The new woodland garden links Helmingham's more formal gardens with the ancient Tudor deer park that contains fabulous 900-year-old English oaks. I have planted decorative 'domestic' trees in the woodland garden such as liquidambar, acer, prunus, malus and sorbus, all genera that would be unsuitable in the park.

The walled garden has trained fruit, expansive vegetable areas and double cruciform herbaceous borders. These borders are deep and long and change in character with the season. I am always taking notes and making improvements, curtailing the thugs and encouraging the wimps!

It sometimes feels like I am painting a picture in my head when I have a plant in my hand and I am guided by the aesthetics of shape, texture and structure, whether at work or home. I always like to do the planting myself, as whatever one has planned on paper things can change when you are outside. The design is the picture; getting the placing right is the mounting, framing and hanging.

Running along the walls I have experimented with borders that have a more contemporary theme. There is a potager; we produce all the vegetables from seed in the greenhouses as well as plants for the house, annuals and half hardies and dahlias. Then there are the rose gardens, knot and herb gardens, let alone the wildflower gardens, coach house gardens and the new woodland garden. All require a high level of maintenance. The mowing alone takes up to two days. We have three full-time gardeners, some invaluable work experience help and me.

I have undergone a transformation, learning to accept and love plants previously snobbishly disregarded. Fashions in plants and garden design come and go, as you can see leafing through images of Chelsea or Hampton Court flower shows. But these are theatre and only exist for five days; I know because I have created them. I have grown to love grasses, to feel the texture of ferns, to admire the barks and stems of trees and shrubs and to lie on my tummy looking up at a snowdrop.

Just being lost in wonder at sweeping landscapes and admiring the intricate work of Gerry building my Chelsea garden led me to take a course in digger driving. So I now make humble mini-creations of my own at home, emulating the work of Charles Jencks and Kim Wilkie.

But I just plant on. I will always love roses, lavender and box. This doesn't put me in the 'boring' box, because there is always room for much-loved plants. That doesn't mean you can't be daring, innovative and cutting-edge with ideas. The important thing is that the garden fits in with the surrounding landscape, the art and architecture of the house and the lives and interests of the people who live there. Gardens must be lived in and loved. Every age should enjoy the garden, even if it results in raids on the strawberries. There should be places to sit and views to admire. There must be quiet places where less is more.

My favourite place in the garden at home is under an old almond tree, sitting on oak cubes carved from an ancient Helmingham tree around a home-made fire pit. There, amid the wildflowers, trees and water we can cook, eat, drink, talk or contemplate. I doubt if previous generations did that, and hopefully next generations will find other pleasures within our garden.

BELOW: Old-fashioned roses are grown as standards and over pyramidal metal hoops in the rose garden with hedges of *Rosa gallica* 'Versicolor' and *Nepeta* 'Six Hills Giant'. A small thyme lawn is spread beneath the statue of Flora

THIS PAGE LEFT AND BELOW: The much-copied ornamental gourd tunnel at Helmingham is grown with an ever-changing array of smooth and warted varieties

OPPOSITE ABOVE: The red and white bicoloured runner bean, *Phaseolus coccineus* 'Painted Lady', grown as when it was introduced to Europe in the sixteenth-century as an ornamental plant with a seat designed by George Carter

OPPOSITE BELOW: A yew-backed urn on a pedestal is the focal point to the intoxicatingly scented sweet pea tunnel

OPPOSITE: Morello cherries ripen against an ancient brick wall

ABOVE: Beautiful old wooden wheelbarrows are taken to the orchard for apple harvesting

OVERLEAF: In June the long borders that bisect the walled garden are awash with pale pink and mauve oriental and opium poppies, lupins, *Salvia nemorosa* 'Caradonna' and *Persicaria* x *fennica* 'Johanniswolke' with tall creamy plumes

Spye Park

BROMHAM, WILTSHIRE

Georgina Enthoven

WHEN MY HUSBAND wanted me to follow his hunch that an estate near Melksham where the house had burnt down in the 1970s was 'the one', I must confess that my hopes weren't high as we set off on yet another house hunt. However, from the moment we drove through Spye Arch via tunnels of overgrown laurels through which plantations of ancient trees rose skyward, we sensed something very special. Then the park opened out onto a panorama stretching as far as the Bristol Channel on the horizon, with a 500-foot drop in the foreground. This landscape felt as close to the veldt as anything we could have dreamed of, and the Jacobean coach house and ramshackle farm buildings suited us much better than the gargantuan Victorian house that had burnt down and which Lord Methuen from nearby Corsham thought such a blot on the Wiltshire landscape he chronicled his horror in a letter to *The Times*. All that remains from this edifice was another arch in brick and without the startling provenance of the entrance gates that had been gifted by Catherine of Aragon to the Bayntun family.

The Victorian arch presides over a flat piece of ground that is a veritable graveyard of earlier houses and gardens. We can tell the position of the Jacobean house that John Evelyn stayed in as a guest of 'the humorous old Knight' Sir Edward Bayntun from his diary on 19 July 1654: 'On the precipice of an incomparable prospect . . . a long barn (with) not a window on the prospect side.' They must have stood on that spot before building started on a blustery day and decided the house should turn its back on the wind that roars up the Avon Valley. That house was transformed into an exquisite and quintessential eighteenth-century neoclassical British Georgian building for which Stephen Switzer created *allées*, cascades, parterres and fountains. All now sunk without a trace, just an eerie residue and the strong sensation that this site needed some sensitive handling.

OPPOSITE: Rose 'Albéric Barbier' tumbles over an entrance wall to the Coach House at Spye Park, the large rectangular reflecting pool visible in the courtyard

PREVIOUS PAGE: The infinity meadow merges into the horizon

It is strange taking on a garden where there are the buried ghosts of so many houses and past inhabitants. This chequered history of disasters and destruction needed exorcising through the restitution of the landscape.

Luckily we knew that Pam Lewis was the person to turn to. Pam had worked for my mother-in-law so we were used to her idiosyncratic ways; all she requested was 'the shed' where she can stay when she is here for more than a day. For those of you who haven't read Pam's book *Making Flower Meadows*, or been to visit her garden at Sticky Wicket in Dorset, how can I begin to describe this extraordinary gardener – entomologist, lepidop-terist, shaman, diviner, magician? I joke not. The journey we are on with Pam is not the usual garden designer/client relationship where plans are submitted and handed to a team of contractors. Pam reads and rereads the site on a monthly basis, getting under the surface of Spye's skin, and in most places having the surface scraped away altogether . . .

We work collaboratively. Pam likes to keep in mind our original brief to regard her work here as primarily a conservation initiative and to keep the gardening activities informal and on the wild side, supporting the natural woodland, wetland and grassland habitats. She created a remarkable team including Nori and Sandra Pope, before they returned to live in Canada, who inspired and advised in the early days, and Ed Brooks who is still very closely involved and who brilliantly interprets Pam's schemes with his remarkable landscape engineering skills. Nick Lewis now heads up a team of five others, all of whom share the same ethos of conservation; Pam's creative vision couldn't happen without their practical input.

My priority was to grow our own produce, so the kitchen or 'secret' garden became our first project. It earned its name because of the months it took before we penetrated the brambles to reveal the remains of glasshouse ranges and cold frames that a friend had a hunch were lurking behind a thicket of thorns when we were clearing and making bonfires in our early days here. This protected corner is always balmy while the rest of the garden is blasted with wind. It was rapidly transformed into a haven of cut flowers and vegetables and has been a rock of constancy as we have played musical chairs moving between the buildings during a decade of restoration and construction.

Pam sees Spye in its entirety, and though she may be renowned as a meadow maker her remit here covers everything from opening up 'windows' of views of the landscape to creating interesting features set amongst an oasis of species-enhanced vegetation. She has 1000 acres of forestry, grazing, meadows and garden in that order of priority to keep a 'shepherd's eye' on.

Plants are added to fulfil a role in creating a diverse mosaic of habitats that will in turn supply pollen, nectar, berries and habitat for the garden wildlife that was conspicuous by its absence when we arrived. Pam's moment of revelation while watching Dame Miriam Rothschild on television in the 1970s is echoed by the continuously revelatory experience we have watching her at work.

Diversity and regeneration are constantly on all our minds, from the programme of tree planting that began on our arrival and continues each year as we propagate native trees, especially oaks, of strictly Spye provenance, to finding novel ways to provide pheasant food and cover that will banish the terrible airstrips of corn that scar the landscape. Pam is planning to experiment this year by burying a mix of chopped-up willowherb and aster roots amongst whips of native trees and shrubs. Knowing Pam she is on to something.

There are so many schemes that significantly show her powers at work, but the one that always makes us laugh at ourselves is the 'infinity meadow'.

For a couple of years we looked out over a lunar pan of broken-up concrete from what had been a farmyard and to which Pam had added not soil but nuggets, both large and small, of snow-blinding chalk. To our tentative enquiries as to when the meadow might materialise Pam would simply reply, 'When it's ready.' Well, ready it became. Now we all just gasp in amazement when surveying the miracle she has procured from rubble. Swallows swoop across the Wiltshire equivalent of an alpine meadow. From early summer swallows behave here as they do over a pond preparing to migrate back to Africa, and all the seed heads are an Arthurian bird table in autumn and winter. No wonder the keepers are happy to let her play with chopped-up willowherb roots.

Pam cajoles out of bare earth concoctions of wildflowers that are so absorbing and intoxicating, as much for us as a family as they evidently are to insects. However we are fully cognisant that while Pam is painting these extraordinary canvases it is not really us she is doing it for. Not many houses have every species of cotoneaster outside their main doors. Google cotoneaster/bees and you will soon see why there are so many species and varieties at Spye.

Many of the 'gardened' areas are protected against deer and rabbits, and mad though this may sound to most gardeners there are several patches of meadow where rabbits that selectively graze grass have become more of an ally than unselective mowers! The bugloss meadow is an area where construction traffic parked for a decade, leaving naked, compacted ground, is now a haze of bird's foot trefoil and viper's bugloss, some spontaneous but always under the careful ministrations of the team. Orchids only started appearing a few years ago, but now as you meander down the serpentine paths in the main meadow you are hard pushed to find an area that doesn't have orchids.

The project at Spye is all about achieving balance, and we are not coy about dealing with invaders. When we arrived giant hogweed amassed in colonies that made large areas of the park impenetrable. Fields were infested with docks, thistles and nettles, and old boundaries were loosely defined by a jumble of tangled fences and broken gates, but this was nothing compared to this encroaching invader. Glyphosate is used but only applied directly to the plant it is intended for; there is no blanket spraying at Spye. The common weeds are topped to rein in their threshold, and an annual programme of techniques is carried out to eradicate a proportion of those that are most intrusive. If the weeds are not imposing a threat to finer

ABOVE: A rose pergola designed and made by Ed Brooks divides the kitchen garden where self-sown opium poppies are allowed to occupy space until it is needed, here amongst edible artichokes

species or intruding on the immediate landscape, and are meanwhile providing food or shelter for wildlife, we leave them to fulfil their supporting role. The entire family is aware of the need to prevent ragwort seeding and we all snap off emerging flower heads as and when we see them. The team have a wonderful way of focusing in on problem hotspots that show up from year to year with a more intensive management regime, and they prefer doing as much weeding as possible by hand so that the impact of their workings leaves a light footprint.

Meadows are a significant feature of the landscape here, but there are many other aspects and textures in the Spye tapestry. The Spiral Garden is an ingenious raised mound that partially conceals a neighbouring house while making a mesmeric platform on which ornamental grasses sway in a sea of cranesbills, toadflax, scabious, knautia and eryngium rising out of ground-hugging thymes and oreganos. It is an original and sympathetic solution that keeps our neighbours, and us, happy, inspired and amazed. The banks around it are a sea of bird's foot trefoil. In the bee garden *Phacelia tanacetifolia*, a sensational source of nectar and

pollen for bumble, mason, solitary and honeybees, is the primary plant, more important than the soft-pink-flowered David Austin roses such as roses 'Saint Cecilia' and 'Sharifa Asma' that float above its mauve carpet.

The entrance courtyard, by contrast, has an intentional scarcity of plants and is the Spye that anyone coming to visit us at night leaves with a memory of. We did not want cars clogging up the architecture or the exquisite cobbles outside the coach house where we live so a large rectangular reflecting pool deters entering traffic, who cannot see that it is all of a couple of centimetres deep. For something that looks so simple and effortless, of all the projects we undertook at Spye this was the one that taxed the engineers to the limit, and in the end all the cobbles needed lifting and realigning. The shallow skein of water is dynamic when children's bicycles splash through it, or contemplative and reflective, contributing hugely to the newfound harmony that now appeases the ghosts of earlier generations of Spye inhabitants, and gloriously nourishes our own.

LEFT: Birds-foot-trefoil *Lotus corniculatus* and viper's bugloss *Echium vulgare* flourishing on the site compacted by building trucks, now the backdrop to local cricket matches

RIGHT: Field poppies, corncockle and ox-eye daisies in the meadow

ABOVE AND BELOW: Common spotted orchid *Dactylorhiza fuchsii* migrate around the various areas of meadow and significantly increase year on year

Howick Hall

ALNWICK, NORTHUMBERLAND

Charlie Howick

OWICK IS THE family home of the Greys, the best known of whom was Charles, Second Earl Grey, who, as Prime Minister, forced through the Great Reform Bill of 1832 (and for whom Earl Grey tea was created). The house is one mile inland from the coast of Northumberland and is about halfway between Newcastle and Berwick. The soil is a good medium loam for the most part, mainly neutral but with some lime in patches. The neutral parts occur over whinstone extrusions between the underlying limestone strata. The climate is mediocre; summers are often cool, but the sea moderates the temperature in winter, delaying the onset of spring and thus often avoiding the problem of late frosts.

In the early 1800s the Prime Minister planted many of the old trees which still surround the house and furnish the banks of the small valley containing Howick Burn, known as the Long Walk. The burn runs through the garden and down to the sea in a long S-bend for about a mile and a half past beeches coming to the end of their lives, oaks in their prime, a few tall limes, sweet chestnuts, ash and disease-free (so far) horse chestnuts, mixed with older yews and younger Scots pine.

We have no detailed accounts of the nineteenth-century garden but it seemed to follow the Victorian fashion for sweeping lawns, parterres and borders around the house, with a large kitchen garden providing fruit, vegetables and cut flowers for the household.

It all changed when my grandparents, Charlie and Mabel Grey, inherited in 1917. His mother was Alice Holford from Westonbirt, while Mabel was a Palmer from Blackmoor, a family with botany in their genes. Both were formidable gardeners and they were heavily influenced by William Robinson; away went the formality and in came a much more natural style throughout the fifteen acres surrounding the house.

Mabel's great interests were bulbs, and herbaceous and mixed borders. For years she planted daffodils and snowdrops by the thousands, with autumn colchicums another favourite since

OPPOSITE: The south-facing front of Howick Hall in Northumberland with a naturalised carpet of *Narcissus* 'Seagull' that was originally planted in the 1920s

she loved their rich green leaves in spring amongst all the daffodils. Soon after the war she started to plant single-colour late tulips in the long grass, but this stopped when she died in 1957 and was picked up again by my mother in the 1970s. I have always found it curious that she did not also plant more bluebells or cyclamen, but she didn't, apart from some Spanish bluebells in the woodland garden that have mostly found their way to the bonfire. She liked South African bulbs and planted crinum, watsonia and schizostylis on the top terrace while there is a lovely row of deep blue agapanthus along the top of the wall above the next terrace, which consists of the best forms of the original 'Headbourne Hybrids' bred by her brother, Lewis Palmer, from seed sent to him by Kirstenbosch Botanic Garden in Cape Town in about 1948. Their rich colours look vibrant in the the August sun with wands of *Dierama pulcherrimum* waving in the wind on the terrace above; they have survived all our winters without any protection, and regular dividing has kept them going for over sixty years. Another South African feature, also from Lewis Palmer, is a small yew enclosure filled with *Kniphofia* 'Lord Roberts' around a large urn; they are tall, scarlet and splendid in late September and early October, but it is a form that seems to have disappeared from nurseries. She discovered that Howick summers do not favour crocuses and that tulips were short-lived. Another surprising omission was the dog's tooth violet which my mother introduced to the woodland garden very successfully in the 1980s: one of my favourite spring bulbs.

My grandfather Charlie's kingdom was the woodland garden. A patch of pure greensand was found west of the house in 1930, the year of his and Mabel's silver wedding, in a wood of old oak, wych elm and Scots pine that was ideal for his rhododendrons and its name, 'Silverwood', has stuck. Many of the early plants came from Westonbirt but, like many of that generation, he wrote little down apart from keeping the odd notebook recording this or that rhododendron being received; where they were planted in Silverwood remains a mystery. Most of the entries before the Second World War were for species rhododendrons of all kinds and particularly the white, pink, pale-yellow and richer purple flowering ones. He loved *Rhododendron decorum, R. oreordoxa* var. *fargesii, R. falconeri, R. campanulatum, R. williamsianum* and the good forms of *R. augustinii*, and many of the old plants still soldier on. He allowed a few of the better hybrids such as 'King George' and 'Penjerrick'. Colour fills the wood in April and May with azaleas following on in May and June, particularly the white and paler sweet-smelling ones. He was less fond of red and perhaps *A. arboreum* was too tender then, although he did have some *thomsonii* and *griersonianum* and its hybrids. His favourite magnolias were *M. campbellii* and *M. wilsonii*; there are two magnificent trees of the former a good sixty feet high now, quite a feat for Northumberland, but the original *wilsonii* are dying out, and sadly we lost the National Champion tree in 2012. Fortunately it set viable seed and we have planted a number of its progeny. There are good surviving plants from this era of *Eucryphia glutinosa, E.* x *nymansensis* and *E. cordifolia* mixed in with a few clethra, embothrium, drimys, crinodendron, acer and lacecap hydrangeas. He used bracken as a mulch more to protect the shallow roots in winter than to provide a feed; we continue to do so since it looks so much better than the alternatives.

After Charlie died in 1963 my mother, Lady Mary Howick, took over and continued to centre the garden around Silverwood. She carried on planting the rhododendrons she liked, but from the mid-1970s she steadily built up the herbaceous ground cover. She loved

ABOVE LEFT TO RIGHT:
The emerging foliage
and flowers of: *Betula
calcicola* from Yunnan.
*Illicium simonsii. Acer
caesium. Cercidiphyllum
japonicum* from Sichuan

euphorbias and primulas, particularly the candelabra ones, but as the years went by the ground seemed to get 'sick' and new areas had to be found for them. However pulmonaria, brunnera, hellebores, maianthemum, ajuga and lamium abound, mixed in with meconopsis, geum, dicentra, bergenia and many others. She instilled in me the importance of paying if anything more attention to foliage than to flower, and passed on a suspicion of variegation which often sits uneasily in what is meant to be a 'natural' setting. In the last few years we have continued to expand the ground cover to the point where I sometimes worry that we now have a garden in a wood and not a woodland garden, but walking through it on a late spring evening it is impossible to think of changing it. Silverwood will always be the heart of the garden.

The borders around the house are conventional and the rockery distinctly odd in that it is in considerable shade beneath a large Atlantic cedar and behind a huge beech and lime, which in Northumberland is not desirable. However, as it was built one winter after the war by my grandfather and his two sons-in-law, it would seem disrespectful to move it. Nature will deal with the trees and the light will one day return; in the meantime it is planted with bulbs and plants that will tolerate these conditions.

The real recent change, however, has been the development of an arboretum over the past thirty years. I thought that it would be more interesting and more fun to plant it entirely with trees and shrubs grown from seed collected in the wild, both to make it useful to scientists and because it seemed to fit in better with the Robinsonian ethos of the garden. A chance meeting with Jane Jansen from California, who had similar ideas for her property in the Sonoma Valley (now named Quarryhill Botanical Garden), led to a partnership which started in 1987 and has continued ever since. A deal was arranged with Kew and the Chengdu Institute of Botany in Sichuan which led to twelve expeditions to China from 1988 onwards, which in turn opened up contacts with the Royal Botanic Garden Edinburgh, resulting in further expeditions with them to Japan, North America and the Caucasus, an enduring programme. Bill McNamara, the director of Quarryhill, and I have also collected seed in India and Taiwan, while a touch of megalomania and curiosity also tempted me to collect in Tasmania and New Zealand, not obvious areas for Northumberland. The twenty years after 1985 found me in foreign parts each September

and October, normally up mountains, always in spectacularly beautiful landscapes, and in China frequently completely cut off from the outside world in the days before mobiles became ubiquitous. Age has stopped me and our head gardener, Robert Jamieson, now goes in my place. We have only ever collected seed, never plants, bulbs or other material; the quarantine complications are too complex. The excitement and passion for collecting seed of a plant where Mother Nature chooses to grow it remains as vivid now as a memory as it did as a reality in Sichuan on that first trip in 1988.

The arboretum occupies about sixty acres at the moment and continues to expand into old softwood plantations and woods. I have planted it in geographical sections and, if the shelter has been right, the plants have flourished for the most part. The best part is the Long Walk, which holds most of the Chinese and Japanese sections. I get enormous pleasure each year as more plants flower and fruit for the first time, particularly if I can remember their parents in their native mountains.

The Chinese wingnuts are my favourites since I did not know them at all beforehand and did not expect them to flourish at Howick, which they undoubtedly do. *Pterocarya macroptera* var. *insignis* is the best, with racemes almost a metre long hanging down from the walnut-like leaves, and I wait for the younger *P. macroptera*, *P. hupehensis* and *P. paliuris* to follow. Another surprise has been *Eleutherococcus* (syn. *Acanthopanax*), a genus normally found at fairly low altitudes but apparently quite hardy here. *E. henryi* and *E. giraldii* are both covered with hand grenades of round black fruit, often left alone by the birds until well into winter. A group of three *Malus prattii* from Sichuan's highest mountain, Gongga Shan, flower and fruit prolifically each year. The *Abies delavayi* group are just beginning to show their purple cones above their silver-banded dark-green leaves, while the Asiatic birches with their multitude of coloured barks, maples and sorbus in great variety provide many of the smaller trees. The main shrubs are rhododendrons, deutzias, viburnums, cotoneasters, berberis and roses, but the last do need a hotter summer than we can give them and you must go to Quarryhill in California to see them in all their spectacular glory. Indeed it is of great interest to compare the performance of so many identical plants from so many expeditions in the three completely different habitats of Kew, Howick and Quarryhill.

ABOVE TOP ROW LEFT TO RIGHT: *Cercidyiphyllum japonicum* from Sichuan, *Acer caesium, Acer henryi, Acer maximowiczii*

MIDDLE ROW LEFT TO RIGHT: *Sorbus koehneana* from Sichuan China, *Berberis pruinosa, Rosa setipoda*, drooping clustered berries of *Eleutherococcus leucorrhizus* var. *setchuanensis*

LEFT: The golden autumn leaves of a mature beech tree

RIGHT: Howick Burn in spate in autumn

One unplanned spin-off for us has been all the herbaceous seed which the botanic gardens collected on our expeditions. I have concentrated it all into one area surrounding a small pond in the garden and it has proved very popular. It is at its peak in July and August with still more to come in September, and is therefore of great benefit to what is essentially a spring and early summer garden. The spikes of *Rheum alexandrae* are always a talking point while *Primula poisonnii*, *P. bulleyana*, *P. sikkimensis* and *P. florindae* spread themselves freely around. The other primulas have proved short-lived. Other favourites are *Nepeta govaniana*, white and pale-mauve *Astilbe chinensis*, the white *Anemone rivularis* and the red fruits of *Arisaema consanguineum*, all growing together with many other species in a lightly gardened jungle.

The garden and arboretum are now owned by a charity so their future is secure. Three generations of enthusiastic gardeners have left their imprint and it will soon be time for the fourth to take it all on to the next stage, whatever that may be.

OPPOSITE: The path to the sea with overhanging branches of *Fagus sylvatica* and naturalised petasites

BELOW: The bare branches of *Juglans cathayensis*, a Chinese walnut beside the North Bank of Howick Burn

OVERLEAF: The North Sea coast at Howick Haven from the mouth of Howick Burn

Cothay Manor

GREENHAM, SOMERSET

Mary-Anne Robb

WHEN FIRST I came to Cothay, I climbed the spiral stairs in the tower and looked out on the browns and greens of Somerset, changed little since medieval times, when the old house was built in the fifteenth century. Cothay lies near nowhere on the Somerset/Devon border, set deep within the high-banked lanes, on the banks of the River Tone. The old garden has long since vanished, but the secret link between time and eternity linger on. When Colonel Reginald Cooper, who was a friend of all the gardening grandees of that era, came to Cothay in the 1920s, little remained of the earlier garden. Cooper laid the garden out in the Arts and Crafts manner, the dominant feature of a yew walk 200 yards long, off of which are many small garden rooms.

When I came to Cothay two decades ago the old garden had an ethereal feel, holding its breath as if watching and waiting. Little remained of interest except Reggie's original strong design; no plans existed. One should not become distracted from change; making a garden is like a journey. I was free to begin again, leaving the lovely old bones to work within.

We gutted the inside of all the garden rooms, and much of the surrounding park and meadows that had been fenced off were brought in as part of the garden. A small lake was dug, and the earth from it used to build a mount in the north meadow where in spring thousands of black tulips 'Queen of the Night' bloom, and are added to each year along with camassia and alliums. The long meadow grass has paths cut through, and now it's like walking through fairyland with all the wildflowers and grasses blowing in the wind.

Cothay is above all a romantic garden that wraps around the house with a dreamlike quality, at its best in late spring and summer. In summer there is no earth to be seen, the garden full to bursting with the soft colours of perennials and shrubs which I like so much.

I find many people can't be bothered to grow annuals, but I feel they are an essential part of any garden, for when the perennials have had their day the gaps they leave can be filled with these elegant plants. I usually grow white annuals, the frilly flowered cosmos, which if

OPPOSITE: The terrace outside the entrance to the garden has a formal structure of box domes that in summer are engulfed by self-seeding blue-flowered tree lupin *Lupinus arboreus*, *Geranium* x *oxonianum* 'Claridge Druce' and *Campanula persicifolia/ latiloba* as well as *Nepeta govaniana* and the alpine wood fern *Dryopteris wallichiana*

ABOVE: An urn encircled by *Erigeron karvinskianus* is filled for summer with *Argyranthemum* 'Jamaica Primrose', trailing sweet peas, *Bidens ferulifolia* and *Helichrysum petiolare*

dead-headed I find lasts well until the first frosts. The tall tobacco plant *Nicotiana sylvestris* is so useful for shining a light in shady spots. Above all I love the American spider plants *Cleome hassleriana*. Each year, despite my efforts, this gorgeous plant won't reach my height, which it does in the wild. I'm lucky if it makes two-and-a-half feet. I plant it out everywhere so it runs through the garden as if by some miracle it has self-seeded; my favourite is the white form 'Helen Campbell'. The summer flowering bulbs are also a source of pleasure, especially the tall August-flowering *Galtonia candicans*, which I dot about hither and thither.

To capture even for a moment the perfection of a garden comes tantalisingly seldom. For three short weeks in summer I bask in the glory, only to be brought down to earth with the realisation that in a garden if you live 'above the shop' there is always something to do. As someone once said to me: 'Work is the rent you pay for your time on earth.'

Legend has it that the red and the white roses on the walls of the house adjacent to the terrace were planted to celebrate the end of the Wars of the Roses in the fifteenth century, and when they die are always replanted. Close by, carved in Latin on a stone plaque, is a charming botanical riddle, dating from the twelfth century and originating from southern Germany, where the monks grew roses in their monastery gardens. The riddle has been handed down by word of mouth and so can differ slightly. This botanical riddle refers to the dog rose *Rosa canina*:

> *Quinque sumus fraters in eodem tempore nati sunt duo barbate duo sunt sine barba create*
> *unus et e quinque non et barbatus utrimque.*

BELOW: The view from the terrace

'The five sepals which lie behind the rose petals are five brothers, two of these five sepals have appendages, or "beards" on both edges, two have no appendages or are "beardless" on both edges, the fifth has only one appendage and the other side is plain, in other words it has only half a beard – thus The five brethren of the Rose.'

The terrace is not for sitting on; every crack between the old blue lyre stone slabs is filled with self-seeded plants, brought in by the wind, happy with their roots protected under the old slabs. The enchanting daisy *Erigeron karvinskianus* (known at Cothay by its nickname 'Kevin's arse') flourishes. I hear that it has now been declared an invasive weed, but I love it! The elegant 'Angel's fishing rod', the South African harebell, *Dierama*, have also colonised the terrace. In the midst is a glorious long-racemed wisteria grown as a standard. Some years ago I heard a voice calling 'Help, Help!' Rounding a corner I came face to face with a man holding up the wisteria that had blown over in a gust of wind. He shouted at me, 'Don't just stand there, fetch the gardener and some rope and props.' An hour later, the job finished, I thanked him, saying, 'How did you know what to do, are you an engineer?' To which he replied in a deep American drawl, 'No honey, I'm a brain surgeon'!

Light and shade play an important part in any garden, nowhere more so than in the 'Walk of the Unicorn' Garden, where we planted forty *Robinia pseudoacacia* 'Umbraculifera', high grafted at about ten foot, with a round 'mop' head, underplanted in spring with thousands of tulip 'White Triumphator'. When they fade the glorious thug *Nepeta* 'Six Hills Giant' hides their fading remnants. The name of the avenue originated when I was showing a group of Americans around the garden. 'We are,' I announced, 'in "The walk of the Unicorn." ' 'Why do you call it that?' enquired the leader. 'Because in medieval times the chatelaine would exercise her tame unicorn here.'

ABOVE: The standard wisteria towers above the mix of tree lupins, lavender and dieramas on the terrace

BELOW: Terrace plots with *Argyranthemum gracile* 'Chelsea Girl', *Verbena* 'Homestead Purple', and 'Burgundy' sweetly scented *Lathyrus odoratus* 'Matucana' and *Salvia* 'Christine Yeo'

'Do you hear that girls? Well who'd have thought it, we were always told that unicorns were mythical animals.' 'Sure they're mythical, but if you're a virgin you can always see them,' said a voice from the rear!

I have heard it said the eyes look and the mind sees. I feel a garden should flow; repeat planting makes for restfulness. Looking down the terrace border, I am minded of an old tapestry; the soft colours of catmint, *Anthemis punctata* subsp. *cupaniana* and lavender draw the eye onwards in keeping with our pale English skies.

Each of the garden rooms is colour coded. The white garden known as 'The Green Knight Garden' by a friend, having spent the previous night drinking whisky, she went for an early walk the following morning and swore she saw him riding through. Here tall *Crambe cordifolia*, the wonderfully scented rose 'Blanc Double de Coubert' and the giant-headed *Hydrangea* 'Annabelle' are the dominant tall plants.

Emily's Garden, named for my first granddaughter, is cream and yellow, dominated by an old Kentucky coffee tree *Gymnocladus dioicus*. The early American settlers made coffee from the beans. Here it only flowers after a very hot summer. It is the last tree to leaf up in mid-June and the first to lose its leaves. In Holland it is known as the 'bones-of-a-dead-man' owing to its gnarled bare branches in winter.

The Bishop's Garden is named for my favourite uncle, known to his family as 'glamour gaiters'; the colours here are episcopal purple and scarlet, fabulous in spring when the huge Oriental poppies are in flower, mingling with *Allium* 'Purple Sensation' and the lovely tulip 'Queen of the Night'. In late summer *Verbena bonariensis* and dark *Clematis viticella* together with the annual sweet pea *Lathyrus* 'Almost Black' bewitch this corner of the garden.

Our terracotta pots planted up each year with half-hardy perennials are a Cothay speciality. Cuttings are taken during the summer months and overwintered in our increasingly decrepit greenhouse. Each pot needs about twenty to thirty plants; as I have ten pots it's not such a labour of love but, like the rest of the garden, very high maintenance. On April Fool's Day I start to plant them up from seven-centimetre pots. I know I have enough plants in each pot when I can't squeeze any more in. Glorious tall red salvias *S. elegans* and *S. fulgens* are particular favourites as well as many different varieties of argyranthemum, various felicia and anisodontea, in any colour except orange! The tall plants go in the centre and the trailers at the edge. I love the verbenas bred in the 1930s – 'Sissinghurst', 'Silver Anne', 'La France', 'Homestead Purple' and 'Burgundy' – mixed with masses of the grey-leafed *Helichrysum petiolare*, malvastrum, *Sphaeralcea munroana* with its pretty pink and apricot flowers, and white lobelia. Through all the pots I plant annual sweet peas. The containers are kept in the greenhouse until the danger of frost has passed when out they go, on an old skateboard. They are watered and dead-headed each day, but most important is the weekly foliar feed: a watering can with Chempack No 4, to which a squirt of washing-up liquid is added which works as a wetting agent, keeps them all flowering until November.

OPPOSITE CLOCKWISE FROM TOP LEFT: A *Dierama pulcherrimum* seedling, *Stachys byzantina*, *Trifolium rubens*, *Salvia sclarea*, *Rosa* x *odorata* 'Mutabilis', *Lathyrus sativus*, *Lathyrus tuberosus*, *Lupinus arboreus*, CENTRE: *Morina longifolia*

RIGHT: *Dierama* seedlings in varying shades of pink

'The Walk of the Unicorn' Garden with high grafted
Robinia pseudoacacia 'Umbraculifera' above gravel
paths lined with *Nepeta* 'Six Hill's Giant'

I love climbers, grown everywhere, up walls, through plants and up supports. Nothing to my eye beats the glorious rose, *Rosa* x *odorata* 'Mutabilis'. Grown in a favoured spot up a south-facing wall it has reached twenty feet here and flowers on and off until Christmas. The late great rosarian Peter Beales likened the flower to a host of butterflies; no garden should be without it. Its glorious single flowers are shades of pink fading to apricot. Small-flowered *Clematis viticella* clamber about the garden, trouble-free and easy to grow in any aspect. Another favourite is the eye-catching *Lathyrus tuberosus* with flowers the colour of fresh raspberries. An acquaintance, spellbound when we stopped to admire the Lathyrus, asked for a pod of seeds. 'Sadly it seldom sets seed,' I replied. 'Well how do you propagate it?' she asked. 'By Irishman's cuttings in February.' She looked perplexed, and then with a strong Irish accent said, 'You mean som times it works and som times it doesn't!'

Annual sweet peas fill the garden. We sow most of them before Christmas, planting them out in April; they fill every corner of the garden scrambling through plants, up supports and in pots. The early sown ones last well into August, the later ones sown in January often flower until October. *Vitis coignetiae* and *Ampelopsis brevipedunculata* climb thirty feet up the gatehouse tower. Climbing *Aconitum wilsonii* flowers well in the shade as does *Hydrangea petiolaris* and the scarlet *Tropaeolum speciosum* planted on the north side of a yew pillar; the red flowers show well against the dark green where *Eccremocarpus scaber* also scrambles about. I rather like the climbing alstroemeria relative *Bomarea multiflora* which is quite special. I grow it up twisted metal supports.

ABOVE: 'The Green Knight Garden' where white-flowered plants include the tall *Achillea grandifloria* (above) and (below) the beautiful single rose 'White Wings'

ABOVE: The silvery white foliage of lamb's ears *Stachys byzantina* is repeated as a border, including the single flowered rose 'White Wings', foxgloves, and *crambe cordifolia* with *Asphodelus aestivusus* (seen right)

Over the years my taste has changed dramatically. I have come to realise how lucky I am to have such wonderful structure to work within. Even on dull winter days the yew hedges planted nearly 100 years ago give to the garden an air of permanence. I try each year to add and improve the evergreen structure and have added many standard *Elaeagnus ebbingei* within the Inner Court. The Kitchen Court is now maturing, although it is an area in which I am constantly changing the planting. Last year I had a round stone set in a path, carved on it in old English 'Friendship outstays the hurrying flight of years, and aye abides though laughter and through tears.'

This glorious garden at Cothay is not the work of one hand; it is a link with the past and our ancestors. Sometimes on a summer's evening I see Reggie Cooper's evanescent form in the dim light of dusk walking towards me; he crosses the lawn and vanishes through an archway he created so long ago.

I have tried to capture in the garden the essence of the medieval mind, for the golden threads of time are woven through our lives, linking the old and the new.

Turkish annual pea
Lathyrus belenensis (left)
and climbing Dicentra
Dactylicapnos scandens
(below)

Tregothnan

St Michael Penkivel, Cornwall

The Hon Evelyn Boscawen

What is a garden – and who is a gardener?

There cannot be a greater ambiguity in establishing these definitions anywhere than here at Tregothnan. In the eighteenth century the area known today as, 'The Garden', was, 'The Pleasure Grounds', and what was then, 'The Garden', is now 'The Kitchen Garden'. The owner was never the gardener! Time moves on, trees blow over, they die, many more are planted. Gardens change with every season and generation as much here as everywhere else.

OPPOSITE: The east façade of Tregothnan seen through an arching canopy of *Rhododendron arboreum* and a large specimen of the white-flowered *Rhododendron* 'Boddaertianum' near the house

It is this understanding that gives us the confidence to do what we do at Tregothnan. We follow a simple philosophy: where once the garden was great but has now seen better times we aim to recreate a sense of what was there before, in full, not half measures! Where there is failure, one has the opportunity to be creative.

The approach to the house is down a long carriageway beside a tidal tributary to the River Fal. It begins with a new avenue of *Trachycarpus fortunei* palms, then winds through woodland lined with *Quercus ilex* that broadens out into an avenue of *Magnolia* 'Star Wars'. A couple of miles from the lodge a collection of rhododendrons planted in the mid-nineteenth century eventually brings you to the north front of the house. The ends of the drive had become dark and gloomy; and the demise of the diseased beech avenue gave rise to the magnolias, as seen above. At the lodge where the old ilex avenue had fallen into disrepair a decision was taken to make this exciting and different, hence the palms. We removed some old camellias and rhododendrons that, with judicial regeneration, are once again spectacular in recreating the sense of space around the front when the house was built. We like the stimulation of creating something new while maintaining the greatness of what was already there. Also first impressions are most important.

Tregothnan, 'the house at the head of the valley', sits on a typical small Cornish hill 130 feet above sea level, looking down to the River Fal. Immediately below the terrace on

OPPOSITE ABOVE:
Tregothnan, 'the house
at the head of the valley',
looking down to the River
Fal with Robert Myers's
recent grass parterre

OPPOSITE BELOW: The
south façade of the house

ABOVE AND BELOW LEFT:
Magnificent stands of
Rhododendron arboreum
'Cornish Red' and
Pinus pinea around the
Summer House Lawns

the south-facing front of the house was a parterre created in 1845 by Nesfield. By the end of the twentieth century this had become something of a nothing so ideas were sought. My idea was for a flat lawn with some wide straight gravel paths but my wife Katharine suggested we should be more imaginative; her advice was to do it with 'finesse'. Robert Myers was engaged and he produced a design of a grass parterre including two reflection ponds supported by gravel paths. These lead the eye towards the river while at the same time altering the impression of the shape of the house when looking from the opposite direction.

Like all great gardens there are certain elements that enthuse the owner to continue the expression of their predecessors. I am particularly inspired by our *Magnolia campbellii,* an amazing tree of immense beauty planted by my grandfather in 1923, and one of our three greatest plants. It flowers for a month from mid-February; it is big, bold and beautiful. The pureness of these deep-pink flowers having survived the winter and bursting into bloom is the signal that spring is here and marks the beginning of our gardening year. So much of what we do is spurred on by this one tree, and, remembering a seedling does not flower for twenty years, we make certain that we have plenty of youngsters from that same strain coming along. We are planting for generations ahead, not ourselves! This tree is situated midway along the Quarter Mile Walk which starts at the Bowling Green and ends at the Summer House Lawns.

The Bowling Green is shown on a seventeenth-century plan and until recently was surrounded by a wall of laurel, having lost its surrounding trees in the massive storm of 1979 when the wind felled thousands in the woods and garden, which went like dominoes. We have just cleared one side and are in the process of creating a magnolia and cornus bank that will stand alongside existing magnolias including *M. campbellii, M. dawsoniana* and a seedling given to my parents when they moved here in 1962 by Julian Williams of Caerhays Castle.

At the other end of this path are the Summer House Lawns. These are a landscape design feature formed around paths and lawns in the shape of a shield by my great-great-grandfather's brother. On three sides the plantings consist of *Rhododendron arboreum* 'Cornish Red', *Quercus ilex* and *Pinus sylvestris* forming a backdrop that jumps from 30 to 60 to 90 feet high. Not only do we get the rhododendron flowers in April and May and the lovely red bark of the Scots pine that lights up particularly beautifully in evening sunlight, we also gain a substantial windbreak. At the bottom of the Lawns is an enormous mass of *R.* 'Cornish Red', unsurpassed anywhere else and here echoed by yet more in enormous clumps on the lawns. There are some Stone pines *Pinus pinea* planted to mark royal visitors at the end of the nineteenth century.

So much damage was done in the storm of 1979 that my parents concentrated on recovering those areas that were taken out overnight, leaving the surrounding damaged areas standing. This included tracts of beech trees that had become shady, giving us enormous opportunity for creative replanting. In one we have established a magnolia plantation that will be visible from the south-facing bedrooms in the years to come, quite a sight to wake up to in March.

Another area destroyed by the same storm was the Oval Bed, which contained original introductions by Sir Joseph Hooker, in particular *R. sinogrande* and *R. falconeri.*

It was perhaps plants from this bed that gave me my first interest in the garden when I entered a competition at the Cornwall Flower Show with a class on different rhododendron leaves. While it was a long time ago, I remember they ranged from *R. sinogrande* (the largest) to *R.* 'Blue Tit' (the smallest). Over the years we have tried to recreate this fabulous bed but without success – whether through dirty ground or it becoming too dry for rhododendrons we were never sure – so instead have amassed a tree peony collection inspired by a planting Katharine and I saw at the Ming tombs in China. We originally planned a pagoda for the middle but have ended up planting the unusual deciduous softwood conifer *Taxodium distichum*.

The second of my three favourite plants is *Camellia reticulata* 'Captain Rawes', named after the captain of the clipper *Warren Hastings* who brought the plant to England from Whampoa, Canton, in 1820. Our original plant, long since gone, had astonishing dimensions remembered by many. We have a few sizeable plants from our original. On the back of this we are putting together a collection of *Camellia reticulata* with plant material we have sourced from around the world. They are just getting to noticeable size, having survived the five pests that are our scourge: deer, grey squirrels, badgers, rabbits and, last but not least, poor operators of mowing equipment. Fortunately, we have had a brilliant operator on board for the past few years.

Off the east side of the North Front is Farm Drive, from where we removed existing stands of imposing *Camellia japonica* to a new location, we have established a new collection of the daintier *Camellia sasanqua*, many of which we brought here from a monk's collection in Kyoto. These start to flower prolifically in November with delicate scent and butterfly-like flowers.

When Katharine and I swopped houses with my parents in 1999 the first project we undertook was to restore the *Luma apiculata* avenue which had become swamped by laurel and thus starved of light. To have something which flowers here in late summer is a rarity for us, and the blooms are a delicious bonus to the beautifully coloured stems: it is much enjoyed.

Our attention was then drawn to the fact that the two main grass avenues, one flanked by luma and the other by *Dicksonia antartica*, did not interlink with any other paths, so Katharine set out a new circuit around the garden that encompasses both these avenues. It was somewhat surprising in the process to discover many things we did not know existed here! We also took this opportunity to improve the tree fern avenue, sourcing new plants from a garden nearby that had been created by a relative so the ferns are all descended from the same original 1845 import. Near the bottom of the tree fern walk is a glorious *Cercidiphyllum japonicum*. This delightful deciduous thirty-foot-high tree has the most beautiful shape, the most lovely round leaves and, unusually for us, wonderful autumn foliage that has the strong and distinctive smell of caramel at leaf fall.

The tree fern avenue leads to the Camellia Bank, and behind that the arboretum. This forms a crucial windbreak from the south-east and since the 1970s has been a repository for some tender or endangered trees and shrubs of botanical interest from Edinburgh Botanical Garden. Below this lies the earliest outdoor planting of *Camellia japonica*, first planted near the house in the early nineteenth century and moved in about 1920 when a new border was planted next to the house with plants from Kew, from which an early introduction of *Osmanthus delavayi* remains.

OVERLEAF LEFT:
Magnolia campbellii
seedling

OVERLEAF RIGHT:
(clockwise from top)
Magnolia 'Charles Rafill',
Magnolia 'Star Wars',
Magnolia sprengeri var.
diva and another 'Star
Wars' bud

THIS PAGE LEFT TO
RIGHT: *Rhododendron*
'Loderi King George',
Camellia 'Donation',
young shoots picked
for Tregothnan tea
from *Camellia sinensis*,
the white-flowered
Rhododendron ciliatum

OPPOSITE TOP: Looking
up into the canopy of
the splendid cork oak,
Quercus suber, detail of
its bark below right

OPPOSITE BELOW LEFT:
One of many tree ferns
that line the avenue of
Dicksonia antarctica
underplanted with
naturalised *Crocosmia* x
crocosmiiflora

OVERLEAF: Early morning
sun streaming through
the speciment *Thuyra
plicata* where the Quarter
Mile Walk opens up
to the Summer House
Lawns

Finally, at the bottom of the garden is the Himalayan Valley, formerly known as the Ponds. To be more in keeping with the overall scale of the garden we have recently restored the ponds and enlarged the expanse of water. There is more moisture in the ground here and it is extremely sheltered, so we are putting together a new collection of species rhodos collected in the main by Tom Hudson of Tregrehan. Alongside this we have also planted about 400 plants of *Camellia sinensis*, the tea plant, as guests continually ask us if they can see some of our tea plantations that are used for the now famous Tregothnan tea!

The Himalayan Valley abuts the new South American collection that has been put together by our gardens director Jonathon Jones. He made a trip to South America following in the footsteps of William Lobb, a Cornish plant collector who, amongst other things, was responsible for the commercial introduction of *Araucaria araucana*, the monkey puzzle tree, some of which can be seen in the arboretum. Amusingly, we have planted a glade of these just outside this part of the garden as you would see them in Chile. They form a first line of defence against the wind. The geographical tour continues further up with a new planting of southern-hemisphere plants including another member of Araucariaceae, the Wollemi pine *Wollemia nobilis*, a remarkable plant of very narrow distribution that was only known as a fossil until 1994 when it was discovered growing in a steep-sided gorge less than 100 miles from Sydney. Ours is busily producing male and female cones.

I have mentioned little and forgotten much, but there is one tree that is a real favourite of mine: *Quercus suber*, the cork oak. The Tregothnan specimen is a truly majestic tree larger than any to be found in southern Europe as it has never been cropped for its bark, that shows up in a myriad of soft colours in the evening sun.

I mention my third favourite plant here at the end for the simple reason that it is our last great rhododendron to come into flower. *Rhododendron griffithianum*, formerly *R. aucklandii*, whose emerging flowers start out pink followed by some very powerful leaf shoots. This magnificent rhodo ends up as a wonderfully large white-flowering specimen.

I began by asking the questions 'what is a garden' and 'who is a gardener?' I am certain at Tregothnan that gardens are things of great beauty, and gardeners mere pupils dedicated to the enshrining of nature.

Pettifers

Lower Wardington, Oxfordshire

Gina Price

IN THE SUMMER of 1984 James and I moved into Pettifers, a seventeenth-century farmhouse built of mellow, honey-coloured Hornton stone, set back from the village street but facing the church of Lower Wardington in North Oxfordshire. Behind lies a rectangular garden of one-and-a-half acres, facing north-east. The land drops away from the house in a couple of shallow terraces and plunges you into a long view of wooded hills with horses grazing. In winter it is reminiscent of a medieval landscape with long shadows on the ridge-and-furrow fields. What lies behind the house is so unexpected that people exclaim when they see it for the first time.

I knew almost nothing about gardening in those early days, but I was very lucky to have the support and encouragement of three unique, kindly and very talented women: Dianey Binny of Kiftsgate, her sister Betsy Muir and my aunt, Beryl Hobson. They used to come over and look at my garden about twice a year to advise and criticise! They were quite fierce with me, and taught me a lot, often without my realising it. 'No mingy borders Gina,' Dianey used to say. One time when she cross-questioned me on what roses I had and I replied 'Peace' and 'Superstar' the riposte came swiftly: 'My two *most* hated roses.'

I was learning the hard way about taste and fashion in gardening. Dianey did not really like clematis, and loathed ivy; they collectively got furious about forget-me-nots in borders. I was told to write everything down and put the list on my dressing table where I could look at it before I went to bed.

Betsy hated plants that 'ran' and she once rapidly dismissed a small curved bed near the house as 'A damn dull bed Gina, just a lot of aquilegias and not even special ones.' I was also learning the lesson of plants that seed everywhere. The funniest remark Betsy ever made, while looking at my hostas, was, 'Is that hailstone damage?' I still laugh when I think about it!

I remember once Dianey taking me to a lecture by Penelope Hobhouse who said that when she was in a garden she wanted to feel near to tears. Dianey almost audibly announced

ABOVE: The contrasting partnership of sea hollies and red hot pokers is repeated in several areas of the garden. Here with *Eryngium bourgatii* 'Picos Blue' and *Kniphofia* 'Jenny'

ABOVE: A trio of allium 'Purple Sensation', *Persicaria bistorta* 'Superba' and tulip 'Black Parrot'

'Stuff and nonsense!' but I know what Penny Hobhouse meant. Very few gardens make you feel that: the inimitable nature of a good garden that perhaps people now call a 'sense of place'.

So although I did not agree with them about absolutely everything, they did make a fascinating pair: Dianey and Betsy, with their memories of how their mother, Heather Muir, created Kiftsgate during the era of great garden making with Lawrence Johnston nearby at Hidcote and Vita Sackville-West at Sissinghurst. I sometimes wonder what Dianey and Betsy would think of my garden now; we do not have rooms (which I know they would recommend) and there are so many new plants, almost too many. I would love to hear their reaction to all my ornamental grasses.

About ten years ago I decided to change the garden from top to bottom. My taste had slowly been forming. I had totally fallen in love with perennials and grasses. I wanted an all-year-round garden, and most of all I wanted the garden to flow into the landscape. I no longer liked huge shrub roses or, come to think of it, the majority of shrubs that I grew. The roses looked so ugly in the winter and to my eyes the shrubs were large and lumpy. The garden was very bitty and I had started to see the merit of having large sections of the same plant. Now when I do new borders they all have a different theme and, on the whole, different plants. I have favourite plants that crop up in several borders. Sedums, veronicas- trums, grasses, aconitums, agapanthus, eryngiums and alliums all feature repeatedly. I have started planting ferns and named snowdrops near the house.

Graham Gough of Marchants Hardy Plants – who I have been going to for about twenty-five years – has been a big influence, and I adore the plants that he sells. Whenever I go to see him I wonder why I go anywhere else. Apart from everything he stocks being unusual they are very well grown and flourish once they are in the ground. A recent Marchants' find that excited Polly, my current gardener (she had wanted to get hold of it for years) is the liquorice plant *Glycyrrhiza yunnanensis*. It has wonderful spiky brown balls of seed heads up its stems in autumn and winter. Polly and I also often go to Bob Brown of Cotswold Garden Flowers who we are so lucky in having nearby. The way he rates the plants 10 out of 10 is incredibly helpful.

The wonderful Polly has been with me for seven years and is by far the best gardener I have ever had, which makes such a difference to the garden (and me). We like the same plants and she has good ideas of her own. She is marvellous when we have people round the garden and very generous with her knowledge. It was Polly's idea that we should have a website and we now do a blog that we both find great fun. She writes 'Plant of the Month'. The garden has come on in leaps and bounds since Polly arrived although she cannot really see that as she is in it all the time. From the word go her talent for clipping has been transformative. It is not easy; I have tried neat clipping but am just an embarrassment. Luckily one of the nicest things about working with Polly is that we have a lot of laughs.

When we first came to Pettifers there was a large weeping willow at the end of the lawn. Backing the main lawn a vast privet hedge; a walnut tree at the bottom of the lawn, and a big poplar tree in the paddock… all these bit the dust. This has been the saving grace of the garden; we would have seen nothing in the distance had they been allowed to stay. In the early days too there was so much stone near the house that it sometimes took a good couple

of hours to plant something. A huge beech tree that had been badly topped was casting a lot of shade and taking up the moisture from the ground. All this was very unpromising. My main mistake, at first, was to plant things without preparing the ground properly and then wonder why they did not thrive. Luckily quite early on I met Clive Jones who was the gardener for Mrs Cavendish of Holker Hall, a marvellous garden in Cumbria. He was horrified to learn that I did not have a compost heap. When he came to see my garden the only thing that really excited him was a large pile of donkey manure over the fence in my neighbours' garden. He also taught me the benefits of putting a thick mulch on your borders in spring. Hellebores were one of his favourite plants and he introduced me to Washfield, Elizabeth Strangman's nursery in Kent, where I first met Graham Gough. I think he liked my enthusiasm.

On the left side of the garden we had what can only be described as a grassy track running slowly downhill with a dozen leylandii ending in a turning point for cars and a garage. Peter Chappell of Spinners Nursery (who called my garden 'your little patch') came to spend the night, and on leaving looked at my garage and said 'What an eyesore!' We had become quite used to it. The leylandii came out quite easily and we spent six months paving the grassy track with old stone setts that had come from a farmyard in Yorkshire. For the top end we had some large solid wooden gates made and painted them blue. Backing Dianey's so-called

ABOVE: A foreground of urns and barrel-shaped box topiary echo the form of trees in the distant landscape seen across a simple rectangular lawn. The narrow path is lined with purple betony *Stachys macarantha* 'Superba'

OVERLEAF: Allium 'Globemaster' and topiary seamlessly merge into the backdrop of rolling Oxfordshire countryside

'mingy border' was a wide privet hedge that we replaced with one-year-old yews that took about seven years to make a substantial hedge.

In 1992 we made the parterre, or picking garden. This is not visible from the house because of the lie of the land; you have to walk to the end of the lawn in order to see it, and it makes a lovely surprise. I used *Buxus sempervirens* 'Handsworthiensis' which has quite an upright habit so I kept tipping its new growth for it to bush out. Both the yew and the box are cut on a batter, wider at the bottom with sloping sides so that the light reaches it evenly and keeps the bottoms thick. In the centre of the parterre on both sides I planted tiny plants of *Phillyrea angustifolia* that has been used for topiary since Tudor times, and they quickly became great round domes.

It is important to think about your garden in winter. Pettifers faces north-east, and the main lawn is mostly in shade for three months. At the bottom of the steps is the half-moon crocus lawn, with drifts of crocuses in February including *C. chrysanthus* 'Blue Pearl', *C. c.* 'Prince Claus', *C. c.* 'Cream Beauty', *Crocus tommasinianus* and *C. t.* 'Ruby Giant'. They make a beautiful splash of colour with intermingling shades of cream and amethyst. I have been lucky and have never lost any to grey squirrels or mice, possibly because we always have a cat in the garden.

In our first winter here masses of buttercup-yellow aconites and double snowdrops emerged from underneath a carpet of snow and they have increased hugely. I love spring and have made what we call 'The Botticelli Meadow' at the bottom of the garden. *Fritillaria meleagris, Anemone blanda*, various narcissi and bluebells all carpet underneath three magnolias with a mown grass path curving through them. In the paddock there are more crocuses – *C. vernus* 'Vanguard', 'Pickwick' and 'Queen of the Blues' – that unfortunately do get nibbled by pheasants. It is hard to believe it, but did you know it is considered to be unlucky for snowdrops to be brought into the house? There is a wonderful family story of the time my husband's brother, Robin, took his ageing maiden aunt, Aunt Ivie, to lunch at his home, Rhiwlas, near Bala in North Wales. It was January and as they came up the drive Aunt Ivie commented on how beautiful the snowdrops were. Robin replied that there were a few in the house to which she resolutely stated that she therefore refused to step indoors as it was very unlucky. It was raining hard, and after some pleading he left her chain-smoking in a rapidly misting-up car. She refused to budge so back she went to her nursing home in Llandderfel!

We have had the garden at Pettifers for almost thirty years now and there is still room for improvement. The last five years we have been putting in more structure. Some huge *Rosa nutkana* 'Plena' at the end of the lawn have gone and two domes of yew have taken their place. I found large bearded irises very high maintenance with weeds constantly working their way between their rhizomes. I now find them really ungainly compared to the species of which I grow just a few. Solomon's seal bit the dust because of the sawfly all over it, but I still grow the variegated form as it does not seem to be affected. I love delphiniums but find them difficult to grow well: I have no idea why they are so tricky. I am not going to give up on them, though, as they are totally beautiful with a marvellous range of colours. I do not grow hostas anymore!

Gardens never stop changing or evolving, and one always strives for them to get better. They provide endless happiness and something to think about, not only for those who create them, but also (one hopes) for anyone who sees them.

OPPOSITE ABOVE: Seats under a rose embowered apple tree sit in long meadow grass that is studded with a succession of spring bulbs. *Geranium* 'Mrs. Kendall Clark' makes a naturalistic transition from border to meadow

OPPOSITE BELOW: In autumn, yew and box topiary are set against the golden leaves of *Betula utilis* var. *jacquemontii* and a young *Parrotia persica* with *Aster* 'Little Carlow' and the red hips of *Rosa glauca* 'Rubrifolia'

OVERLEAF: Bands of *Euphorbia griffithii* 'Fireglow' and allium 'Purple Sensation' ribbon through a wide border at the onset of summer

Spilsbury

TISBURY, WILTSHIRE

Tania Compton

ON THE SEPTEMBER day fifteen years ago my botanist husband Jamie and I moved to our house in Wiltshire, a regatta of cotton-wool puffball clouds drifted lazily across a panoramic canopy of cerulean blue. The eve of our five-year-old daughter Sophie's first day at school, and of our leg-limpet-son Fred's at playschool. That late summer cloud formation unfailingly conjures a sense of profound elation. Our borrowed landscape became an Iron Age hilltop studded with the buried treasure of rare Tisbury coral whose summit we could reach by walking from the oxbow bend of our stream over a stile and up, up, up through an ancient, steep-sided, ferny holloway.

This backdrop did not call for the spell-breaking fuss and frill of a formal garden. Barbed-wire-topped fences and the tarmac drive had to go. The sheep farmer whose flock had grazed all but docks, brambles and nettles to extinction came with a spray canister sloshing on the back of his quad bike and an expectant smile, but blanket pesticides didn't match our idealistic vision of children running without boundaries and making dens. We wanted lawn to meld into meadow, meadow to pond to nut walk to oxbow, and beyond. We didn't want to have to leap any fence, and there certainly weren't the funds for a ha-ha.

With six acres we had twenty-five times more space to tend than in our previous garden but still with Henry Johnson, our then gardener, helping one day a week plus contract mowing half a day. The space needed lateral thinking, but I didn't then have much time to think so there was no miracle master plan. Instead the garden has grown a bit each year as a result of meandering, perusing and ruminating. The overall structure is now much as I originally imagined it in my mind's eye, a mind that likes geometry and pattern but knew they had to be applied with a light touch in this setting. We have ended up with a bipolar garden. There is manic fecundity with mere hints of form in summer but sharp lines and shapes in winter. It has to look good from windows in all months but, more importantly, feel good when we are in it.

OPPOSITE: Old tin wash tubs filled with a succession of scents from hyacinths to dianthus to night-scented stocks are positioned at nose level by the entrance; rose 'Madame Isaac Péreire' and *Vitis coignetiae* grow up the house

ABOVE: The main axis of the garden is aligned on an old forked oak tree. *Euphorbia palustris* forms spurge green mounds around the fastigiated hornbeams *Carpinus betulus* 'Frans Fontane'

Jamie grew up a gardener. He won prizes at prep school for his exquisitely curated patch, he did the Kew Diploma and spent a decade as head gardener of the Chelsea Physic Garden. I grew up with pavement, not pasture, under my feet. Then a few years after I married my swashbuckling plant collector he swapped gardening for academia and went wildly off-piste for a decade of immersion in the world of ancient Chinese porcelain. His current obsession with wisteria seems to have got his garden-grafting mojo back and he has a new area we teasingly dub 'The Playpen' where he is starting a congregation of his wild collected wonders. So responsibility for the garden has until now been pretty much left to me.

The object that had sparked the Damascene conversion of my life from clubbing to cuttings was anchusa, spotted on a walk along the stony Phoenician tracks of Ibiza where I lived in my early twenties. On the edge of a meadow I spied flowers glinting in the very same way as a particularly prized, very 1980s, Guerlain eyeshadow in shades of lapis lazuli richly flecked with gold. I got to know the sprawling field edge the anchusa inhabited well with its garland of cistus and convolvulus, ballota and euphorbia, fennel and rosemary, asphodel and helichrysum. In late spring the cultivated meadow's heart burst into pink and red with alliums and poppies, gladioli and corncockle. There was barely a member of the Mediterranean flora that didn't put in an appearance, from the February eruption of gynandriris and crocus to autumn squills and cyclamen, each identified closely from my grandmother's copy of Keble-Martin's *Concise British Flora*. I brooked endless showers of spit through the mouth-with-few-teeth of the very chatty Ibicenco farmer who allowed me to collect armfuls of everything to carry back up the track.

I had since been longing to recreate the atmosphere and exuberance of this mind-altering meadow but our gault clay, grey as pewter, heavy as lead and descending to the earth's crust, had little in common with free-draining limestone. We can pull rank with the odd chemical and if we failed to give the meadow an annual topping sometime before October it would rapidly be re-appropriated by the oaks, hazels and field maples that encircle it. As one day, post *Homo sapiens*, they inevitably will. For now various forms of hornbeam – columnar, pear-shaped and cubed – that are aligned between magnificent oaks and a voluminous willow in a neighbouring field signal order amongst the chaos. Nature firmly has the upper hand.

BELOW: A plan of the garden

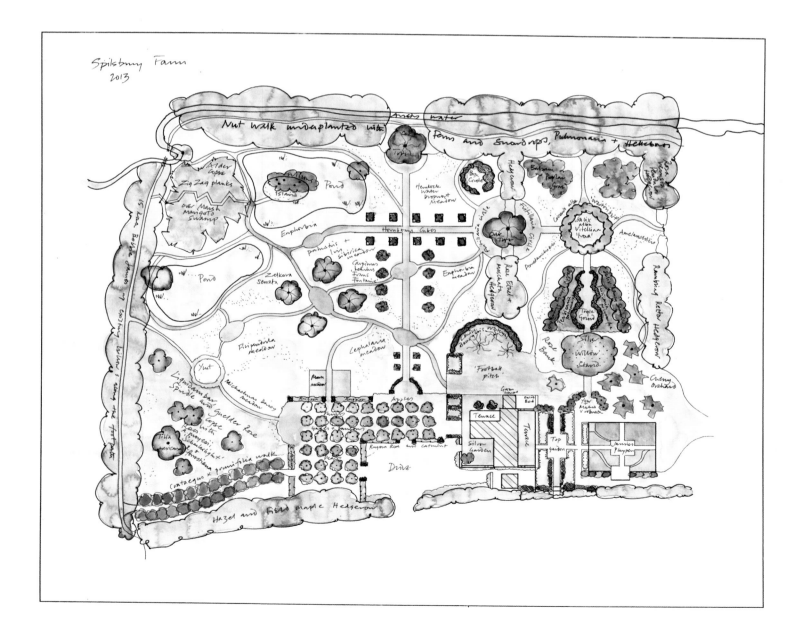

LEFT: Self-seeders such as white *Lychnis coronaria* 'Alba', parsley and tragopogon migrate around *Cornus sanguinea* 'Midwinter Fire' and foxtail lilies in a bed near the house

ABOVE: Roses 'Ispahan' and 'Blairii Number Two' need ducking under in midsummer

BELOW: *Helichrysum angustifolium, Perovskia* and *Santolina pinnata* subsp. *neapolitana* 'Edward Bowles' in the entrance garden with white pots made by Alexander Macdonald-Buchanan

In a bid to faintly echo the Mediterranean meadow camassia stands in for asphodel, *Cephalaria gigantea* for scabious, *Centaurea macrocephala* for *C. nigra* and *Iris sibirica* for gynandriris. *Euphorbia palustris*, the undisputed star of the meadow, subs for characias. Goat's rue and aruncus, cranesbill and bistort, white willowherb and sanguisorbas, monkshoods and Michaelmas daisies all fight their corner with the much better adapted and beefier resident grasses. Bulbs are seen at their very best in grass that conspires to hush up their dying leaves. So while squirrels nick our nuts I am squirrelling kilo boxes of buried treasure into the ground.

The meadow was intended as a time-saving exercise. It wasn't then an act of conscious conservation. It may have been an *unconscious* attempt to make amends for the failure of previous generations to prevent the annihilation of 97 per cent of our native meadows, a landscape every bit as precious and vulnerable as the Masai Mara. I now see just what has been sacrificed. The number of reasons to stop endless mowing and spraying start going off the radar when you look into the bees, butterflies, beetles and spiders, grasshoppers and moths a meadow shares its bounty with. Hogweed and hemlock water dropwort, though edited, are not to be sniffed at when you see the number of creatures that revel in and rely on them.

Damselflies dart across the euphorbia like electric-blue fishes on a coral-reef dive. Glow-worms light up our paths. They wouldn't step even one of their six feet in too tidy a meadow as their larvae only hatch after two years on a grass stem. I feel like the acrobatic French thief in *Ocean's Eleven* ducking and diving spider threads that criss-cross the meandering meadow paths in autumn. Jamie found a purple emperor at the foot of the sitting-room curtains. Barn and tawny owls, even a nightjar took up residence last summer. It is beyond our wildest dreams.

Not all the garden is given over to meadow. There are more choreographed areas of garden too, and in them I do revert to matron on ward patrol checking hospital corners. The flower garden is the domain of perfectionism. The meadow chimes with the lazier me who would rather be lying with a book in a hammock waiting to observe the kingfisher than tying in clematis. The meadow feels collaborative and abstract, the garden areas more figurative.

Bridging the two is the orchard. This was a present from friends for Jamie's and my joint fortieth and fiftieth birthdays. Its fecundity is phenomenal. Hot on the heels of 'Warwickshire Drooper' and 'Bryanston' gages come buckets of 'Victoria' plums and early apples like 'Discovery' and 'Spartan'. In September and October I get tennis elbow from stirring: damson prune cheese, 'Langley Bullace' ice cream, quince paste and 'Pitmaston pineapple' jelly. The children's friends love pear tarts and Jamie apple snow. Bad months for work and waistlines.

Vegetable growing comes and goes in cycles as it gives the devil on my shoulder a valid excuse to condone weeding rather than working. Gardening is a wondrous but pernicious habit. Who wouldn't rather be listening to long-tailed tits flit and chat, conversing with a robin, tidying up crispy pelargonium leaves or handling crumbly worm-laden leaf mould than staring at a screen? I am the mistress of prevarication in every area other than going outside and losing track of time and myself in the garden. So although we could supply

restaurants with our surplus cut-and-come-again salads and herbs we now largely rely on our local pick-your-own. Apart than certain staples, squashes and potatoes to romp through the compost heaps, Sungold tomatoes are compulsory for the heaven of smelling their leaves when pinching out and picking warm, and Jamie's rows of peas that never make it to the kitchen. Rainbow chard is an essential for looks as much as flavour. Laying seed drills and sowing between the start of BBC Radio 4's 'Classic Serial' and the end of 'Poetry Please' is my dream Sunday afternoon. We have also completely cut down on the greenhouse so we can travel in spring. No more auriculas, a fanaticism that chimed with the demands of small children when I could tend a few at a time before going back to build another Playmobil castle. The vine weevils guessed when I gave up Provado's 'Ultimate Bug Killer'.

To be honest I probably walk around the garden as much as work in it; each hour of each day something wondrous is coming or going. Dusk and dawn, frost or heatwave . . . but Spilsbury is at its most magical and graphic by moonlight. Clear full-moon nights elicit obligatory family walks that end up with us lying on the trampoline in the willow circle.

The willow circle is what we may opt to keep when Jamie and I get too old and creaky, when flower borders go feral and the orchard stops being pruned. It started as a dozen rootless wands in 1999 but was a double ring of mature pollarded willows within a decade, monikered the 'Ring of Fire' as its scarlet stems are set ablaze by slanting winter sun. We leave the annual pollard until as late as possible, and this has become a ritual spring wassail, done by Fred and his friends armed with music, beer and a cat's cradle of ladders. The cue for the willows was John Stefanides's circle of pleached limes at Cock Crow, a garden whose match we have yet to experience for chic and atmosphere. Fred and his friends are also dab-hand topiarists, and we dread the day they are no longer students in search of the odd summer job.

Box is the backbone of the garden, both loose and shaped, and we now leave it to get big and old before touching it. Any blight (and we are by no means immune) is burnt and clipping stops in that area for a couple of years. I don't know what the secret is but it seems to be curing itself. The same has happened with euonymus scale and viburnum beetle in the autumn copse where an understorey of spindle and guelder rose anchor groups of liquidambar, *Acer rubrum* and *Rhus typhina*. Five years ago it was devastated, each leaf shredded punk lace. I decided to lie on the hammock and read instead of spraying. Cutting out dead wood a couple of years later everything was sprouting from the base. You couldn't move through the dense psychedelic seed-laden branches this autumn. Plants want to live as much as we do.

There is a reassuring repetitiveness to the gardening year. From snowdrops in spring to the late-autumn-flowering *Galanthus reginae-olgae*, these bookend plants each signal the start and finish of a cycle in which there is always something flowering, fruiting, berrying or in bud to satisfy the insane desire and longing and appreciation that all fellow plant obsessives will be able to identify with. Each emerging spectacle relates us to nature's cycle as together we all make our annual spin around the sun on an ellipsoidal trajectory travelling half a kilometre a second at 1,000 miles an hour in a limitless universe. Life is a miracle.

OPPOSITE ABOVE: The willow circle of pollarded *Salix alba* var. *vitellina* 'Nova' is surrounded by *Cornus alba* 'Sibirica'

OPPOSITE BELOW: Planted together young *Malus* 'Evereste' and yew grow into a two-tiered hedge of evergreen structure and spring blossom followed by fruits feasted on by fieldfares in winter

ABOVE: The house seen from the edge of the pond with hemlock water dropwort, a beautiful nuisance

LEFT: A path through the meadow with *Euphorbia palustris* and *Camassia leichtlinii* subsp. *suksdorfii*

OPPOSITE: A collage of meadow dwellers including yellow rattle, *Geranium pratense* 'Snow Queen', *Centaurea macrocephala*, *Euphorbia* and *camassia* as before, knapweed, meadowsweet, the giant scabious *Cephalaria gigantea* and white willowherb

OVERLEAF: Looking across the open meadow in spring to the pond, alder copse, nutwalk and distant landscape

Acknowledgements

I T FEELS LIKE a cast of thousands has helped with this book, the owners, their gardeners, the photographers, garden designers, assistants and spouses. Everyone has contributed with such gusto so thanks go to each and every one of you for your time and enthusiasm.

As always collaborating with Andrew Lawson and Sabina Rüber has been utter joy and to all of you who have been wonderfully magnanimous in photographing the gardens that Andrew or Sabina could not reach, thank you: Tim Brotherton and Katie Lock, Val Corbett, Marcus Harpur, Paul Highnam, Jason Ingram, Andrea Jones, Tim Kahane, James Kerr, Marianne Majerus, Andrew Montgomery, Clive Nichols, Clay Perry, Allan Pollock-Morris and Jo Whitworth.

Jamie Compton, constantly interrupted from his own book, is the unsung hero of nomenclatural perfection and proof reading. To Sophie and Freddie Compton, Clare Weldon, Rosie Templeton, Mark Lole, Kris Olejnik, Christopher Woodward, Claudia Downes, Jane Pendry and Claudia Rothermere, thank you all for your vicarious and invaluable support.

The end result would be a mere shadow without the ministrations of the Art Director Rich Carr. Thank you Rich for patient indulgence of many layout alterations.

Claire Chesser at Constable, is now an expert botanist, thank you Claire, and grateful thanks to Linda Silverman and Grace Vincent.

Andreas Campomar has indulged my every editorial whim, dogged in our determination to make a book that Nick Robinson would have been as proud of as *The Domesday Book of Giant Salmon*.

OPPOSITE: Spilsbury
OVERLEAF: Trematon Castle

Image Credits

Some of these gardens are now open to the public (although all of the houses remain private). Please visit the websites listed below for more information.

Ferne Park
Page 4 ©Paul Highnam
All other images ©Andrew Lawson

The Barn
www.tomstuartsmith.co.uk
Pages 22-3 ©Tom Stuart-Smith
Title page and pages 20, 24-7 ©Andrew Lawson
Pages 2-3, 29-33 ©Andrea Jones

Plaz Metaxu
Page 37, garden plan by Liane Payne
All other images ©Jo Whitworth

Hilborough House
All images ©*Country Life*

Bury Court
www.burycourtbarn.com
All images ©Andrew Lawson

Ven House
All images ©Andrew Montgomery

Petworth House
All images ©Tim Brotherton & Katie Lock

Boughton
www.boughtonhouse.co.uk
Pages 100 and 106 ©By kind permission of
   The Duke of Buccleuch, KBE
All other images ©Jason Ingram

Eaton Hall
www.eatonestate.co.uk
Pages 112, 117, 118 (bottom),
   119-125 ©Allan Pollock-Morris
Pages 114, 118 (top) ©Lady Arabella Lennox-Boyd
Page 116 ©Andrew Lawson

St Paul's Walden Bury
www.stpaulswaldenbury.co.uk
All images ©James Kerr

Folly Farm
All images ©Jason Ingram

Hatch House
Page 160 ©Tom Stuart-Smith
All other images ©Andrew Lawson

Farleigh House
Pages 168, 170-3, 176-9 ©James Kerr
Page 175 ©Jo Whitworth

The Old Rectory, Naunton
www.danpearsonstudio.com
Page 182 ©Dan Pearson
All other images ©Andrew Lawson

Crockmore House
www.crockmorehouse.com
All images ©Andrew Lawson

The Vineyard
All images ©Andrew Montgomery

Mount St John
Page 216 ©Tom Stuart-Smith
All other images ©Andrew Lawson

Wychwood Manor
Pages 226-8, 234, 236 (top),
  239 ©Andrew Lawson
Page 230 ©Isabel Bannerman
Pages 232-3, 235, 236 (bottom),
  237-8 ©James Kerr

Stavordale Priory
Pages 246 (bottom), 250-1
  ©Michael Le Poer Trench
All other images ©Jason Ingram

Wyken Hall
All images ©Clay Perry

Fonthill House
www.fonthill.co.uk
Page 266 ©Tania Compton
All other images ©Sabina Rüber

The Old Rectory, Alphamstone
All images ©Marcus Harpur

Haseley Court
All images ©Andrew Lawson

Trematon Castle
www.bannermandesign.com
Pages 304-6, 310-11, 316-17 ©Andrew Lawson
Pages 312-3, 454-5 ©James Kerr

The Old Rectory, Duntisbourne Rous
Page 318, 320, 322-3, 328-31 ©Marianne Majerus
Pages 324-7 ©Andrew Lawson

Malplaquet House
www.tlg-landscape.co.uk
Page 334 ©Todd Longstaffe-Gowan
All other images ©Andrew Lawson

Gresgarth Hall
www.arabellalennoxboyd.com
All images ©Allan Pollock-Morris

Rockcliffe
www.rockcliffegarden.co.uk
Pages 354, 356, 358, 359, 366-7 ©Clive Nichols
Pages 360-5 ©Andrew Lawson

Helmingham Hall
www.helmingham.com
Pages 368, 371, 373, 375,
  376-9 ©Marcus Harpur
Page 370 ©Tim Kahane/Trigger Air
Page 374 ©Allan Pollock-Morris

Spye Park
All images ©Andrew Lawson

Howick Hall
www.howickhallgardens.co.uk
All images ©Andrea Jones

Cothay Manor
www.cothaymanor.co.uk
All images ©Sabina Rüber

Tregothnan
www.tregothnan.com
All images ©Sabina Rüber

Pettifers
www.pettifers.com
All images ©Andrew Lawson

Spilsbury
Page 441 ©Tania Compton
All other images ©Sabina Rüber

OVERLEAF: Petworth House